DEMONS OF STRESS AND ANGELS OF PEACE

A WAR WITHIN

Vikas Gupta

Are you ready to confront your demons and embrace the angels within you?

*Peace is not a destination;
it's a continuous journey!*

CONTENTS

Title Page

Chapter 1   7

Chapter 2   16

Chapter 3   39

Chapter 4   61

Chapter 5   86

Chapter 6   107

Chapter 7   125

Chapter 8   148

Chapter 9   168

Chapter 10   191

Chapter 11   214

Chapter 12   233

Chapter 13   259

Chapter 14   277

Chapter 15   296

Chapter 16   322

Chapter 17   324

Chapter 18   328

Chapter 19   333

Chapter 20   338

Chapter 21   342

Chapter 22   345

Chapter 23   349

Chapter 24   353

Chapter 25   357

Chapter 26   363

Chapter 27   367

Chapter 28   370

Chapter 29   375

Chapter 30   377

Chapter 31   380

Chapter 32   384

Chapter 33   389

Chapter 34   393

Chapter 35   396

Chapter 36   400

Chapter 37   403

Chapter 38   406

Chapter 39   409

Chapter 40   413

Chapter 41   417

Chapter 42   423

Acknowledgements

To all the incredible people in my life who have taught me the true meaning of life and its many lessons— thank you!

A special thanks to my father and mother, Shyam and Madhuri, the foundation of my life. Their unwavering love, support, and encouragement throughout my upbringing instilled in me a passion not just to live, but to live fully in the present.

To my beloved wife and best friend, Swati—thank you for your endless love, patience, and understanding during all those late nights and weekends I dedicated to this book, time that I should have spent with you and the kids. This book wouldn't have been possible without your steadfast support through both the highs and lows.

To the two brightest stars in my life, my son Viraj and daughter Samara, my lifelong companions—thank you for your constant encouragement and for being my sounding boards during this long, emotional journey. Your listening ears and insightful suggestions helped me find a way forward whenever I felt stuck. I'm truly blessed to have you both in my life.

To my brothers and sisters-in-law, Deepak, Savita, Vivek, and Chhavi—thank you for being my unwavering support system, for adding such joy and strength to my life, and for pushing me forward in every way you could.

To my extended family, Maithili, Savita, Vipul, Shweta, Ajay and Sandhya—thank you for enriching my life with your presence and making it all the more wonderful.

To all the next generation in my family—I feel so proud of each of your unique achievements, and I am continually inspired and learning from you every day.

To all the close relatives and friends who have helped me face life's challenges with courage—your support means the world to me.

And to those whose names I may have unintentionally left out—thank you for your contributions to my life!

Introduction

T hroughout my life, both personally and professionally, there's rarely been a day when I haven't encountered someone talking about stress. It's a constant topic of conversation. Some people discuss how they manage it—or at least try to—while others wonder what they can do about it.

Another thing I noticed was a significant difference in the way I handle stress compared to others, which prompted me to explore this subject further.

Intrigued by this, I began observing how and why people, including myself, experience stress. What I discovered was quite surprising: numerous factors in our daily lives contribute to stress, yet we seldom connect these underlying causes to the stress in our system. I call these contributors "demons," because they quietly disrupt our well-being, feeding into what I call the master demon—stress.

In this book, I aim to introduce an approach to overcoming this master demon stress by bringing its servant demons under control, thereby weakening stress itself. Whether we like it or not, we coexist with these demons, and a constant battle rages between us and them. We unintentionally nourish them, and in return, they feed their master, stress, which is their primary purpose.

Many of the demons I'll discuss will likely be familiar to you, and you may recognize them from your own experiences.

However, there will also be others that might not immediately come to mind as demons that haunt you and contribute to your stress.

If we can learn more about these demons that significantly impact our lives—and especially if we can find ways to control them—we can lead a life with much less stress, though achieving this is easier said than done.

Interestingly, while these demons are mostly harmful, they sometimes have a brighter side, which makes it difficult to completely eliminate them. However, despite their occasional benefits, we cannot allow them to take control, as their dark sides often outweigh their bright sides.

The key, then, is to live with these demons in a state of control, where we can benefit from their positive aspects while keeping their negative traits in check. The central message of this book is that trying to fight stress directly is futile; the real battle lies in weakening the servant demons that empower stress.

In addition to exploring these demons, I will also delve into some of the "angels" within us, whose role is to protect and support us in our war against stress and its servant demons. Just as all demons serve their master, stress, these angels work to strengthen their guardian, peace. Peace is a state of bliss, the ultimate source of inner strength, and the essence we all strive to achieve in our lives.

Furthermore, I'll share various theories I've developed over time that have helped me in my own struggles against these demons. Each chapter will offer a few mantras for dealing with specific demons—strategies that have worked for me but may not fully resonate with everyone. Even if they don't work entirely for you, they'll still provide valuable insights in this context.

Finally, I want to set some expectations for readers and include a few disclaimers. The human mind is incredibly complex, and when billions of minds interact, the complexities multiply exponentially. Living a stress-free life in today's world, with its challenging social fabric, is not easy.

The motivation behind this book comes from my own experiences as an ordinary person who has learned a lot about stress and its servant demons. I want to share these insights with the world. Since my learnings are based on personal experiences, I cannot cover every demon that haunts humanity, nor can I explore every detail about the ones I do discuss.

I believe that readers, much like myself, have their own experiences and can relate to my insights in various ways. Whether they agree, somewhat agree, or completely disagree with my thoughts, my goal is to provoke thought. My readers don't have to agree with everything I say, as their minds work differently, shaped by their own experiences. They are welcome to challenge my ideas.

My hope is that, even if I can't solve all their problems, if I can help guide their thoughts toward a life with stress under control, I will consider my efforts a success.

And finally, even when we know everything, sometimes we just need a little reminder.

CHAPTER 1

The Source of All Demons

B efore delving deeper into this book, it's important to shed light on the origins of these demons in our system and address questions such as, "Where do these demons come from?" or "How are they born?"

If we examine the full spectrum of our lives, it essentially consists of five interconnected worlds: the Inner world, Personal world, Professional world, Social world, and Fabricated world. We navigate through these worlds daily, often switching seamlessly from one to another, with no clear boundaries between them. In fact, there is significant overlap among these realms.

This chapter emphasizes a crucial point: the source of all demons within us arises primarily from the struggle to navigate smoothly among these five worlds we inhabit.

While our Personal, Social, and Professional worlds are heavily influenced by external factors, over which we have limited control, the Inner and Fabricated worlds are somewhat unique.

Our Inner world is particularly special because we are always present in it, regardless of where we are physically. This world continuously processes and reflects everything from the other worlds we traverse.

Similarly, our Fabricated world is unique because it is a space we consciously create—often as an escape from reality. This imagined realm is our refuge, where we exclude negativity and maintain complete control, shaping it into a sanctuary where we can retreat and recharge.

An interesting fact is that we adopt different personas in each of these worlds, effortlessly switching between them several times a day. Although these personas vary, they are interconnected and influence one another. In reality, these personas are simply different reflections of the same underlying personality.

Often, the experiences we undergo in one world don't remain confined there; they spill over and affect our other personas. For instance, a bad day at the office in the Professional world can spoil our evening at home in the Personal world. Similarly, personal struggles at home can impact our performance at work, our interactions in the Social world, or even our moments of solitude in the Inner world.

It's important to understand that these different personas in various worlds are not a matter of choice but a necessity for living what we consider a "normal" life in today's complex society.

The Inner world is the truest reflection of who we are. It's the world where we are always present, connected to our deepest thoughts and emotions. This world is like a black box, storing every experience, thought, and memory from our entire life, accessible only to us. Others can only speculate about what lies within based on our behavior, but no one can truly know for sure. The Inner world captures the entire spectrum of our life and remains with us throughout our journey.

The personal world is where we connect with people from our biological family and those we've chosen to be part of our lives, such as loved ones who hold a special place in our hearts and minds. This world is anchored by the bonds we share with these individuals, bonds that begin the moment we are born into a family, forming the foundation of this realm. It is here that we experience the warmth of family, creating cherished memories as we grow together.

These connections are largely determined by the circumstances of our birth and the people we choose to include in our personal lives. They are often unconditional, rarely questioned, and are followed with a sense of inherent duty and responsibility. The pillars of this world are built on love, care, sacrifice, trust, and responsibility, supported by numerous other elements that create a strong support system. While this world evolves, its growth tends to be slower compared to others.

The social world is the realm where we cultivate our friendships and social connections. This world is the most dynamic in terms of its structure, continually expanding as we meet new people and form new relationships throughout our lives. The connections in this world are primarily by our own choice, as we typically decide who we want to be friends with —at least, for the most part. In today's environment, where social media plays a dominant role, this world often becomes the one where we spend the majority of our time, often engaging with people we barely know in reality.

The connections in this world are usually driven by our needs, wants, and desires, aiming to enhance the quality of our lives by surrounding ourselves with like-minded individuals. While the closeness of relationships in this world generally ranks second to those in our personal world, there are exceptions where friendships can even surpass the bonds we share with family. Friendship is the lifeblood of our existence as social beings in this complex world we inhabit.

The professional world is where we manage the entirety

of our professional life. This world is centered around the work we do to earn a living. It is composed of the people we interact with at work, including colleagues, clients, and other professional contacts. These relationships are often formed out of necessity rather than choice, driven by our professional needs and obligations. Occasionally, some of these connections may cross over into our social world as we form more personal bonds with certain individuals.

Although the professional world exists primarily to meet the demands originating from other aspects of our lives, it has become the most crucial realm for ensuring our survival in today's competitive environment. It's fair to say that in our modern world, we begin preparing for our role in this sphere from a very early age, continuously learning and developing skills that eventually lead us to a chosen profession. This is the role we play for most of our lives, often until retirement. Without a doubt, the professional world has the most significant influence during our formative years, as we strive for success and fulfillment throughout our lives.

The Fabricated world is perhaps the most fascinating of all. It's a realm we create, blending reality with fiction, filled with imagination, aspirations, experiences, infatuations, and ideals. This world is characterized by gray areas and blurred lines between reality and imagination, and is shaped by our experiences in the other worlds, as well as by the books we read, the movies we watch, the stories we hear, and the places we visit. It's a realm we design according to our own desires and inclinations, serving as a refuge where we can find moments of calm and a space to dream and recharge.

The introduction of these worlds into our lives happens at different stages. The personal world begins the very day we are born, as connections with our family start forming immediately. However, we only become aware of this world after gaining self-consciousness. Soon after, we leap into the social world, forming new connections as we interact with others. Our inner world, though always present, only becomes noticeable once we realize our existence in this world.

The journey into the professional world typically starts when we step out of our homes to begin our formal education, often as early as kindergarten. This marks the beginning of our professional journey, which continues to evolve as we grow.

As we navigate these five worlds, our fabricated world starts to take shape, drawing its elements from all the life experiences we encounter in the other realms.

Each of these worlds has its own rules, expectations, and obligations, with some overlap between them. A strategy that works well in one world may fail in another. Unfortunately, in today's society, our lives are not defined by who we truly are —a reflection of our Inner world—but rather by how well we navigate and balance these multiple worlds. Those who master the art of juggling these worlds, navigating their chaos and challenges, emerge as the winners.

The root cause of much of the turmoil in our lives lies in the roles we play in these worlds and the constant juggling required to maintain equilibrium among them. The conflicts and challenges we face in these worlds give rise to the demons that haunt our system. As we navigate through these worlds, we find ourselves constantly battling various demons—some specific to one world, others spanning multiple worlds.

In the following sections, I will discuss some common life situations and how they serve as breeding grounds for these demons. While these are just a few examples among countless others, they illustrate the core idea that the demons within us are born from the structure of our modern lives. In the end, we are the architects of our own struggles.

Family and Relationships

Family is one of the greatest gifts to humanity, and it's

fair to say that many of us live for our families. Similarly, relationships are the lifeblood of our existence, providing us with purpose and setting us apart from other animals. However, just like all good things, family and relationships come with their own complexities and challenges. These complexities require continuous management, and if not handled properly, they can become breeding grounds for numerous demons within us.

The primary reason family and relationships can become sources of demons is that they often involve conflicts with the very people we love and care about. Making decisions that go against the wishes of those close to us is incredibly difficult. Some of the demons that arise from family and relationships include expectations, comparisons, ego, over-encouragement, worry, and guilt, to name just a few.

Expectations of Each Other

Within our close-knit circles—such as family members, close friends, and colleagues—people often have various expectations of us, both explicit and implicit. While explicit expectations are usually clear, implicit ones can be hard to discern. The same holds true for us, as we also have a wide range of expectations of others, as well as of ourselves.

The reality is that not all expectations can be met, which creates fertile ground for many demons within us. These expectations come in various forms and intensities, and they will be explored further in the chapter dedicated to the demon of expectation.

The Burden of Responsibility

The sense of responsibility is a commendable human trait, but it often demands significant sacrifices. Unfortunately, responsibilities are rarely clearly defined, and people may not always understand or fulfill them as expected. Balancing responsibilities with the other chaos in our lives can be challenging.

When we fail to meet our responsibilities, the guilt demon emerges. Similarly, if others do not fulfill their responsibilities toward us, our expectations are unmet, giving rise to frustration and disappointment. Worry is another demon born from responsibility, as we constantly fret over those we feel responsible for. This feeling of responsibility has the potential to create several other demons within us as well.

The Habit of Comparison

Humans have a tendency to constantly compare themselves and others, sometimes intentionally, other times unconsciously. While comparison can be a useful tool for decision-making, it can also be a curse, breeding numerous demons when used inappropriately in daily life.

A common example in a family setting is when parents compare their children to others, giving rise to various demons in both the parents and the children. Comparison is a significant demon and a source of many others, which will be discussed in detail in its dedicated chapter.

Social Life and Pressure

As social animals, humans thrive on social interactions. However, this enjoyment comes with its own set of hidden costs, including the constant pressure to meet societal expectations. Whether we acknowledge it or not, we are always under social pressure—stemming from society's expectations of us and our own desire to be perceived as successful by the world around us.

This pressure is present at every level of society: when we are at a lower level, we feel pressured to climb higher, and once we reach higher levels, we face the pressure to maintain our status. This relentless social pressure becomes a breeding ground for numerous demons within us.

The Pursuit of Money: Need, Want, and Greed

Money is undeniably one of the most important aspects of our lives, especially within the context of society, as it influences many aspects of our social standing. We interact with money on three levels: need, want, and greed. While the need for money is entirely justified, and the want for money may be somewhat acceptable for the happiness it provides, the greed for money is a root cause of many evils.

When greed becomes the primary driver in our pursuit of money, it spawns a multitude of demons within us. Although money is essential for a happy life, an excessive pursuit of it can also lead to misery. Managing the balance between these two truths is a significant challenge that often results in the emergence of various demons.

Survival in a Competitive World

In today's complex and competitive world, Darwin's theory of evolution—where only the fittest survive—applies to every aspect of life. This struggle for survival can lead to the loss of friendships, the creation of enemies, and the emotional toll of love and hate. We may start with many companions at the bottom, only to find ourselves standing alone at the top.

These are just a few examples of the costs we pay in the race to get ahead in life. This ongoing battle for survival generates numerous demons within us as we navigate fierce competition. As resources become scarcer, competition intensifies across all fields. While healthy competition is beneficial and drives progress, the cutthroat nature of the rat race, where people seek to outdo each other at any cost, often results in the birth of many demons within us.

The Consequences of Inaction

Inaction is a major contributor to the proliferation of demons within us, allowing them to grow unchecked when they could have been controlled through decisive action. Inaction also creates new demons in our system.

It occurs when we intend to do something but fail to follow through, as our good intentions are not matched by our actions. A common example of inaction is making New Year's resolutions but failing to act on them, allowing demons like procrastination and regret to take hold.

And the List Goes On

Given the complexity of our lives today, there is no shortage of situations that serve as breeding grounds for demons within us. The examples above are just a small fraction of the countless sources of inner turmoil. Now that we have discussed the complexities of life and the demons they produce, let's delve deeper into these demons to understand how they are born and what we can do to manage the chaos they create in our lives.

CHAPTER 2

Ego: The Demon of Inflated Self

Many of us might not realize that "ego" is the Latin word for "I," which explains a lot about the nature of this demon. When a person frequently uses words like "I," "me," and "my," it indicates they are under the influence of this demon known as ego.

So, What Is Ego?

Ego is our false self that forces us to become a person who seeks superiority over others while assuming that everyone will still like and admire us. In other words, it's a misguided belief about who we are, far from the reality. Ego creates a sense of separation between ourselves and others, and fosters a belief in our own superiority.

Ego is something that's not a constant or fixed entity, but a constantly evolving phenomenon throughout our life. It's a collection of beliefs we've accumulated since we began making sense of the world, often filled with all kinds of contradictions and chaos.

A quick way to detect the presence of the ego demon within you is to observe your reaction when someone tries to correct you. If you feel offended, regardless of how justified the correction is, it's a sign that you are under the influence of this demon.

This demon pretends to be our friend, convincing us to adopt a superiority complex and frequently use "I" and "me" in our speech. It isolates us with our emptiness, preventing others from filling those voids by making us believe they are better left empty.

Ego negatively impacts our relationships and is one of the leading causes of relationship issues. Quite often, small actions could prevent or fix damages in our relationships, but this demon stands in the way, stopping us from taking those actions.

Sometimes, we realize our mistakes and want to make amends with positive actions, but this demon intervenes and prevents us from acting. Similarly, there are times we can proactively improve our relationships, but this demon creates roadblocks by provoking thoughts like, "Why should we be the first to act?"

I can continue describing what ego is, but to stay within the scope of this book, let's explore what makes ego a demon, how it haunts us, and what we can do to deal with it.

Ego Obscures Our Perception of Reality

Ego clouds our mind with the dust of false beliefs, preventing us from seeing things as they truly are. It distorts our perception, making us believe that our interpretation is the absolute reality.

Often, our thoughts about something differ significantly from its true reality. However, this demon prevents us from any fact-checking and convinces us that our perceptions are accurate, and there's no need for any validation.

Ego Inflates Us With False Overconfidence

Ego fills us with false overconfidence, convincing us that we are the best at whatever we do. Even in the face of failure, it prevents us from accepting reality and reflecting on the reasons behind our shortcomings. Instead, it persuades us that the failure was unavoidable and that no one could have done a better job. This leads to an overestimation of our abilities and an underestimation of others'.

In reality, no matter who we are, there will always be people more knowledgeable and skilled than us in many areas. It is beneficial to listen to and learn from them. However, this demon hinders this opportunity by making us believe that we already know enough and that there is no room for further learning. Ego convinces us that no one around us could be more knowledgeable than we are.

This false overconfidence leads us to stop learning and results in a dangerous stagnation.

Ego Makes Us Believe We're Flawless and Entitled to Criticize and Judge Others

Ego convinces us that our work is flawless and superior, leading us to believe that anything done by others is likely to be inferior and flawed. This sense of superiority gives us a perceived right to criticize and judge others.

This demon hinders our ability to be self-critical, which is crucial for identifying and correcting our own flaws before they become apparent to others. Ego rejects the reality that no one is flawless, preventing us from acknowledging our own imperfections.

Ego Makes Us Manipulative, Inflexible, and Rigid

Ego shapes our personality so that we always want things done our way and expect results that meet our expectations, regardless of what others may think or want. This "my way or nothing" attitude drives us to manipulate those around us to achieve our desired outcomes.

This demon instills a belief in us that we are always right, leading to an inflexibility that prevents us from accommodating others. This rigidity forces others to yield if they want things to move forward.

Quite often, we find ourselves at a disadvantage when dealing with someone whose ego is even larger, leading to inevitable clashes of egos.

Ego Creates a Constant Need for Praise

Ego instills in us an implicit desire for constant praise from others, leaving us feeling empty when that praise is absent. In reality, no matter how well we perform, there will always be people who don't appreciate our work. These individuals may not only withhold praise but might also criticize us and our efforts, when given a chance.

This insatiable desire for continuous praise is impossible to achieve, leaving us in a state of unrest.

Ego Gives Us a False Sense of Toughness

Ego provides a false sense of toughness, creating an outer shield that hides a weak inner core. This demon makes you appear as someone with an "impossible to please" personality. However, the true reason behind this facade is your tendency to reject all ideas, no matter how excellent, because you believe none of them surpass your own.

Under the influence of this demon, you may seem tough, but in reality, you're missing out on much while confined within the cocoon of your perceived toughness.

Ego Limits Our Growth by Confining Us Within Ourselves

Ego convinces you that you are superior to everyone else, creating an impenetrable cocoon around your thoughts and actions that rejects all suggestions or inputs from others, regardless of their excellence. This makes it impossible for you to see beyond your own confinement.

When your thoughts try to cross that boundary to seek external validation, this demon intervenes, persuading you that your ideas are the best and nothing outside can match them. This significantly hinders your progress, as you can only grow so much with your own knowledge without any external input.

This demon confines your growth to the limits of your own understanding, making you like a frog in the well of your own thoughts, unaware of the vast possibilities beyond.

And This List Could Go On Forever

Ego manifests in countless shapes and forms, and there are hundreds or even thousands of ways this demon can harm us. The examples mentioned above are just a few, and this list could literally go on forever.

Ego, Confidence, Pride, and Arrogance

Though these terms may seem similar, they have distinct differences. Pride and confidence are positive aspects, while ego, arrogance and overconfidence are negative ones. Despite their differences, they are interrelated, with overlapping traits that can affect us in various ways. The lines between them are very thin, and under the influence of ego, pride can quickly turn into arrogance and confidence into overconfidence.

Pride is a feeling of deep satisfaction that people get from their own achievements, as well as those of others they are very close with, but it can seamlessly transform into arrogance when these achievements lead them to extreme sense of self importance and superiority over others.

Confidence is a powerful ingredient for success, that can bring a "can do" attitude and become a magnet attracting the trust and respect of others. On the other hand, its dark side, overconfidence, repels people and deters support. The transition from confidence to overconfidence is subtle, so it is crucial to remain vigilant to avoid crossing this thin line.

The Good Side of Ego

There's no doubt that ego is mostly a bad demon that is often seen as a negative force, causing stress and conflict, and it might seem like eradicating it entirely from our system would be the best course of action. However, like many other demons discussed in this book, ego possesses some good qualities despite its generally negative nature, making it a complex and sometimes beneficial presence in our system.

When we dissect our ego, we find it to be composed of both positive and negative self-esteem. The negative self-esteem represents the dark side of this demon, which we have been discussing throughout this chapter so far.

On the other hand, positive self-esteem is a solid, healthy, and strong sense of self. It acts as an invisible force that helps us stay on the right path, even in unfavorable situations. A healthy ego boosts our self-confidence, drives us forward, and gives us the backbone to face and overcome our fears, helping us set and exceed high expectations.

In times of adversity, when we are on the verge of giving up, it is the positive side of ego that gives us the courage to face and conquer the toughest challenges, emerging victorious. This good side of ego offers many benefits, providing us with the strength and resilience needed to succeed.

However, despite these positive aspects, it is essential to remain vigilant about the negative side of this demon. While it has good qualities, ego is primarily a troublesome force, and we must keep it under control to prevent its darker aspects from taking over.

Dealing With the Ego Demon

To win the war against the ego demon or at least bring it under control, we need to fight two battles: one against our own ego and the other against the egos of others. Let's start by discussing a few mantras to manage our own ego, and then we'll explore how to handle interactions with people who have inflated egos.

Mantras for Dealing With Our Own Ego

Before you can effectively deal with your ego, the first and most crucial step is to acknowledge and accept the presence of this demon within yourself. Many people are unaware or unwilling to admit that they are influenced by ego, despite the harm it causes in various aspects of their lives. Recognizing and accepting this is essential for any progress in dealing with this demon.

Mantra 1: Bring Your Ego Under Control by Reducing "I" and "Me"

The first step in bringing your ego under control is to reduce the use of "I" and "me" to a healthy level. To achieve this, you'll have to stop considering yourself as the center of the universe and avoid giving excessive importance to what others think about you. Mastering this mindset is already half the battle won.

Additionally, make a habit of giving credit to others, even when you feel your contribution was the most significant. This'll encourage you to use "we" instead of "I" and "me." In reality, most accomplishments are the result of teamwork, with all members making required contributions, and the whole team wins as one team sharing the fruit of success.

Furthermore, as we'll explore in the "Past, Present, and Future" chapter, the concept of "I" and "me" is fundamentally flawed. We are constantly changing. Today's "I" is different from yesterday's and tomorrow's "I." When referring to past actions, they were performed by a different version of yourself. The same applies to future actions, emphasizing that the self is ever-evolving.

The mantra is to reduce the usage of "I" and "me" and give others proper credit for their contributions to bring this deadly demon under control.

Mantra 2: Accept That the World Is Not All About Us

Ego creates the misconception that the entire world revolves around us, making us feel indispensable and overly important. However, the truth is that everything in this world existed before us and will continue to exist after we are gone. Nothing stops whether we are here or not and our presence only makes a tiny dent in the grand scheme of things.

The reality is exactly opposite where our existence depends significantly on the world around us, and if the world were to end, it would take us down with it. While people and things may rely on us, this dependency is mutual and primarily due to our coexistence with them.

The mantra is to realize and accept this fact, and the sooner we understand that we are just a part of the world, not the center of it, the quicker we can move towards an ego-free self.

Mantra 3: Go Against Your Ego and Start Accepting Your Mistakes

No one in this world is perfect. While some may excel more than others, even the best make mistakes because it is human nature. Your ego creates a false image of perfection, making it difficult for you to acknowledge your mistakes. It tells you that you cannot make mistakes because you are perfect in everything you do.

To break free from the influence of your ego, recognize that mistakes are a natural part of being human and are essential for learning and growth. Accepting that you are prone to making mistakes, just like everyone else, will help reduce this demon's hold on you.

Own your mistakes by taking responsibility for them, as admitting your mistakes is the first step toward rectifying them. Our society has given us a magical concept of saying "sorry", which allows us to acknowledge our mistakes and ask for forgiveness. Apologize sincerely when your actions hurt others, as a genuine apology can heal wounds and restore trust.

Unfortunately, the usage of "sorry" has become so common that this magical word has started losing its credibility. Be mindful not to overuse "sorry," as its overuse can dilute its sincerity and impact. Use it when truly necessary to ensure it retains its credibility.

The mantra is to go against your ego and accept your mistakes, as it is a powerful way to grow personally and strengthen your relationships. By recognizing your imperfections, taking responsibility, and offering sincere apologies, you can overcome the negative influence of this demon.

Mantra 4: Be Open to Advice From Others as You Don't Know Everything

There are mainly two approaches to doing things: "inside out" and "outside in". Our ego persuades us to take the "inside out" approach, convincing us that we are experts in everything, leading us to impose our views on others rather than considering theirs.

In reality, experts in every field have achieved their status through dedicated time, energy, and effort. While you may have a solid understanding of certain subjects and may even be better than some people, it's almost impossible to match the expertise of those who have specialized deeply.

With millions of subjects in the world, no one, including yourself, can be an expert in all of them. Our world is full of smart people, and many of whom are within our reach, offering a great opportunity for learning if we are open to it.

Unfortunately, under the influence of ego, we rarely listen to others. Even when we do hear them, we often reject their ideas or advice outright, as this demon finds reasons to dismiss others' ideas, regardless of their merit.

The mantra is to put your ego aside and be open to advice from others, to grow and learn. Ignoring good advice can mean losing opportunities for growth and learning, and it may even result in significant losses, so embrace the wisdom and insights that others offer.

Mantra 5: Stop Looking for Flaws in Others While Ignoring Your Own

The truth is that no one is perfect, and the ego demon exploits this by urging us to focus on the flaws of others, knowing that we will inevitably find them. This fact includes you as even you are not without flaws. However, the ego demon convinces you that you are an exception.

As long as you concentrate on the flaws of others, you will never fully accept their views, no matter how beneficial they might be. This demon will continue to control you by keeping you focused on the imperfections of others.

To counteract this growth-inhibiting ego demon, start

accepting people and their views despite their flaws. Don't let their imperfections become barriers to your acceptance. Additionally, acknowledge your own flaws that may be hindering your progress toward your goals.

There's nothing wrong in seeking perfection, but it can become a blocker as it is not realistic.

The mantra is to stop looking for flaws in others and start accepting your own. This practical and progressive approach will keep you moving in the right direction for growth, effectively keeping your ego in check.

Mantra 6: Ease Off Your Desire for Control Over Everyone and Everything

Ego has a strong affinity for control, and under the influence of this demon, you develop an insatiable desire to control everything and everyone around you. This causes distress when things don't go your way.

In reality, it's impossible to control everything and everyone for numerous reasons. This constant falling short of expectations creates disturbances within you. Control gives you a feeling of power, and this demon uses that feeling to deepen your desire for more control.

To weaken this demon's grip on you, you need to bring this desire for control to a healthy level initially and work towards eventually letting it go. As you reduce this excessive need for control, you'll experience less internal disturbance. You won't feel troubled by the inability to control situations or people.

The mantra is to reduce and eventually get rid of your desire to control everything and everyone around you, if you want to weaken the influence of this demon on you.

Mantra 7: Adopt a Beginner's Mindset to Stay Relevant

A beginner's mindset is one that continuously seeks and

embraces opportunities to learn new things. As we grow, our ego grows with us, and at some point, it can become so inflated that it hinders further learning by convincing us that we already know everything and there is nothing more to learn.

This is when we stop growing and become like a frog in a well. The world is constantly changing, often drastically, so if we don't keep our minds open to learning new things, we will quickly become obsolete.

The mantra is to set aside our ego and adopt a beginner's mindset to continually learning new things, as it has become a necessity for us to stay relevant and effective in our ever-changing world.

Mantra 8: Don't Hide Your Failures to Keep Your Ego Intact

Life is a series of successes and failures. While every success should be celebrated, every failure should be treated as a learning opportunity. However, our ego often prevents us from accepting our failures in front of others, making us believe that failure signifies weakness.

Your ego pushes you to hide your failures instead of openly accepting and learning from them. It convinces you that exposing your failures will damage your reputation. As a result, you start making excuses to hide your failures, which often leads to further complications and chaos as one lie leads to another.

As long as you view your failures through the lens of others' opinions, you will keep running from them. This might preserve your ego, but it will also cause you to miss valuable learning opportunities.

The mantra is to openly accept and learn from your failures instead of hiding them, as this approach will help you break free from the clutches of this demon and foster personal growth.

Mantra 9: Recognize the Negative Impact of Ego on Your Relationships

Ego has a profoundly negative influence on the quality of our relationships. This demon drives us to actions and behavior that damage our connections with others.

Relationships thrive on warmth and mutual acceptance, but ego obstructs this process. A person controlled by ego has high expectations of others and refuses to compromise, creating undue pressure on their counterparts. This imbalance prevents the development of genuine relationships, benefiting only the ego.

No one enjoys the company of someone with a big ego, and such relationships rarely last. They are one-sided and survive only as long as the other person continues to compromise.

The mantra is to reduce your ego to healthy and acceptable levels, ultimately freeing yourself from its grip. This will help you maintain and enjoy meaningful and balanced relationships.

Mantra 10: Recognize That Ego Can Be a Major Source of Anger in Our System

Ego can be a significant source of anger in our lives, triggered by others or originating within ourselves. When our ego feels challenged or threatened, it often responds with anger as a defense mechanism. This demon convinces us that our self-worth is under attack, leading to feelings of frustration and rage.

Under the influence of our ego, we develop high expectations of people and situations, often without any willingness to compromise. However, not all of our expectations can be met, especially when we are inflexible. When people or situations fail to meet our expectations, anger arises within us.

Sometimes, issues can be resolved through action, but our ego prevents us from taking those steps. This conflict, where our mind agrees to necessary actions but our ego blocks us, results in anger over the situation.

Anger itself is a formidable demon that must be dealt with in its own way. However, we can control anger stemming from ego issues by overcoming our ego. To manage this demon effectively, it's crucial to understand how ego fuels it. By recognizing the connection between ego and anger, we can address the root cause of our emotional responses. Lowering our ego helps reduce anger, allowing us to respond to situations more calmly and rationally.

The mantra is to acknowledge the role of ego in generating anger and work towards keeping this demon in check. Start by challenging your ego, lowering your expectations, and being ready to compromise to accommodate people and situations. This approach will lead to a more peaceful and balanced state of mind.

Mantras for Dealing with Others With Big Egos

Now that we've explored mantras for dealing with the ego demon within ourselves, let's focus on how to handle others who are possessed by this demon. Whether we like it or not, we'll encounter people with big egos in all aspects of life. Whether by choice or necessity, we'll need mantras to navigate their egos.

It's crucial to understand that just because you've managed to overcome your own ego, you can't expect the same from others. It is their choice whether to break free from the grip of their ego or remain its captive.

Some of the following mantras might seem like I'm suggesting you bend to those with big egos rather than confronting them, even if they are in the wrong. The reason behind this approach is that you have chosen to keep these people in your life despite their behavior or actions, and for that you'll need to be ready to compromise if you want to maintain these relationships. And sometimes, you have no other choice.

And it's you who must determine the extent to which you're willing to compromise when dealing with those possessed by this demon. Like everything else in the world, there is a limit to the one-sidedness you can tolerate to preserve your relationships, and for your own sanity it's essential to communicate your expectations once this limit is crossed.

Mantra 1: Limit the Use of "I" and "Me" Around These People but Don't Expect the Same From Them

Just as reducing the use of "I" and "me" is essential in managing our own ego, it is equally important when dealing with people with big egos.

The reason to avoid excessive use of "I" and "me" is that these individuals often heavily use these pronouns themselves and may get easily offended if you do the same. This can lead to a clash of egos, which you must avoid at all costs.

Regardless of whether your use of "I" and "me" is intentional, they may perceive it as a threat to their position and existence, prompting them to protect themselves fiercely. They may see you as competition and resort to any means, including dirty tactics, to satisfy their ego.

The most important thing to understand here is that even after reducing your use of these pronouns, you'll only win half the battle. You still have to deal with their frequent use of "I" and "me."

The mantra is to control your own use of these pronouns while adjusting your temperament to accept their continued usage. You cannot expect them to change just because you did.

Mantra 2: Be Extra Careful to Avoid Hurting Their Ego

For people with big egos, their ego is the focal point of their lives, and they are obsessed with satisfying this demon in their system. Whether deliberately or accidentally, if you hurt their ego, the outcome will be unpleasant.

Unfortunately, it's quite easy to offend them, as they have very little patience and no room for compromise in their expectations. It often seems like they are looking for opportunities to be offended, and inevitably, you may do something that upsets them, hurting their ego.

It's very important to keep in mind that you must be extra careful and vigilant when dealing with them to avoid any actions that could hurt their ego, even unintentionally. If something does happen to offend them, which is not unlikely, be proactive in calming the situation.

The mantra is to remember why you are with these people, even if being around them takes you out of your comfort zone. That reason should motivate you to be extra cautious and ensure you don't offend them.

Mantra 3: Make Sure to Be Fully Engaged When You're With Them

People with big egos demand your full focus and undivided attention when you're with them. While it can be challenging, given the constant distractions and need for multitasking in our busy lives, it's essential and an unspoken requirement to meet their expectations. Moreover, you cannot completely silence all the thoughts running through your mind while you're with them.

They require a level of attention that can read between the lines, hear the unspoken, and understand their implicit demands. If they sense you're not fully engaged, their ego gets hurt, as they take everything personally. Essentially, they demand your constant and undivided attention during conversations.

The irony is that while they expect your complete attention, they may not reciprocate. Nonetheless, you must stay vigilant, even when they seem disengaged, as they can quickly turn their focus back on you and take offense if you're not attentive.

Your actions should show commitment, but also make them aware of the extra efforts you're putting in to meet their expectations. Gradually, start communicating where they fall short in fulfilling yours. Over time, aim to align their ego to better accommodate you.

The mantra is to ensure you're fully engaged with them during interactions, but don't expect the same level of engagement from them.

Mantra 4: Keep Your Arguments Under Control When in Conversation With Them

People with big egos are often control freaks who see their word as the final say in any situation. Ironically, they want you to engage in conversation but dislike hearing anything they disagree with, taking your arguments as direct insults. For your own peace of mind, avoid arguing with them as much as possible.

While they may not care if you follow everything they say, they simply do not want their thoughts countered. This includes any attempts to correct them, even when you feel a suggestion is necessary.

In reality, conversations naturally include differences in opinions, making arguments almost inevitable. Two people's thoughts can never completely align on every topic, so disagreements are bound to happen.

Dealing with such people is challenging because they cannot stand arguments, yet it's nearly impossible to avoid conversations with them altogether. Therefore, you must keep your arguments in check, limiting them to absolute necessities - only in extreme situations where they cannot be avoided.

The mantra is to remember that arguments can offend these individuals, so avoid them unless absolutely necessary. Always think twice before bringing up any points of contention with them.

Mantra 5: Avoid Challenging Their Authority in Public

People with big egos are particularly sensitive about their public image and hate being challenged publicly. Fanatical about maintaining their authority and shining image, they work hard to create an illusion of control and importance, and they will go to any lengths to protect and preserve that image.

To deal with their demand for authority, you need to be tactful. While you don't have to fully accept their authority, you also shouldn't openly challenge it. Sometimes, ignoring their authority can be beneficial.

Even when you strongly disagree with them, avoid expressing your differing opinions publicly. They will perceive it as a challenge to their authority. Instead, control your urge to speak out against them in public and wait for a private moment to share your thoughts.

The mantra is to recognize their need for a positive public image and avoid challenging it in any situation.

Mantra 6: Don't Take Their Behavior and Actions Too Seriously

While previous mantras focused on how to manage interactions with people with big egos, this one emphasizes protecting yourself from being affected by their negative behavior and actions.

People with big egos often lack empathy for others, caring only about their own feelings. Without a second thought, they may hurt your feelings without even realizing it. It's not always their primary intention to hurt you; they simply don't think about you. Their focus is entirely on themselves, and in satisfying their own needs, they may inadvertently cause you pain.

Regardless of their intentions, their actions can end up hurting your feelings. Since they don't care about how you feel and don't hesitate to say or do things that may hurt you, you shouldn't give much weight to their actions or let them affect you.

You need to master the art of ignoring them and not take their behavior more seriously than necessary. Even when they are in conversation with you, their thoughts are centered on themselves. So, if they speak harshly or criticize you, it's often not personal - they're simply not thinking about you at all.

The mantra is to acknowledge that, as a human, you may still feel hurt at times, as it's impossible to ignore everything. However, by mastering the art of ignorance, you can gradually reduce the impact of such moments and handle them with greater ease.

Mantra 7: Don't Expect Any Immediate Change in Them and Be Persistent

People with big egos are deeply attached to their own perspectives and come with many preconceived notions. For them, their thoughts are final and unchangeable, and they believe their viewpoint is the only correct one.

They are so consumed by their own ideas that it's almost impossible to introduce new ones unless they come up with the ideas themselves. You might tolerate their behavior to maintain the relationship, but their rigidity can make it challenging to adjust to them. Sharing your perspective might seem futile, as the chances of influencing a change in them are slim.

You shouldn't have high expectations for them to change, especially not immediately, as this will likely lead to disappointment. Set your expectations low to avoid being let down.

While there's no harm in trying to present other points of view, don't expect them to accept these perspectives right away, or even ever. In fact, they're more likely to reject your views outright without considering them, as their minds are closed to new ideas.

The mantra is to understand that if you want them to change, even a little, you'll need to be persistent in presenting your viewpoints, maintain low expectations, and hope for gradual results over time.

Mantra 8: Empathize to Understand the Source of Their Ego

So far, the mantras have mainly focused on your actions when dealing with people with big egos, outlining what you can do to make those interactions successful without expecting much change or accommodation from them. This mantra encourages a different approach: empathizing with them to understand the real source of their ego.

Often, people with big egos are masking their insecurities, fears, or complexes by creating a false image of themselves and resisting anything that challenges this facade. By showing empathy, you may gradually gain their trust and access to their core, allowing you to understand the roots of their ego.

Start by pretending to understand them, even if you don't fully, to gain their trust. As they open up, you'll have the chance to learn where their ego stems from. This mantra goes beyond superficial interactions, encouraging you to form a deeper connection to help identify the source of their ego and potentially assist them in overcoming it.

This mantra is driven by a long-term vision and should be used selectively, as it requires significant effort and involvement from your side. Apply it with a chosen few, focusing on building a meaningful connection and understanding the source of their ego.

Mantra 9: Define Your Limits and Be Ready to Disengage if Necessary

While previous mantras focused on your actions to maintain relationships with people with big egos, this one emphasizes setting boundaries to avoid tolerating a one-sided relationship indefinitely.

Even if you choose to stay around these individuals, don't completely surrender your own needs and expectations. Dealing with ego-driven people often requires significant compromises, but your own interests should not be sacrificed.

Such relationships inherently lack equality and can make you suffer during every interaction. While you may have valid reasons for maintaining these relationships, it's important to define your limits to prevent endless suffering.

Clearly establish your boundaries and expectations, ensuring their ego doesn't dominate or disrespect you indefinitely. When necessary, express yourself respectfully but firmly.

Sometimes, despite your best efforts, dealing with someone with a big ego may remain unproductive or harmful. In such cases, it may be necessary to consider whether continuing the relationship is worth it. As a last resort, be prepared to disengage from a relationship that is impossible to manage despite all your efforts and compromises.

However, remember to leave the door open for possible reconciliation, as it's a small world full of surprises. Circumstances may change, and you might need to reconnect with people you once distanced yourself from.

The mantra is to define your limits when dealing with people with big egos and be ready to disengage if necessary to prevent indefinite suffering from these one-sided relationships, while leaving the door open for reconciliation in future.

Mantra 10: Sometimes, You Simply Have To Accept People As They Are, Without Question

In general, it's wise to navigate interactions with people who have big egos in a way that reduces friction. However, there will be times when none of your strategies or mantras will work. In those moments, you'll need to accept people with inflated egos just as they are, because there's a reason you're in their life or they're in yours.

This applies to personal, social, and professional settings, where you may have to deal with relatives, friends, or colleagues who are difficult because of their outsized egos. Unfortunately, this is a reality of life, and there's little you can do to change it. Not everyone will adjust to fit your expectations or needs.

What's important to remember is that, in some cases, you need these people in your life for various reasons. That awareness alone can provide you with the motivation to tolerate their ego-driven behaviors. Life won't always align with your desires, and this is one of those instances where compromise becomes essential. Accepting them without trying to change them is the middle ground for navigating these challenges.

The mantra is to understand that learning to accept people with big egos without trying to change them is a crucial life skill. While it may not always feel fair or easy, understanding that certain individuals play a necessary role in your life can help you find the patience to deal with their difficult traits. Not every situation will align with your preferences, and compromise is often the key to maintaining harmony. By accepting others as they are, you free yourself from unnecessary frustration and allow yourself to focus on what truly matters.

CHAPTER 3

Expectations: The Demon Fueling Disappointment

One of the most detrimental forces that has happened to humanity is none other than the expectation demon, a powerful beast capable of single handedly spawning countless other demons within our system. While there is nothing wrong in having expectations and they are not inherently harmful, the way we wield them and attach them to various aspects of our lives transforms them into a deadly force. We amplify the power of this demon by allowing it to dominate our emotions and actions, leading to a constant disturbance within us.

Under the possession of this demon, we relinquish control by completely surrendering to it, making our happiness entirely dependent on fulfilling these expectations. When they go unmet, we deny ourselves any chance of joy. The expectation demon manifests in countless ways, constantly tormenting and feeding on us.

This demon begins its insidious work by setting benchmarks for ourselves and others, and when results fall short, it conjures additional demons like disappointment, anger, and frustration, shattering our inner peace.

Expectations are present in all the worlds we live in, yet their nature, impact, and working style vary across different contexts.

Everyone harbors a unique set of expectations of others and everything else; only the type, nature, and intensity differ from person to person. This demon maintains a strong grip on us, present in almost every action we undertake, and there's hardly anything in our lives that's not intertwined with expectations.

Expectations are diverse, coming in various forms, shapes, sizes, and intensities. Also they are not static and evolve over time. A particularly menacing aspect of this demon makes it a double edged sword with its dual impact on everyone involved in the game of expectation. Those who harbor expectations feel distress when they are unmet, while those expected to meet them experience pressure and subsequent disappointment when they fail to do so.

Another significant problem with expectations is their variability among different people where everyone has a different set of expectations of us, often leading to contradictory demands. This forces us into difficult decisions, unsure of whose expectations to prioritize. Those who strive to meet everyone's expectations suffer the most, unable to say no and becoming entangled in this destructive cycle of demanding expectations, finding no escape from it.

Another facet of this demon is the correlation between higher expectations and the likelihood of failure and disappointment. Conversely, lower expectations set a lower benchmark, reducing the chance of disappointment but potentially leading to lower-quality experiences.

Understanding the depth of this demon's influence is crucial to learning how to manage and mitigate its effects. Let's delve deeper into the nature of the expectation demon to uncover ways to confront and overcome its hold on our lives.

The Expectations Others Have of Us

People harbor all kinds of expectations of us, making us susceptible to this powerful demon in our system introduced by their demands. These expectations vary in form and intensity, primarily shaped by our relationships with them. Some expect a great deal, others are more moderate, and some expect nothing at all. Their levels of tolerance toward us also differ widely.

Our lives are filled with various individuals—family members, friends, relatives, colleagues, managers, and partners—each with their unique set of expectations of us. At any given moment, we are surrounded by an ocean of these expectations, and attempting to satisfy all of them is like swimming in all directions; it exhausts us without making much progress, eventually causing us to drown in that ocean.

The biggest issue is that their expectations are not truly from you but from a version of you they have created in their minds. This gap between their imagined version and your real self makes it nearly impossible to fulfill all their expectations satisfactorily.

Moreover, their expectations are centered on their desires, not yours, even when they believe they are for your own good. Trying to meet these expectations often feels like living someone else's life and chasing their dreams, neglecting your own in the process.

Another complication arises from the fact that nothing remains constant. People, their expectations, and even we ourselves are continually changing, making it impossible to maintain a consistent alignment with everyone's evolving expectations.

In our professional world, expectations are supposed to be well-defined and tied to our job profiles, making it relatively easier to understand and meet them. However, in reality, expectations often extend beyond what is officially documented, including implicit ones based on industry norms and the unique dynamics of our teams and companies. This discrepancy breeds many demons in our professional lives.

Conversely, in our personal lives, there are no clear-cut definitions of expectations, making it harder to comprehend what exactly others want from us. Implicit expectations based on social norms and the diverse nature of people further complicate this already intricate ecosystem.

Our past performance can also influence others' expectations of us. Exceptional past achievements can lead to higher expectations, and failing to meet these elevated standards results in disappointment.

The key to navigating this complex landscape of expectations is to thoroughly understand and assess what is expected from us, rather than making assumptions. Moreover, we need to regularly reassess these expectations, given their constant evolution.

Failing to manage these expectations properly can easily overwhelm us. Striving to please everyone by fulfilling their demands often leads to a scenario where no one is truly happy, including ourselves.

The Expectations We Have of Others

In this manifestation of the expectation demon, we are the ones responsible for introducing this demon into other people's system, making them victims of our expectations. By tying our happiness to these expectations, we also become victims ourselves.

We harbor various expectations of different people in our lives, and while they are the ones expected to fulfill these demands, our emotions and actions remain closely linked to the outcomes. Thus, we find ourselves entangled in a web of these expectations amid an ocean of other kinds of expectations at any given time.

Having expectations of others is not inherently bad and is, in fact, perfectly human. However, when we make our emotions and actions heavily dependent on how others meet these expectations, we end up spawning numerous demons within ourselves.

When we set expectations for someone, these expectations are usually tied to specific actions they must perform. The results of these actions dictate our reaction, which can be either happy or sad, depending on whether our expectations were met.

The problem arises because we set expectations based on our perception of someone and their abilities, not their true nature. Additionally, we may hold several preconceived notions about them, which might not be accurate. This creates a high likelihood of setting wrong expectations, setting them up for failure from the start.

Wrong expectations can arise in various ways, such as over-expecting from an average or underperformer, expecting results from individuals with inadequate or irrelevant skills, or parents having unrealistic expectations of children who may not be as competitive.

Another issue is the dynamic nature of our expectations, which can change over time. Others may be unaware that our expectations have shifted, continuing to fulfill outdated expectations and thus setting up for failure.

Understanding that wrong expectations of others can breed many demons in both their and our lives is crucial. By being mindful and reassessing our expectations, we can cover this issue to some extent.

By removing some wrong expectations and recalibrating others to be more realistic, we can reduce or even eliminate the introduction of several demons in both our system and that of others. This mindful adjustment can lead to healthier relationships and a more balanced emotional state.

The Expectations We Have of Ourselves - Self-expectations

Another intriguing form of the expectation demon is self-expectation, where we become both the source and the victim of this demon within our own system. We all have certain expectations of ourselves, and this trait is fundamental to self-awareness and motivation, driving us toward success.

Self-expectation is essential for our progress and it involves various activities within our inner world, such as setting goals, making promises, plans, resolutions, and other commitments to keep us moving forward and improving ourselves daily.

The problem, however, is similar to what we have seen with expectations of others: wrong expectations can become a significant source of inner demons. In this case, having unrealistic or misaligned expectations of ourselves is the culprit.

Incorrect self-evaluation often leads to inflated self-expectations that we cannot meet. Outside influences and wrong comparisons significantly contribute to this incorrect evaluation. When we see others achieving success, we might think, "If they can do it, so can I," without understanding the full extent of their efforts and circumstances.

Overconfidence can also result in miscalculated self-evaluation. Additionally, past successes may boost our confidence, leading us to overestimate our current abilities and forget that different circumstances can yield different outcomes. A past winning performance is not a guarantee of success again.

When we fail to meet our self-expectations, the turmoil occurs within our inner world, and often unnoticed by others. This internal struggle can be isolating and challenging to overcome without external support. Sharing our self-expectations and disappointments with a trusted inner circle can help us navigate through these difficult challenges.

An interesting facet of self-expectation arises when we perceive that some individuals set lower expectations for themselves than their true potential warrants. For instance, we might believe that our children have more potential than they recognize and should aim higher. However, this well-intentioned push can introduce demons into their system if our perceptions are influenced by our desires for their success rather than an accurate assessment of their capabilities.

Even if someone possesses high potential, realizing it often requires significant effort, and not everyone may have the will or desire to pursue it to its fullest extent.

In conclusion, while self-expectation is crucial for personal growth and motivation, it is essential to set realistic and well-informed expectations. By doing so, we can avoid the pitfalls of unrealistic self-demands and maintain a healthier, more balanced inner life.

The Expectations We Have of Situations and Things

It may sound unusual, but just as we have expectations of people, we also have expectations of the situations and things around us. For a smooth life, we often expect situations to be favorable and things to be as we like them, and given our diverse nature, our expectations vary widely.

Here's a good example: an urban dweller and a farmer have opposing expectations for the weather. The urban individual, planning a picnic, hopes for perfect, sunny weather with no rain. Meanwhile, the farmer wishes for rain to nourish his crops. This illustrates a clear contradiction in expectations arising from the same situation.

Another example involves food preferences: adults generally expect their meals to be served hot, while young children often prefer their food cold.

While having expectations of situations and things is natural, their outcomes are unpredictable due to numerous influencing factors. Situations can change and may not always be favorable, and things might not always come to us as expected.

The best approach is to cultivate flexible expectations that can adapt to changing situations and unexpected outcomes. This adaptability can help us navigate life's uncertainties with greater ease and resilience.

Implicit Expectations

Implicit expectations are a unique form of the expectation demon, characterized by their unspoken and assumption-based nature. These expectations are never explicitly communicated but are highly desired to be fulfilled. Their inherent ambiguity makes them challenging to meet, as there is a limit to how much one can understand the unsaid.

In reality, implicit expectations are not based on pure assumptions or wild guesses. Instead, they stem from a collection of unspoken or assumed conventions, customs, norms, behaviors, morals, laws, rules, or standards associated with a particular context or relationship. For example, in a library, you are expected to be quiet. When driving, you are expected to follow traffic rules. Young people are generally expected to respect their elders.

Implicit expectations are prevalent in all of our worlds, and our success and happiness often hinges on how well we understand and meet these unspoken demands.

In the professional world, implicit expectations are about dress codes, work hours, communication, collaboration, continuous learning, and more. For instance, there might be an unspoken expectation for you to dress appropriately for client meetings and respond to customer inquiries promptly.

Similarly, in our social world, there are many implicit expectations about our behavior, conduct, actions, respect, communication, and other social norms.

In the personal world, implicit expectations exist within our relationships and families. These might include roles and responsibilities within the household, communication patterns, cultural traditions, emotional support, and general understanding. These expectations can vary widely depending on factors such as wealth, culture, country, family dynamics, and individual preferences.

It's important to recognize that implicit expectations can sometimes lead to misunderstandings or conflicts, especially when different people have varying interpretations of what is expected. To address this, fostering open communication, clarifying expectations when necessary, and remaining respectful of diverse perspectives and experiences can be helpful.

Due to the very nature of implicit expectations, you may need to go an extra mile to understand them so you can fulfill them to the best of your ability, and reduce potential conflicts.

Expectations Vs Reality

One of the biggest sources of problems related to expectations is the gap between our expectations and reality. What we expect and what actually happens are often two different things, and there is almost always a discrepancy between the two.

In many cases, our expectations are far from reality because they are shaped by our own desires, assumptions, and preconceived notions. Problems arise when our expectations exceed what is realistically possible given the situation or circumstances.

Expectations that are far from reality have a high probability of failure, and simply waiting for these expectations to be met often leads to disappointment. It is essential to assess your expectations against reality. If they seem unrealistic, you must either recalibrate them to align with what is possible or prepare yourself for potential disappointment.

Expectations and Acceptance

When discussing the relationship between expectations and acceptance, it's important to acknowledge that while there are many approaches for managing expectations, the art of acceptance stands out as one of the most powerful weapons against this demon.

There are times when we realize that some of our expectations of others are too high and difficult to meet. Our initial reaction might be to lower our expectations, often without considering that this might involve significant compromise on our part.

Instead of immediately lowering our expectations, we should first accept the results as they come, without measuring them against our preset expectations. This approach allows us to analyze what went wrong and determine the appropriate course of action regarding our expectations.

It's crucial to distinguish between lowering your expectations and accepting the results. Lowering your expectations implies compromising your standards by setting lower benchmarks for others, which should only be done if you are certain of the other person's inability to meet your expectations.

On the other hand, accepting the results without comparing them to your preset expectations means approaching situations realistically without compromising your standards. You continue to expect others to meet your established benchmarks but are willing to accept inferior results if there are valid reasons for them.

Even after mastering the art of acceptance, you have only won half the battle against the expectation demon, and the remaining half can be even more challenging. Once you embrace acceptance, an implicit expectation may arise within you that others should also stop expecting from you, simply because you have done so.

In this context, controlling your own expectation demon is one thing, but attempting to control the demons of others is another challenge entirely.

The Good in Expectations

After exploring the many negative aspects of expectations, we might wonder whether we should rid ourselves of this demon entirely or allow it to remain in our system. Surprisingly, like some other demons discussed in this book, the expectation demon also possesses a few redeeming qualities that justify its presence within us.

When others have expectations of us, it can make us feel valued. Conversely, when no one expects anything of us, it can lead to feelings of worthlessness. Thus, expectations contribute to our sense of self-worth.

Expectations can also serve as motivating forces, propelling us towards our life goals and providing a sense of direction. They act as catalysts for growth and progress, driving many of our daily decisions. Often, our expectations become the driving force behind the good things we do in life. For example, without expectations of positive results, returns, or profits, we would never invest our time, money, and effort into various ventures.

Similarly, by setting self-expectations, we create a direction for our lives. Sometimes, others set high expectations for us because they see potential in us, and rising to meet these expectations can push us to achieve heights we might never have imagined on our own.

Our expectations of others can also guide them to make positive choices in life. Although this may create pressure for them, it often works out for their benefit. In the professional world, we remain employed as long as the company has expectations of us. In the social world, expectations play a significant role in maintaining social connections.

When we expect something bad to happen, it gives us an opportunity to plan and prepare for potential adverse situations. If we didn't have such expectations, we would have nothing to plan or prepare for and would have to handle everything spontaneously, which doesn't always work well.

Despite these positive aspects, the negative side of expectations often outweighs the good. Therefore, while we allow this demon to stay within us, we must keep it on a tight leash to prevent it from causing harm.

Now that we have delved deeply into the nature of expectations, let's explore a few key mantras for managing this demon effectively.

Matra 1 - Don't Compromise on Your Expectations but Keep Them Flexible

In reality, most of our expectations won't be met at the level we set for them, leading to some degree of disappointment. Therefore, we need to find ways to handle these disappointments caused by fully or partially unmet expectations.

One approach is to eliminate expectations entirely.

However, since we saw some value in having them, we don't want to get rid of this demon completely from our system.

Another way to manage these situations is to accept outcomes as they are and try not to feel disappointed. While this is easier said than done, it is definitely a good practice.

As long as we are human, we will have expectations, as it's impossible to remove all expectations of ourselves and others completely. Even if we somehow manage to suppress them, they may still exist in a dormant state, ready to re-emerge.

Also the story of expectations in our system won't end there, as suppressing or eliminating our expectations doesn't mean others won't have expectations of us. We can't control others' expectations, and trying to do so is a recipe for disappointment.

Another option is to lower your expectations of others. By doing this, it becomes easier for others to meet them, reducing the chances of disappointment. However, this can lead to a feeling of compromise. While this approach can be practical at times, it shouldn't be the default for every expectation you have.

Since every expectation is unique, its outcome should be dealt with in its own unique way.

Therefore, the mantra is to keep your expectations high without compromising but remain flexible if they don't turn out as expected. Don't measure outcomes against a preset benchmark for your expectations. Set limits on a case-by-case basis and lower them when absolutely necessary, maintaining a practical approach. Treat the outcome of every expectation uniquely, considering its type, importance, nature, and the person or situation it involves.

Matra 2 - Understand What's Truly Expected of You and Keep That Understanding Current

People, including yourself, will have all kinds of expectations of you. But do you really understand them in their full context?

While you may have a relatively clearer grasp of your own self-expectations, understanding others' expectations can be challenging. Most of the time, you'll only have a partial understanding, and often this is only for the explicit expectations. Implicit expectations are even harder to grasp, and your incomplete understanding can lead to failing to meet those expectations.

In the professional world, expectations are generally clearer as they are mostly explicitly stated, and you can infer the implicit ones based on general norms. However, in other areas of life, expectations are more complex, often unclear, and highly dependent on the individuals involved.

Assumptions, though unavoidable, play a significant role in failed expectations. It's common to assume what others expect and what will make them happy, but acting on these assumptions can lead to failure when they prove incorrect.

Therefore, it's better to validate your assumptions before acting on them. All the efforts you put into fulfilling someone's expectations may go to waste if based on incorrect assumptions, resulting in disappointments.

For self-expectations, it's crucial to judge your capabilities accurately. Over-expecting can lead to failure, while under-expecting can restrict you from reaching your true potential. Also keep your self-expectations flexible to accommodate deviations from your set levels for them.

Additionally, expectations evolve over time. If not recalibrated regularly, you may end up with a wrong understanding of what others expect from you. Similarly, your own capabilities evolve, requiring a reassessment of your self-expectations on a regular basis.

The mantra is to truly understand what's expected of you, including self-expectations, as this is the first step towards successfully meeting them. Additionally, you need to keep assessing and updating your understanding regularly to stay current.

Mantra 3: Communicate Your Expectations Clearly

We all have various expectations of others, and how well we communicate these expectations significantly impacts their successful outcomes. If we fail to clearly state our expectations or if others misunderstand them, the expectations will likely fail, leading to disappointment.

When setting expectations, express your needs and desires clearly and straightforwardly. Avoid vague language to help others understand your perspective and reduce the chances of miscommunication. Being direct and honest—without sugar-coating or beating around the bush—ensures that everyone is on the same page regarding what is expected.

After expressing your expectations, check to confirm that the other person comprehends what you've communicated to prevent assumptions and clarify any confusion. Encourage others to share their thoughts and feelings about your expectations, and be receptive to their feedback, willing to adjust your expectations if necessary.

Additionally, make sure your expectations are realistic and achievable given the circumstances, as unrealistic expectations set the stage for disappointment. Be prepared to adapt your expectations as circumstances change. Life is dynamic, and flexibility in your expectations can prevent unnecessary frustration. Communicate any changes in your expectations promptly to keep everyone informed and aligned.

The mantra is to communicate your expectations clearly to foster better understanding, minimize conflicts, and build stronger, more cooperative relationships. Additionally, don't forget to update others if there are any changes in your expectations of them.

Matra 4 - We Should Regularly Recalibrate to Align with Changing Expectations

This mantra builds on the phenomena that expectations are constantly evolving, as briefly mentioned in the previous mantra. Change is inevitable, and this applies to expectations as well. Just like everything else in life, expectations are not set in stone and shift over time, whether they are our own or others' expectations of us.

As we journey through life, we grow and learn, transforming into different versions of ourselves. This personal evolution brings changes in our expectations as well. Likewise, the expectations others had of us in the past may no longer be valid as their perspectives and needs might have changed.

To stay on track in fulfilling expectations, we must understand these shifts and keep recalibrating accordingly. It's also essential to communicate our evolving expectations to those who are impacted by them, ensuring they can adjust as well. Failure to do so can lead to disappointment, which would be unfair to those who were unaware of the changes.

Similarly, even our self-expectations are also subject to change, requiring regular reassessment and adjustment. It's important to remember that while having expectations is natural, clinging to them in their current form for too long can be detrimental.

The mantra is to regularly recalibrate to align with the changing expectations to ensure that everyone remains updated and expectations are met effectively. As time progresses, adapt to changes by updating, adding, or removing expectations, ensuring they align with your current reality and personal growth.

Mantra 5: Make Sure You're Aware of Your High Self-expectations

Self-expectations are common, as we all have various expectations of ourselves. However, in a non-ideal world like ours, some of these expectations might exceed our capabilities, leading to failure. Such failures can make us feel terrible and, in extreme cases, have catastrophic consequences.

Having high self-expectations is not inherently bad; in fact, they can be powerful motivators, pushing us to stretch beyond our known limits and try harder. The issue lies not in the high expectations themselves but in our unawareness or incorrect assessment of our abilities to meet them. Often, we set high self-expectations without realizing we lack the necessary skills or capabilities.

When we understand our limitations but still set high self-expectations, we are consciously stretching ourselves. Even with a risk of failure, these expectations motivate us to try harder, as we take calculated risks rather than shooting in the dark.

Setting expectations higher than our abilities involves a mix of doubt and implicit hope. We have a belief that we can meet these goals, but are still focused on learning and developing the skills needed to reach them. High self-expectations give us the courage to explore new territories beyond our usual limits, opening doors to new opportunities and growth.

The mantra is to thoroughly understand our abilities before setting self-expectations. While it's acceptable to set them higher than our current capabilities, we should be fully aware of this and prepared for unexpected outcomes.

Mantra 6: Be Vocal About Your Inability to Fulfill Others'

Expectations

We live in a world where people have all kinds of expectations of us, and we usually try our best to meet those we are aware of. While this effort is commendable, sometimes we have to stretch far beyond our comfort zones, only to discover that certain expectations are beyond our abilities.

The reality is that many people will have different expectations of us at any given time. Even if we try our best, it's practically impossible for us to meet all of them, especially since some expectations are implicit and unknown to us, while others are clear but difficult to fulfill. Consequently, some expectations are bound to be unmet.

We have two options: attempt to fulfill all expectations and inevitably let some fail, or analyze them, identify those we cannot meet, and communicate this to others. The latter approach is more graceful and responsible.

Attempting to meet over-expectations can harm us, as we may not have the courage to say no. Conversely, failing to meet someone's high expectations without explanation can unintentionally hurt them, especially if they heavily depend on us.

The mantra is that when you realize you cannot meet certain expectations, it's better to communicate this to those affected rather than struggling in silence or failing without explanation. Often, people do not realize the pressure their expectations impose on us, so it's crucial to convey your feelings and, in extreme cases, learn to say no.

Mantra 7: You Can Lower Your Expectations of Others but Shouldn't Expect Them to Do the Same

In my opinion, this is one of the most important mantras for dealing with the challenges posed by this demon. After recognizing the potential pitfalls of expectations, you might decide to have no more expectations of others or reduce them to very low levels. This approach can help you reach a state where you're less affected by whether others fulfill your remaining expectations or not.

You might think that by taking this major step, all your expectation-related problems would be solved. However, even after controlling your expectations of others, you are not entirely free from the clutches of this demon.

Once you train yourself to stop having high expectations of others, an implicit expectation may develop within you where you start expecting others to control their expectations of you as well. The reality is that while you can manage your own expectations, you cannot dictate how others should handle theirs.

Just because you have reduced your expectations of others does not mean they will do the same for you. This discrepancy can lead to frustration if not properly managed.

The mantra is to avoid letting these implicit expectations cause further issues. Take satisfaction in the progress you've made in controlling your own demon. If others also reduce their expectations of you, consider it a bonus. If they don't, handle their expectations as you would have otherwise, without letting it disrupt your newfound peace.

Mantra 8: Avoid Expectations That Are Purely Influenced by Comparison

Expectations often arise from comparisons, which can lead to unrealistic and unmet expectations if the comparisons themselves are flawed. When we set expectations based on comparing others to someone else, we assume they should meet these expectations because others have. Similarly, others may set expectations for us based on comparisons, assuming we can fulfill them just like someone else.

This also applies to self-expectations formed by comparing ourselves to others. However, just because one person can do something doesn't guarantee another can, as abilities, circumstances, and numerous other factors vary significantly.

Remember, not everything is everyone's cup of tea. Comparisons are valid only when they are accurate and fair, which is rarely the case. Therefore, while setting expectations based on comparison isn't inherently wrong, they often lack a hundred percent success rate.

The mantra is to avoid having expectations purely based on comparisons, as they are highly likely to go unmet and lead to disappointment. Instead, focus on setting realistic, individual-based expectations that consider unique abilities and circumstances.

Mantra 9: Managing Expectations is Key for Successful Relationships

While managing expectations is crucial for our overall well-being and happiness, it becomes even more important in the context of our relationships. Expectations play a significant role in our interactions with family, friends, and colleagues, and can become a breeding ground for many demons if not handled properly.

Expectations that are not clearly communicated or are perceived as unfair can strain relationships, and a constant effort to meet these expectations can create tension and resentment, negatively impacting the quality of the relationship.

Every relationship begins with some sort of an initial set of expectations. These expectations evolve as the relationship grows, and the smoothness and longevity of the relationship depend on how these constantly changing expectations are managed.

Unmet expectations often lead to disappointment and frustration, negatively impacting relationships, and in extreme cases, they can even cause a breakdown in relationships. By managing expectations realistically, you minimize the risk of these negative emotions and foster harmony in your interactions.

When you consistently meet expectations, it builds trust and reliability. When people know they can depend on you, it strengthens the bond and credibility in the relationship. This trust forms the foundation for strong, resilient relationships.

The mantra is to understand the importance of managing expectations and recognize their direct impact on our relationships. Strive to meet the constantly evolving expectations to maintain healthy, happy, and long-lasting relationships.

Mantra 10: Be Mindful That Our Expectations Can Place Pressure on Others

Our expectations may sometimes create pressure in others. High or specific expectations can lead to a sense of obligation or stress for those trying to meet them. This pressure might create other demons like anxiety, decreased performance, or strained relationships.

Ensure that your expectations are achievable and clearly communicated, considering others' abilities and circumstances, and foster an environment where others feel comfortable expressing concerns or limitations regarding your expectations.

Avoid unrealistic demands. High or unrealistic expectations can lead to stress and feelings of inadequacy.

Keep your expectations balanced. Understand that rigid professional and personal expectations can lead to burnout and decreased satisfaction.

Give others the freedom to fulfill your expectations and avoid micromanaging. Excessive control can be demotivating and lead to frustration.

Be mindful of the emotional burden your expectations may place on others. Expectations related to emotional support can pressure others to act or respond in ways that align with your expectations, even if it conflicts with their own feelings or needs.

Avoid comparisons. Comparing others to high standards can create a sense of competition and stress.

Address implicit expectations by making unspoken expectations clear to avoid confusion and frustration.

Encourage independence by allowing others to develop self-confidence without overly seeking your validation while fulfilling your expectations.

The mantra is to set realistic, achievable expectations, communicate them clearly, and maintain mutual respect and understanding in order to avoid creating pressure in others. Encourage open dialogue and be receptive to feedback, ensuring your expectations are considerate of others' capabilities and circumstances.

CHAPTER 4

Comparison: The Demon of Evaluation

We all have used comparison in one way or another, and it's unlikely that any of us have escaped the grasp of the comparison demon, often in more ways than we can imagine. The concept of comparison is deeply ingrained in human nature, and regardless of where we are or what we're doing, comparison is present. In fact, it has become an integral part of our lives, influencing almost everything we do.

Our perspective plays a significant role in determining whether a comparison is harmful or not. For instance, we can either feel jealous from a comparison or use it as inspiration; it all depends on our perspective.

Some comparisons, even when intended for good, can have negative side effects. A common example is using comparison to teach children lessons. While the intention might be good, such comparisons can often make children feel bad and leave lasting emotional scars in them.

Comparisons play a major role in our lives, as many of our decisions and actions are based on them. When these comparisons are flawed, they can lead to wrong actions and decisions. Many comparisons result in emotional harm or feelings of low self-esteem, and quite often hurt those closest to us.

Depending on which side of the comparison you are on, you can either be the source of this demon or its victim, and in the case of self-comparison, you play both roles. You might also be an observer, witnessing others haunted by this demon, where you're not directly affected but still see the negative impact on others.

Regardless of our thoughts on this demon, the fact remains that comparison is here to stay. We will continue to compare and be compared. Let's delve deeper into the world of this demon to understand it better.

Comparison in All of Our Worlds

This demon has a presence in all of our worlds and is a pervasive aspect of human experience, infiltrating various facets of our lives across different worlds—personal, social, professional, internal and even fabricated. This demon, as we might call it, has a way of shaping our perceptions, behaviors, and emotions in profound ways.

In the Personal World

In our personal lives, comparison often manifests in the form of sibling rivalry. Parents, sometimes unintentionally, might compare the achievements or behaviors of one child to another, fostering feelings of inadequacy or competition. This can lead to a lifelong struggle with self-esteem and self-worth.

In the Social World

In the world of material possessions and societal standards, comparison plays a significant role. The value we place on objects, status, and success is often relative to what others have.

Among friends and peers, comparison is a common social phenomena. We might compare our accomplishments, appearances, relationships, or lifestyles with those of others. Social media exacerbates this by providing a constant stream of curated glimpses into the lives of others, often leading to feelings of envy and dissatisfaction.

In the Professional World

In the workplace, employees are frequently measured against each other. Performance reviews, promotions, and bonuses often depend on how one employee stacks up against their colleagues. This can create a highly competitive environment, which might drive productivity but also foster stress, resentment, and burnout.

In the Inner World

Internally, we often compare our past selves with our present selves. This can be a source of motivation, pushing us to grow and improve. However, it can also lead to frustration and regret if we feel we haven't lived up to our potential or if we idealize the past and undervalue our present achievements.

In the Fabricated World

In our fabricated world—the one constructed from our collective thoughts, values, and societal norms—comparison plays a significant role in shaping our perceptions and behaviors.

This demon is deeply ingrained in the fabric of our fabricated world, influencing our thoughts, behaviors, and self-perceptions. While it can drive ambition and achievement, it often leads to dissatisfaction, inauthentic living, and mental challenges

When We're the Source of the Comparison Demon

There are numerous scenarios where we introduce the comparison demon into the lives of others. This happens when we compare them with those we perceive as better, often doing so right in front of them. Sometimes, we do this intentionally, thinking it will motivate them to improve. Other times, we are completely unaware of the impact our words have.

In some cases, we deliberately use comparisons, especially during moments of anger, to bring others down and make them feel bad. Additionally, comparisons are sometimes used as a misguided attempt to push someone towards self-improvement. For example, a parent might compare their child's performance in school to that of a more successful peer, hoping to inspire better effort. However, this often backfires, leading to feelings of inadequacy and resentment.

On the other hand, quite often, we compare people without realizing the damage it can cause. These comparisons can occur in any setting—personal, social, or professional. When someone is not meeting our expectations, we might compare their performance to others in an attempt to motivate them. Unfortunately, this method usually does not yield the desired results and can even be counterproductive.

When we compare someone's shortcomings to others' strengths, our intention might be to highlight areas for improvement. However, this usually makes the person feel worse about themselves and can breed resentment towards those they are compared with.

What seems like a simple and well-intentioned comparison can be complex and damaging. These comparisons can plant seeds of self-doubt and animosity, both in the person being compared and in ourselves.

The key takeaway is that, knowingly or unknowingly, we often become the source of the comparison demon in others.

By becoming more aware of this tendency, we can take steps to reduce such harmful comparisons. Instead of comparing, we can focus on constructive feedback and encouragement that fosters growth and self-esteem without the negative side effects.

In later sections, I will elaborate more on a specific case: the impact of comparing children to their peers. For now, the essential point is to recognize our role in perpetuating the comparison demon and actively work towards minimizing its presence in our interactions.

When You're the Victim of the Comparison Demon

These are scenarios where you find yourself on the receiving end of comparisons, becoming a victim of this demon. Whether you realize it or not, you have likely been subjected to comparisons on numerous occasions throughout your life, across all aspects of your existence.

In the personal realm, you may have been compared to siblings and cousins by your parents or relatives. These comparisons can shape your self-esteem and sense of worth from a young age.

In the social sphere, comparisons often occur between you and your friends. Sometimes initiated by family members, and other times within your friend circle, these comparisons can affect your social dynamics and personal confidence.

The professional world is a highly competitive landscape where you are constantly compared and evaluated against your peers. Your progress and recognition are often contingent upon these comparisons, influencing your career trajectory and professional relationships.

The parameters of these comparisons vary from person to person, and since we all have unique attributes and circumstances, these comparisons are inherently biased, influenced by the preferences of those making them.

Even in your inner and fabricated worlds, comparison plays a role. Internally, you might compare your past and present selves or measure your achievements against societal standards. These comparisons can be pervasive and damaging, affecting your mental and emotional well-being.

In the professional world, comparisons are often explicit and expected, allowing you to prepare mentally. However, in other areas of life, you may be unaware of implicit comparisons being made by others. This lack of visibility can be particularly harmful, as you may not even realize why you feel diminished or undervalued.

Interestingly, the people who introduce the comparison demon into your life often have good intentions. They might believe that comparisons will motivate you to improve and reach your potential. Despite their intentions, these comparisons can make you feel humiliated and inadequate.

While being a victim of comparison can be painful, it's important to recognize that these situations can also offer valuable lessons. Instead of feeling bad, try to learn from the comparisons, viewing them as opportunities to identify and work on your weaknesses. Think of it as free tuition to improve in your weak areas.

Understanding the impact of being compared can also help you reflect on your behavior towards others. By empathizing with those you might have compared, you can identify and correct any mistakes you've made, fostering a more supportive and encouraging environment.

In conclusion, while the comparison demon can be a source of significant distress, it also holds the potential for personal growth if approached with the right mindset. Recognizing and addressing the negative aspects of comparisons, both as a victim and as a source, can lead to healthier, more positive interactions in all areas of life.

Self-Comparison

There's another scenario where we are both the source and the victim of our own comparisons, which we can call self-comparison. It's human nature to compare ourselves with others, but the outcome can be good, bad, or ugly depending on the context and our perspective.

Self-comparison can be beneficial when done constructively. For instance, comparing yourself with people you admire and aspire to be like can be motivating. This type of comparison can help you identify qualities and habits you want to develop, and guide you towards achieving your goals. Looking up to and comparing yourself with someone good can provide inspiration, as long as it doesn't lead to feelings of inadequacy or envy.

Now let me talk about some of the negative aspects of self-comparison.

Unfortunately, self-comparison often leads to negative outcomes. The parameters on which you can compare yourself to others are countless. You might excel in some areas, but there will always be people who are better in others. Accepting that you cannot be the best at everything is important.

A major problem with self-comparison is that we often compare our worst with others' best, leading to unfair and demoralizing conclusions. For a comparison to be fair, all relevant data points need to be considered, but in real life, it's nearly impossible to gather and evaluate all necessary information accurately.

Another issue is that self-comparison shifts your focus away from yourself to the person you are comparing yourself with. Instead of concentrating on how to improve your own life, you focus on how good others' lives seem to be.

In a professional setting, you might compare yourself

with successful peers whom you believe are less deserving of their success. You may think they took shortcuts or got lucky. However, since you can't account for all factors that contributed to their success, such comparisons are often based on incomplete information and can be misleading.

Let me walk you through this example where you and a colleague are up for a promotion, and despite working hard and believing you are the better candidate, your colleague gets promoted.

Your initial reaction might be shock and disbelief, rooted in your perception that you were the better choice. To calm yourself, you analyze how your colleague could have been promoted over you. It's important to acknowledge that your assumptions about your own suitability might not align with the reality of the decision-making process.

The criteria for the promotion could have been different from what you anticipated. While you focused on impressing in certain areas, your colleague might have excelled in areas more valued by your manager.

Also, remembering your friendship with your colleague is crucial here. You need to understand that their success does not diminish your worth. While it's natural to feel disappointed, try to celebrate their achievement genuinely. Maintaining a positive relationship is important, and your supportive actions can eventually rebuild trust if it was strained by the promotion decision.

Self-comparison extends beyond professional scenarios into all aspects of life. The key is to focus on yourself rather than those you are comparing yourself with. Recognize your strengths and areas for improvement, and use self-comparison as a tool for personal growth rather than a source of negativity.

While self-comparison can sometimes be demoralizing, it can also be a powerful tool for personal development if approached correctly. Focusing on your own journey and using comparisons to inspire rather than discourage can lead to positive outcomes. Understanding both the benefits and pitfalls of self-comparison allows you to use it constructively and avoid the traps of envy and inadequacy.

A Special Case: Where We Make Our Kids Victims of Our Comparison

Though I've mentioned this specific scenario earlier in this chapter, I want to over emphasize on this as this is a super important topic involving the wellbeing of the most important people in our lives, our kids, whom we all love the most.

There is no doubt in this that we want our kids to be successful, and in fact there is a remote section in our heart somewhere that desires them to be the best in whatever they do, and despite understanding and acknowledging that it's not practically possible, we still have this subtle desire.

Also it's not very uncommon for us parents to look at our kids through our own lenses, and inadvertently we push them to fulfill our own unfulfilled desires.

We feel bad when they do not perform well, and we feel more bad when we see their peers or other kids their age are performing better than them.

And these are the situations where we are most vulnerable to being attacked by the comparison demon, and under the influence of this demon we start doing a comparison between our kids and their friends, right in front of them.

And soon you'll admit that despite its good intentions, this approach of comparing your kids with their friends and telling them to improve is the worst possible way of using comparison to deliver a message.

Both you as well as your kids become the victims of many demons spawning as a result of your comparison.

On one hand, this demon makes us feel bad and helpless about this whole situation, as we keep wondering about what in the world we can do to fix this. This demon is aware of our heart's desires, and it uses this knowledge to devour our happiness by giving us false hopes that by doing such comparisons the kids will get better.

And on the other hand, this demon has a very negative effect on our kids when we compare them with their better performing friends right in front of them. Our intent is not for them to feel bad, but to get better by observing what their friends do.

But this is just our side of the story, and there are facts in this story that we never get to see, that only our kids see and suffer from.

The fact is that with our limited exposure to our kid's friends we only see their good sides, while our kids know about their dark sides as well, and as a result they get frustrated as you only know half the story of their "good behaving" friends and are unwilling to hear the rest from them.

Also the friends of your kids will display their best behavior when they're in front of you, so what your kids know about them, you'll never know, and probably you're kids can't tell you that either, and feel suffocated by unable to reveal that.

When we bring up such a comparison, our message is never delivered the way we want to, as our kids will bring up some of the dark sides of their friends in their defense, with the conversation resulting in a confrontation rather than them getting your message.

The harsh truth is that though your intentions as parent are right and best for your kids, and while you hate these comparisons yourself, you still engage in them with a hope that one day your kids will understand you and improve their habits, but that doesn't happen. In fact the opposite happens and kids stop listening to you.

Our Intentions and Desires

There is no doubt that we want our kids to be successful, and deep down, we desire them to excel in everything they do. Despite knowing it's not practically possible, this subtle desire persists within us. As parents, we often see our kids through our own lenses, sometimes pushing them to fulfill our own unfulfilled dreams and desires.

The Vulnerability to Comparison

We feel disappointed when our kids do not perform well, and we feel even worse when we see their peers excelling. These are the moments when we are most vulnerable to the comparison demon, and under its influence, we start comparing our kids to their friends, often right in front of them. Despite our good intentions, this approach is one of the worst ways to deliver our message.

The Impact on Parents and Kids

Both parents and kids become victims of various demons spawned as a result of these comparisons. For parents, this demon amplifies feelings of frustration and helplessness, as we struggle to find ways to help our kids improve. The comparison demon exploits our desires, giving us false hopes that these comparisons will motivate our kids to get better.

Another way the comparison demon haunts parents is when they compare their parenting to others and feel awful and ashamed when they see other parents doing so much more for their children. This can give rise to several demons, including guilt, low self-worth, and worry.

For kids, being compared to their better-performing peers right in front of them can have very negative effects. Our intention is not to make them feel bad but to encourage them to observe and learn from their friends. However, this is only our side of the story.

The Kids' Perspective

From the kids' perspective, things look different. With their closer and more comprehensive view of their friends, they know their peers' flaws and imperfections, which parents often do not see. When kids hear comparisons, they feel frustrated because they know their friends' "good behavior" is only half the story, and parents are unwilling to hear the rest.

Furthermore, kids' friends often display their best behavior in front of adults. This means parents are only seeing a polished version, while kids see the full picture and feel suffocated by the inability to reveal this truth.

The Consequences of This Comparison

When we compare our kids to their friends, the message we intend to deliver is seldom received as we hope. Instead of motivating improvement, it often leads to defensiveness, with kids pointing out their friends' faults, turning the conversation into a confrontation. This leads to frustration on both sides.

The Harsh Truth

Although our intentions as parents are right and meant for the best, and despite our dislike for these comparisons, we still engage in them, hoping our kids will understand and improve. Unfortunately, this rarely happens. Instead, kids often stop listening, feeling misunderstood and demoralized.

Conclusion

In conclusion, while our intentions in comparing our kids to their peers might be well-meaning, the approach is flawed and counterproductive. It's essential to find more positive and constructive ways to encourage our children, focusing on their individual strengths and fostering open, supportive communication. Understanding and addressing the unique needs and perspectives of our kids can help nurture their growth without the negative impact of comparison.

The Good Side of Comparison

While this demon is responsible for many negative aspects of our lives, it also has several benefits that make it a valuable tool and worthy of its presence in our system. When used wisely, comparison can help us make better decisions and improve ourselves.

Comparison is essential when we need to select from multiple options, such as buying a car, house, clothing, or choosing an education path. It helps us evaluate and choose the best option among many, ensuring we make informed decisions. In this context, comparison is a beneficial presence in our lives.

When we use comparison to learn and grow, it serves a positive purpose. Comparing ourselves with others who are more successful or happier can highlight areas where we can improve. This constructive comparison motivates us to work on our shortcomings and strive for betterment.

Comparison helps us filter out bad options, allowing us to focus on the best choices available. As long as we use comparison to identify and eliminate less favorable options, it serves as a useful tool in our decision-making process.

In the professional world, comparison is crucial for progress. Our growth and achievements often depend on how we compare against our peers. By understanding our strengths and weaknesses in comparison to others, we can identify areas for improvement and set goals for professional development.

Even negative comparisons can have positive outcomes. While they might initially make us feel bad, they can also provide valuable insights that we wouldn't have gained otherwise. By reflecting on these comparisons, we can discover areas for improvement and take steps to enhance our lives.

In conclusion, comparison has a good side that can significantly benefit us when used appropriately. It aids in decision-making, facilitates learning and growth, supports professional development, and helps us filter out bad options. By focusing on the positive aspects of comparison and using it constructively, we can harness its potential to improve our lives. The key is to use comparison wisely and avoid letting it lead to feelings of inadequacy or resentment.

Mantras for Dealing With the Comparison Demon

Now, let's explore a few mantras to help you deal with the comparison demon. By embracing these mantras, you can better manage the urge to compare, turning it into an opportunity for growth and self-improvement.

Mantra 1: Don't Compare Your Circumstances with Those of Others

It's common for people to compare their circumstances with those they perceive as happier and more successful, often blaming their own circumstances for their failures. However, the same circumstances that work for one person may not work for another.

Avoid comparing your circumstances with those of others, as each person's life journey is unique, shaped by individual experiences, opportunities, and challenges. Here are a few reasons why such comparisons can be unproductive and how to shift your perspective.

Comparing your circumstances to others' overlooks the unique experiences and challenges that have shaped each person's journey.

What you see is often just a highlight reel, as when comparing circumstances, you only see what's visible or known to you. There may be hidden factors at play, making comparisons unreliable. Everyone has struggles and setbacks that are not always visible.

Compare yourself to who you were yesterday, not to who someone else is today, and recognize the unique challenges you have faced and overcome, as these experiences have made you who you are and contributed to your personal growth.

Be grateful for your journey and experiences, and what they have taught you. Concentrate on your own strengths and celebrate your achievements without comparing them to others. This can help shift your focus from comparison to contentment.

Use others' achievements as inspiration rather than a basis for comparison. Let their successes motivate you to pursue your own dreams without feeling inadequate.

The mantra is that by shifting your focus from comparing your circumstances to others' and instead embracing your unique journey, you can foster a healthier and more positive outlook on life. Remember, your path is your own, and it is shaped by your unique experiences and growth.

Mantra 2: Be Aware of Comparisons That Are Targeted to Make You Feel Bad

In our daily lives, comparisons are inevitable. However, some comparisons are intentionally or unintentionally designed to make us feel bad about ourselves. Being aware of these types of comparisons can help protect your self-esteem and mental well-being.

Some people might compare you to others with the intent to belittle you or boost their own ego. Recognize when someone is making comparisons to put you down rather than to provide constructive feedback.

Quite often, comparisons can be used as a manipulation tool, especially in toxic relationships or competitive environments. Be cautious of comparisons that seem to have an ulterior motive.

Constantly being compared to others, especially in a negative light, can erode your self-esteem and self-worth. It's important to recognize when these comparisons are affecting your confidence.

Negative comparisons can demotivate you, making you feel like your efforts are worthless. Instead of inspiring improvement, they can lead to feelings of hopelessness and frustration.

Protecting yourself from these harmful comparisons is crucial as persistent exposure to them can spawn demons like anxiety and depression in your system.

When faced with a negative comparison, try to focus on what you have accomplished rather than what you lack.

It's important to set boundaries with people who frequently make harmful comparisons. Communicate clearly that such comparisons are not helpful and are affecting you.

The mantra is to be aware of comparisons that are targeted to make you feel bad, as it is essential for protecting your self-esteem and mental health. Recognize harmful intentions, understand their impact, and protect yourself from them.

Mantra 3: Don't Let Comparisons with the Successful and Famous Go to Your Head

By now, you must recognize that you'll be compared to all sorts of people, including famous and successful individuals.

These comparisons might be based on your looks, style, habits, voice, and various other traits.

It's natural to feel happy when you're compared to someone successful and famous, and there's nothing wrong with that—it's a normal human reaction. However, problems arise when you start taking such comparisons too seriously and begin to assume you're the person you're being compared to.

The harsh truth is that these comparisons only highlight superficial similarities between you and the other person; they don't transform you into that individual.

The mantra is to keep your emotions in balance when being compared to someone super famous and successful. While it's great to feel good from such comparisons, don't let it go to your head by taking it too seriously. Stay grounded and focus on your unique personality.

Mantra 4: You Will Always Be Compared

The reality is that comparison is a never-ending process in life, and there's no escaping it. Whether in your personal life, professional career, or social circles, you will always be measured against others.

As you navigate your life, you'll repeatedly find yourself being compared to others, often as part of someone else's decision-making process. This is an inevitable part of the human experience.

Moreover, realistically speaking, it's impossible to emerge as the best in all these comparisons, no matter how you assess yourself. As the criteria for comparison shift, so will the outcomes. For example, you might come out better in comparison to someone at one point, but if compared with the same person again later, you might find yourself coming up short.

For example, in the personal realm, being an only child

might shield you from direct comparison initially. But the moment you have a sibling, comparisons will naturally arise, continuing throughout your life. In the professional world, you might excel in your field or on a specific project, but eventually, someone new might come along who is better, prompting comparisons. Socially, you'll be compared with friends as you explore new experiences together.

The problem arises when you assume that the outcome of a comparison is permanent and become too comfortable with it. When the situation changes, it can lead to discomfort or even distress.

It's crucial to understand that comparisons are fleeting, and they will happen continuously. You might be the best today, but tomorrow, someone better might emerge, or new standards might be set that you can't meet.

The mantra is to accept that comparisons are an inevitable part of life, and you'll encounter them throughout your journey. Understand that the results of any comparison are temporary and will soon be replaced by others as new comparisons arise. Therefore, don't become too attached to any specific outcomes—be prepared to adapt and embrace change. Above all, don't let these comparisons define your worth or limit your growth.

Mantra 5: Don't Expect Every Comparison to Yield Clear Results

When using comparison as a tool, we often aim to make final choices by comparing two or more things. However, reality doesn't always align with this expectation.

When using comparison as a tool, we often aim to make final choices by comparing two or more things. However, reality doesn't always align with this expectation. Comparisons can be imperfect and may not account for all variables, making it important to consider the broader context and individual nuances.

Comparison is a useful tool, but it's not a silver bullet to eliminate all confusion in our lives. Often, the options we are comparing are so closely matched that the results are inconclusive, making it difficult to identify which ones to eliminate.

Additionally, we may sometimes use incorrect or incomplete parameters for the comparison, leading to inaccurate results. This can leave us more confused than before, causing us to regret starting the comparison in the first place.

At times, comparison can become a burden, making us wish we had never begun the process. The plethora of options can make life difficult by forcing us to make hard choices.

The mantra is not to expect every comparison to yield clear results that make decision-making easy. Instead, be prepared for the possibility of confusion as a result of comparisons. You may need to evaluate trade-offs and accept that not all comparisons will lead to a straightforward conclusion.

Mantra 6: Avoid the Pitfalls of Comparing Past and Present

The past undeniably influences our present comparisons, whether it was a period of success or difficulty. We often measure our current self against our past, assessing our progress or lack thereof. This can be particularly harmful when our past was more favorable, leading us to feel a sense of decline.

When our past was better than our present, comparing the two can make us feel as if we are on a downward spiral. This perception of degradation can give rise to various demons in our system such as worry, anger, and frustration. These feelings can be overwhelming, making it hard to appreciate the positive aspects of our current situation.

Dwelling on past successes can create a sense of complacency, where we might feel that our best days are behind us. This mindset can prevent us from striving for new achievements and growing beyond our past.

Similarly, we sometimes remain stuck in our past, especially when it involves negative experiences. We continuously compare those situations to our present, anxiously evaluating the potential for recurrence.

Bad experiences from the past can cast a long shadow over our present. We may live in constant fear of those negative events recurring, leading to anxiety and a diminished quality of life. This fear can paralyze us, preventing us from taking risks and embracing new opportunities.

This constant comparison led by our fear can overshadow our current life, and it's crucial to realize that comparing the past with the present is often an unfair and unproductive exercise.

The circumstances surrounding our past and present are rarely identical. Life is constantly changing, and so are the variables that affect our experiences. What worked or didn't work in the past may not have the same outcome today due to different contexts, people, and environments.

Also, we are not the same individuals we were in the past. Every experience, whether good or bad, contributes to our growth and development. Comparing our current self to our past self fails to acknowledge the growth and learning that have occurred in the interim.

Nostalgia can often cloud our memories, making the past seem rosier than it actually was. This can lead to unrealistic expectations and unnecessary disappointment when our present does not measure up to an idealized version of the past.

To live a fulfilling life, it is essential to focus on the present and future rather than getting caught up in past comparisons, and appreciate your current experiences without the burden of past comparisons.

The mantra is to understand that comparing the past to the present is like comparing apples to oranges. Not only are the past and present different, but their circumstances are different as well. By recognizing this, we can avoid the pitfalls of unnecessary comparison and focus on the unique aspects of our current journey.

Mantra 7: Accept the Inevitability of Comparisons in Every Aspect of Life

Regardless of where you are, comparisons are inevitable, and you'll constantly be measured against others.

In the professional world, comparison is ingrained in your career. Your progression depends on how you stand out, both implicitly and explicitly. New employees bring fresh comparisons, and past achievements don't guarantee future success. The workforce is a continuous cat-and-mouse game of staying ahead.

In the social realm, comparisons with friends are unavoidable due to looks, behavior, achievements, and social etiquette. Social media amplifies these comparisons, often leading to feelings of inadequacy. Dynamics within friend groups can lead to unspoken comparisons about success, popularity, or likability.

In your personal life, you will be compared to your siblings in terms of similarities and differences. Birth order and gender can also influence these comparisons, shaping expectations and perceptions within the family. Parents and relatives might compare siblings academically, creating a competitive environment.

In your inner world, you'll gauge your progress by comparing yourself with your own past. Though this is not entirely a valid comparison—as you and your past self are different personalities with unique challenges and circumstances—it still holds merit. Your past has shaped your current self, so learning from it is not a bad idea.

Sports and movies are fields where comparison is the very essence of the game. Athletes and actors are constantly compared to their peers and predecessors.

The mantra is to recognize that comparisons are inevitable and learn to accept them. Understanding this will help you better prepare for this facet of life. View comparisons as opportunities for growth rather than threats, using them to identify areas for improvement. By acknowledging the inevitability of comparison and adopting a constructive approach, you can navigate its challenges and use it as a tool for personal and professional development.

Mantra 8: Don't Compare Yourself to People Who've Achieved Less Just to Feel Content

Often, comparing ourselves to those we perceive as more successful leaves us feeling envious and inadequate. As a countermeasure, we might be tempted to compare ourselves to those who are less accomplished or fortunate to feel better about our own situation. While this may provide temporary relief, it is neither healthy nor constructive.

Comparing yourself to those who have achieved less creates a false sense of contentment. You might feel better momentarily, but this does not address your true desires or goals. It's akin to running away from what you truly want and prematurely accepting defeat.

By pretending to be content, you miss out on the motivation and the chance to achieve what your heart desires. Continually comparing downwards risks accepting mediocrity, which can prevent you from reaching your full potential and achieving your genuine aspirations.

Feeling superior to someone less accomplished does not lead to actual self-improvement. It can stagnate your personal and professional growth, as it encourages a mindset of complacency.

Look at those who have achieved what you aspire to, and let their success inspire and motivate you, using their achievements as benchmarks for your own goals.

Reflect on what truly makes you envious, as this feeling often indicates what you genuinely want to achieve.

The mantra is that while there are exceptions, most of the time, what makes you envious is what you want to achieve. Comparison validates that feeling by making you witness a live example of your desires. Therefore, comparing yourself to those who have achieved less, just to feel better, is counterproductive. It diverts you from your true goals and potential. Instead, use comparisons as tools for inspiration and growth, helping you achieve your true aspirations.

Mantra 9: Recognize That Only a Few Comparisons Are Truly Apples to Apples

We use comparisons in nearly everything, but not all comparisons are perfectly valid. While apples-to-apples comparisons might be possible in experimental settings, achieving such perfection in real life is almost impossible.

For a comparison to be perfectly valid and apples-to-apples, an ideal environment and complete information are necessary. This includes both visible factors and hidden ones. In real life, we seldom have access to all relevant information.

Also many comparisons involve subjective judgments influenced by biases, perspectives, and emotions, which can skew results.

Each person has unique circumstances, experiences, and backgrounds, making accurate comparisons impossible.

Additionally, personal strengths and weaknesses vary widely, making comparisons unfair and inaccurate.

Furthermore, we often lack full information about others' challenges and advantages, leading to misleading conclusions.

When comparisons make us feel bad or inadequate, it's important to remember their limited validity. Basing our self-worth on such comparisons can lead to negative emotions and diminished self-esteem.

The mantra is to understand that most comparisons are only partially valid. Therefore, placing complete trust in them and feeling bad as a result doesn't make sense. Recognizing their inherent limitations helps maintain a balanced perspective, allowing us to focus on our unique paths and growth.

Mantra 10: Develop Gratitude to Shift Your Focus from What You Lack to What You Have

When you compare yourself to others, it's easy to focus on what you feel is missing in your life. However, those same comparisons can also shed light on what you already possess. The key is to use this insight constructively. Gratitude serves as a powerful tool for redirecting your attention from what you lack to what you already have. By acknowledging your blessings and accomplishments, you can counterbalance the feelings of inadequacy that often arise when comparing yourself to others.

When comparisons arise, consciously shifting your focus to your existing strengths and successes can diminish the impact of negative emotions. In fact, gratitude doesn't need to be triggered by comparison at all; it can begin with simply recognizing the value in your own experiences and achievements. This shift in perspective may even reduce the desire to engage in comparisons in the first place.

Moreover, not all of life's valuable accomplishments are material. Personal growth, lessons learned, and moments of happiness are just as meaningful as any tangible success. Embrace the full spectrum of your journey, including the challenges, as they are crucial in shaping your growth and resilience.

Instead of fixating on others' success, focus on your unique strengths and the progress you've made. Setting healthy boundaries can also help you avoid excessive comparisons, which often lead to stress and dissatisfaction.

The essence of this mantra is understanding that gratitude for your journey—with all its highs and lows—enables you to appreciate every step. By focusing on what you have achieved and the value in your experiences, you can minimize the negative effects of comparisons and cultivate a deeper sense of fulfillment.

CHAPTER 5

Worry: The Demon Fueling Anxiety with Future Fears

I t'll not be an overstatement to say that there'll hardly be anyone in this world who has not become a victim of this demon. In today's world, people are constantly worried about something or someone. Worry is one of the most insidious demons, feeding on our insecurities and fears of the unknown, which are all too common in our lives today.

Rarely will there be a moment when everything in life is perfect. There will always be things that bother us, and this demon thrives on these disturbances. Ironically, worry often frightens us about things that haven't even happened, convincing us they will, despite the possibility that they may never occur.

One interesting thing about worry is that this demon grows as we grow. As infants, we are unaware of worries. Babies have no concept of possession and thus no worry about losing anything. As children, we start to value things and worry about losing them, like favorite toys. As students, we worry about education and the future. When we start working, job and career worries take over.

As single adults, we worry about ourselves and our existing

family members. Marriage adds a spouse to our worries, followed by children and the entire family's wellbeing. With each stage of life, we accumulate more possessions and responsibilities, leading to more worries about losing them.

This phenomenon of increasing worries continues as we progress through life's journey.

Worry operates by projecting problematic situations and keeping us under constant stress about their potential occurrence. Interestingly enough, we humans seem to be unable to live without worry. When we have no immediate worries, we often find new ones.

When we have nothing, we worry about acquiring possessions. Once we start acquiring them, we worry about losing them. The worry of having nothing is often less intense than the worry of losing hard-earned possessions, to which we become deeply attached.

Worry takes many forms and seizes countless opportunities to disturb our peace in today's complex world. This demon manifests in various ways, each representing a different kind of worry. Recognizing this can help us manage and deal with its impact on our lives.

Let's explore a few of them below.

Self-Worries: Worries About Our Own Self

There's a form of worry where we become the subject of our own concerns, often referred to as self-worry. This occurs when we worry about the bad things happening to us or the potential for such events in the future.

Self-worry highlights potential negative outcomes, and how we react to these scenarios is crucial. We can either succumb to depression or accept life as it comes, preparing ourselves to deal with unwanted situations.

Modern life is filled with complexities, providing plenty

of reasons for self-worry. While most self-worries are detrimental, not all of them are entirely bad. In fact, some self-worries can be beneficial.

For example, worrying about gaining weight, increasing blood sugar levels, getting lower grades, or losing hair are forms of self-worry that can be positive. Although these concerns highlight negative possibilities, worrying about them can motivate us to take proactive steps to improve our situation, provided we don't let the worry consume us.

On the other hand, there are self-worries that fall into the negative category, such as fearing job loss while currently stable, dreading failure before attempting something, or worrying about past events repeating themselves. These worries are problematic because they are open-ended with no certainty of occurrence. They might happen or they might not.

While these worries can prompt us to prepare for worst-case scenarios, they should not be assumed to be inevitable outcomes. Instead, consider them as possible outcomes and be ready to face them if they do occur.

Self-worry can motivate us to go the extra mile to handle uncertainties and unwanted outcomes. However, the downside is that self-worry often creates disturbances in our lives. It's impossible to address every problem this demon presents, leaving us in a state where we recognize problems but feel powerless to solve them, leading to frustration and helplessness.

In summary, while self-worry can offer a chance to prepare for the worst and motivate us to take action, it often ends up being more harmful than helpful. Balancing these worries and focusing on constructive responses is key to managing self-worry effectively.

Worries About Others

In this form, our near and dear ones become the subjects of our worries. Our lives are full of situations that lead us to constantly worry about them, such as their health, well-being, school grades, finances, and countless other aspects of their lives. We worry about their losses, failures, and pains, and anything bad that can happen to them. This is natural and perfectly normal, stemming from the care and responsibilities we feel for them.

However, one thing we often overlook is that our worries about others are mostly based on our own perceptions, which may not always be accurate. Instead of worrying based on our assumptions, we should try to understand if they truly need help and offer assistance in the way they want, not the way we think is best.

A positive aspect of this form of worry is that it often compensates for the lack of self-worry in others, reducing their risk exposure. Some people might not worry about certain things, making them vulnerable. Our concern for them can cover these gaps.

On the downside, while we can address the problems we perceive, there will be many issues in their lives we may never know about, leaving them exposed. Additionally, everyone must learn to identify and manage their own issues, as there will be times when help is not available.

While worrying about others can be beneficial, it can also create disturbances in both our lives and the lives of those we worry about. Sometimes, our worries become burdens for the people we care about, who might prefer to handle their issues independently and on their own timeline.

Worrying about others often reveals several problematic situations. When we see our loved ones in trouble and cannot find solutions, it leaves us feeling helpless and frustrated. This state of concern, while well-intentioned, can sometimes lead to more stress for everyone involved.

Worries About the Past, Present and Future

Worrying about the past, present, and future is quite a common theme in the world of this demon, covering our entire life spectrum and providing countless opportunities for it to haunt us. A saying that comes to my mind is quite relevant here: "Worrying doesn't take away tomorrow's troubles; it takes away today's peace."

We often worry about everything happening in our everyday lives. During good times, instead of fully enjoying the moment, we worry about when it might end. During bad times, instead of focusing on overcoming the situation, we worry about the possibility that it might never improve. Regardless of our situation, this demon finds a way to disturb our peace.

The worst thing about this demon is that it spoils our present moments by reminding us of potential future problems or past bad experiences.

When it comes to the past, we worry that if something bad happened before, it might happen again. This demon brings up bad memories and shows us the possibility of them repeating, haunting us with past experiences, whether our own or others'.

For the future, we worry about many possible events and want to be prepared for them, which is why the entire insurance industry exists. While preparing for future insecurities is crucial, we often overdo it under the influence of our worries. Many people I know are victims of this worry, constantly anxious about the future, losing the enjoyable moments of the present, and forgetting the good times they had in the past.

It's important not to worry too much about unfavorable things that haven't happened yet. Think about them and prepare for them, but don't start believing they are inevitable.

The best approach is to reach a mental state where we are not bothered by our past or future and can live freely in the present.

The biggest problem with worrying about the past, present, and future is that it creates chaos within us when we mix things from three different states of time that can never coexist. The present only comes into being after the past has gone, and it lasts only until the future arrives.

What-If: Another Face of This Demon

This demon often torments us by making us dwell on all kinds of "what-if" scenarios, drawing our attention to numerous bad things that could happen, even those with a very remote chance. Though "what-if" isn't limited to the future, this demon frequently haunts us by highlighting future "what-if" scenarios.

In the context of worry, "what-if" allows us to explore all possible scenarios that could result in unwanted outcomes and potential bad things that might happen in the future, so we can prepare to deal with them proactively. However, instead of viewing these as mere possibilities, we start believing they will definitely happen, which fuels our anxiety.

In other words, using "what-if" can be like finding reasons to worry, even when there are none. Sometimes it seems we engage in this for some kind of perverse pleasure, getting surrounded and overwhelmed by worries.

Not all "what-if" scenarios are baseless and some do originate from real events. However, they are still projections with only a certain percentage of truth in them. We shouldn't over-worry about scenarios with a very remote chance of happening, as they might never occur. Instead, we should focus on more pressing ones.

Here's an interesting "what-if" story I want to share: a

conversation I had with my daughter when she was a toddler a few years ago.

One day, I was sitting with my 8-year-old daughter during a thunderstorm. The lightning and thunder were loud and frightening, and she was very scared. Usually, we used to divert her attention to make her comfortable, but that day I decided to talk with her about it. Here's a snippet of our conversation:

Me: "Are you scared?"

Her: "Yes, Daddy, I'm very scared."

Me: "And why are you scared?"

Her: "I'm very scared of thunder and lightning. What if the electricity goes out and it's all dark?"

Me: "Oh yes, that's not a good thing. But you have Daddy and Mommy next to you, and we have flashlights in case of an electricity failure, right?"

Her: "That's correct, but I'm still scared."

Me: "I understand why you're scared. But can you make the thunder and lightning stop?"

Her: "No, Daddy, I can't."

Me: "Exactly. If you can't stop them, they'll do what they can, and you can't stop that either, right?"

Her: "Correct, Daddy."

Me: "But you can stay safe by staying away from the windows, unplugging devices, not taking showers, and keeping flashlights ready, right?"

Her: "That's correct, Daddy."

Me: "Then don't worry about the thunder and lightning. Take precautions and do what makes you feel better. Don't worry about the electricity going out; just be prepared."

Her: "I get that, Daddy."

Me: "Great! So, you're not scared of thunder and lightning anymore?"

Her: "Well, just a little, but I feel better thinking this way."

This conversation has a message that can ease many "what-if" worries. There are countless "what-if" scenarios that haunt us with their potential to become reality. This demon convinces us that our imaginations might materialize anytime, and if we're not prepared, we'll suffer.

For those who want to enjoy today over worrying about tomorrow, this demon creates a significant obstruction, making them constantly worried about possible future issues. It highlights various paths of failure in anything we attempt, leveraging the fact that success is never guaranteed and uncertainties are always present.

Despite its negative aspects, the "what-if" demon can offer several benefits. It acts like a friend warning us of possible failures before we start anything. Understanding these possibilities has merit, but focusing solely on them can be demotivating.

"What-if" is a tool to brainstorm potential issues and develop alternative plans if Plan A has uncertainties. Using it to prepare for unwanted or unanticipated events is good, as long as we don't overdo it. By thinking about possible problem situations, we can better prepare to face them if they happen.

In short, it's like insurance that covers us during bad times. While there are many examples of the good side of this demon, they are few compared to the bad ones. Although the "what-if" demon helps us prepare for eventualities, it's impossible to prepare for every potential problem. Some unresolved "what-if" issues will always linger, creating disturbances. Therefore, it's crucial to draw a line, stop overthinking, and move forward with some hope. We can never cover all our exposures raised by the "what-if."

The Good Side of Worry

The worry demon, by its basic nature, is often perceived as negative. However, much like other demons discussed in this book, worry has some redeeming traits that make it valuable and worthy to be present in our system.

In its beneficial form, worry acts as a catalyst for analysis and the creation of action plans to address our concerns. Without worry, we might not engage in the necessary analysis or develop strategies to handle potential problems. This could lead to chaotic situations where we are unprepared and forced to improvise solutions on the spot.

One positive aspect of this demon is its ability to make us aware of problematic situations and dark spots. It alerts us to the severity of our current or potential future circumstances, prompting us to find ways to extricate ourselves. Without worry, we might remain oblivious to these challenges and lack the motivation to develop solutions.

Another advantage of worry is that it reminds us that even during good times, things can change unexpectedly. This prevents us from becoming too complacent and losing our readiness to handle disruptions that might catch us off guard.

Worry also supports us during difficult times. The action plans it encouraged us to create in anticipation of trouble can help us navigate through challenging periods. Additionally, when we are already in a bad situation, worry helps us comprehend our predicament and think of ways to improve it.

Moreover, worry motivates us to take necessary actions. Concern for others can lead us to help reduce their risks, especially if they are not sufficiently worried about their own situations, essentially covering for their lack of self-concern.

Just as we explored the benefits of the "what-if" side of this demon, we can see that despite its inherently negative nature, worry has significant merits.

In conclusion, while worry may be a demon at its core, its positive traits make it a valuable presence in our lives.

Mantras for Dealing With the Worry Demon

And now let's go over a few mantras for dealing with the worry demon. By adopting these mantras, you can transform the worry demon from a hindrance into a helpful guide, leading to a more balanced and proactive approach to life's challenges.

Mantra 1: Don't Attempt to Handle All of Your Worries on Your Own

We all carry various worries in our system, and while we can manage some, others can leave us stumped. The key is not to handle all your worries alone; instead, share them with trusted individuals who might be able to help.

The goal is to seek assistance by sharing your concerns with people who might suggest solutions you haven't thought of. Often, others can offer valuable insights or experiences that may be helpful to you.

Also two minds are better than one, and collaborating with others can lead to better problem-solving. Sometimes, a fresh perspective is all it takes to find a solution.

When worried about others, it's better to clarify misconceptions. Sharing your concerns with them can reveal that they are already addressing the issue, or that your worry is based on a misunderstanding.

Similarly, many worries stem from our own perceptions, which may not reflect reality. Doing a reality check by sharing these worries can help you see things more clearly.

You should follow a selective sharing for your worries.

Share only selective worries with a trusted few. Over-sharing can lead to being labeled as someone who "worries too much," which may diminish the support you receive.

Confide in a few trusted individuals who form your inner circle. These should be people you trust and who understand you well.

The mantra is to avoid tackling all your worries alone. Seek support from your trusted circle when you need help dealing with worries you can't manage by yourself. Bringing in outside help can make a significant difference in overcoming the worry demon.

Mantra 2: Visualize the Worst Possible Scenario and See if You Can Survive It

Worries can make our lives feel like a living hell, constantly showing us all the bad things that might happen. The best way to stay realistic is to plan for the best but be prepared for the worst.

Often, we worry that things might go wrong, even when everything is going perfectly and there's no sign of any trouble. This worry often stems from the fear of losing what we have, even if there's no concrete reason for it. During tough times, this feeling intensifies and can even keep you awake at night.

While worries can motivate you to prepare for the worst, unnecessary worries can ruin your present moments over irrelevant issues and should be avoided. There are many techniques to deal with such worries, and here's a method that helps me maintain my sanity.

Try to imagine the worst possible scenario, breaking things down to their lowest point. Next, think about what you would do to survive in that situation. Remember that extreme situations bring out extreme measures, and your survival instincts will naturally push you to work harder during pressing times, increasing the likelihood of your survival.

If you can survive the worst, you can definitely handle anything less severe. It won't be a smooth ride and certainly not something you'd choose if given a choice, but remember, it's not your choice but the circumstances that bring you there.

Once you gain confidence that you can survive the worst possible situations, do some preparation for that scenario and then stop worrying about it.

The mantra is to think a little pessimistically about the worst possible scenarios you might face and see if you can survive them. If you can, there's no need to worry much. If not, your worries reflect the reality that you need to work extra hard to prepare for handling bad situations.

Mantra 3: Worry About Your Actions, Not Their Results

This mantra, inspired by a famous lesson from the epic Bhagavad Gita, teaches us to focus on our actions rather than their results. This wisdom is so profound that I couldn't resist including it in my list of mantras. Here's my elaboration based on my understanding of this lesson.

"Action" in this context doesn't refer to a single act but a series of actions taken to achieve a result. Each action in this series has its own intermediate result, which feeds into the next action, continuing the cycle until the final result is reached.

Focusing on your actions instead of their results means concentrating solely on the series of actions and not their individual outcomes, whether they are intermediate successes or failures. This also includes not fixating on the final result.

When you focus on results, their success or failure begins to influence and sometimes dictate your actions, which is the opposite of what should happen. If you're preoccupied with the fear of failure, your motivation suffers. This fear affects your performance because you can't put in your best efforts without strong motivation. Additionally, any intermediate failures further demotivate you, making you believe that failure is inevitable.

The fear of failure often leads to creating a plan B. While it's good to have a fallback, it can weaken your commitment to plan A.

Similarly, if you're overly confident in your success, you might prematurely believe in that success and lose the fear of failure, weakening the efforts still needed to achieve it. Intermediate successes might make you complacent and overly confident about your final success.

However, when you focus solely on your actions, intermediate results won't negatively impact your actions. Instead, they fuel your efforts toward your end goal. By continuously working on your actions and learning from both intermediate failures and successes, you increase the likelihood of eventually achieving ultimate success.

The mantra is to start with your actions, not the results. Don't worry about intermediate failures or get too excited about intermediate wins. Instead, learn from them, apply these lessons to subsequent actions, and keep moving toward your final goals.

Mantra 4: Prioritize Your Worries Before You Start Acting on Them

At any given moment, your mind is likely filled with all kinds of worries. Some of these worries will be very important, others less pressing, and some may even be inconsequential. However, regardless of the category, unattended worries will continue to affect you negatively.

Moreover, worry is not the only challenge you'll be facing; in fact, you'll be battling multiple demons simultaneously.

When it comes to managing worries, the key is to prioritize them before taking action. This approach helps you focus on what's truly important and prevents you from becoming overwhelmed.

Start by listing all your worries, then prioritize them based on their impact and urgency.

High Impact, High Urgency: These worries, if not addressed immediately, could lead to significant consequences. They should be your top priority.

High Impact, Low Urgency: These worries are important but not immediate. Plan to address them after dealing with the urgent ones.

Low Impact, High Urgency: These are pressing but won't cause serious issues if left unattended. Handle them quickly, but don't spend too much time on them.

Low Impact, Low Urgency: These are the least important. They may not need your attention right now, or perhaps at all.

Next, evaluate how much control you have over each worry. If you can control it, take action according to your prioritized list. If not, consider letting go or finding ways to mitigate its impact.

Additionally, regularly reassess your list, as priorities can change and new worries may emerge.

However, there are times when exceptions are necessary. For example, when on a plane, you're advised to secure your own oxygen mask before helping others. Similarly, while worries for your loved ones may seem more urgent, you must secure your own well-being first before attending to theirs.

The mantra is to understand that before acting on any of your worries, analyze and prioritize them. Stay mindful of exceptions that might overrule your priorities, and adjust as needed.

Mantra 5: Don't Worry About Your Bad Past Repeating Itself

This mantra connects deeply with the past, present, and future demon, and is discussed in detail in that chapter, but it's worth emphasizing here as it directly relates to the worry demon.

As we journey through life, we encounter both good and bad experiences. It's often the bad experiences that leave lasting impressions, creating demons that haunt us as we move forward. These bad memories from our past can trigger worries, making us constantly fearful of them repeating themselves.

The truth is, there's always a possibility of something bad happening, but that doesn't necessarily mean it will be a repeat of something from your past. Even if similar events occur, it may be purely coincidental. The circumstances this time will be different, making any repeated mistakes part of a new and unique set of challenges.

While it's important to remember past mistakes and the lessons learned from them, don't let them scare you. Those past experiences have already served their purpose and can no longer harm you.

The mantra here is to not worry about the repetition of past mistakes. Instead, focus on the lessons learned and use them for your benefit and the well-being of those you care about. It's incredibly rare for the exact same thing to happen in precisely the same way, so let go of the fear and move forward with confidence.

Mantra 6: Don't Let Excessive Worry About the Future Ruin Your Present

We humans have a natural instinct to save energy and resources for the future, rather than using everything up in the moment. This trait is not unique to us; some animals also stockpile food for the winter, while others live solely for today, without any worries for tomorrow.

The future is filled with uncertainties, and this unknown can create anxiety. It's perfectly natural to have some concerns about what lies ahead. In fact, a certain level of worry about the future can be beneficial, as it motivates us to prepare for potential challenges and risks.

However, while planning for the future is important, excessive worry can take away from our ability to enjoy the present. When we become too preoccupied with what might happen, we risk sacrificing the joy and opportunities available to us right now.

Worries about the future should serve as prompts to prepare for potential risks, but they shouldn't consume our present happiness. Unfortunately, many of us struggle to cover every possible future risk without compromising our current well-being.

That's why it's important to find a balance between living in the present and preparing for the future. This balance allows us to enjoy life today while still being mindful of what may come. However, this balance is not fixed—it evolves as we grow and change over time. It's also highly individual, varying from person to person based on their circumstances, priorities, and life stage.

As we navigate through life, our needs, wants, and perspectives shift. The balance that worked for us at one point may need to be adjusted as we and our situations evolve. For some, the balance may lean more towards living fully in the present, while for others, it may tilt towards safeguarding the future. Ultimately, it's up to you to decide what balance works best for you. However, when faced with tough decisions, it's often wise to give a bit more weight to the present, ensuring that you're not missing out on the life you're living now.

Since this balance is unique to each individual, it's crucial not to compare your current life and future plans to those of others. You only see what's visible on the surface and can only guess at what lies beneath.

The mantra is that while it's good to be aware of future uncertainties and to prepare for them, don't let them overshadow the present. Worries about the future are simply indicators of potential challenges, not guarantees. So, while it's important to stay informed and prepared, don't let these concerns rob you of the moments you have today.

Mantra 7: Don't Blindly Trust Your Worries, as They May Not Reflect the Full Truth

Our minds are often filled with a myriad of worries, but it's important to recognize that many of these concerns may be mere products of a mix of facts, imaginations, observations, and perceptions. Not all of our worries are valid; in fact, many may be nothing more than figments of our imagination.

The only worries that truly hold validity are those grounded in pure facts. However, it can be difficult to discern which worries are based on reality, as our imaginations and perceptions are often deeply intertwined with the truth, making them almost indistinguishable. Additionally, worries about the future can never be guaranteed to be valid, as the future is inherently uncertain.

A significant number of our worries are based on assumptions without solid evidence to support them. However, the scenarios our minds create can be so distressing that we often avoid confronting them, allowing these baseless worries to disturb our peace of mind.

Additionally, many worries arise from negative events happening around the world. Although these events may not directly impact us, their negativity can be powerful enough to trigger unnecessary worries.

Despite the questionable authenticity of some of these worries, we often accept them as truths, believing that whatever is causing our anxiety will inevitably become a reality. It's understandable to take a worry seriously when there are ways to verify its accuracy, but more often than not, we lack the means to confirm its validity. As a result, we shouldn't allow these worries to dominate our present moments.

The mantra is to understand that not all of your worries are valid. Avoid trusting them blindly without further investigation to determine their legitimacy. Otherwise, you may find yourself consumed by fears that are nothing more than figments of your imagination, with no real possibility of coming true.

Mantra 8: Don't Let Worries About Others Destroy You

It's natural to worry about our loved ones when they're going through tough times, facing challenges, or not living up to their potential. This concern is rooted in care and responsibility, and there's nothing wrong with that. In fact, it shows that we deeply care for them.

While we may worry about them, the reality is that we often have only a partial understanding of their problems and limited influence over their thoughts and actions. Additionally, what we see as a significant issue might not be as serious to them, making our worries less justified.

When we see someone struggling, we can offer advice based on our understanding of the situation. But ultimately, whether they choose to act on our suggestions is entirely up to them. Additionally, our advice may not always be fully applicable, as it may not align perfectly with the reality they are experiencing.

If we persist too much in trying to help, it might push them away, leading them to distance themselves from us and ignore our advice altogether.

While it's challenging to be completely at peace in such situations, it's crucial not to let these worries consume you, as your ability to help is often limited.

This doesn't mean you should give up or abandon them, especially if you see them heading toward a difficult situation. Do what you can to help, but avoid insisting that they solve their problems exactly as you suggest if they're not receptive. Look for other ways to support them.

The mantra is to recognize that you and the person you're worried about are two separate individuals, both mentally and physically, connected by a bond of care. It's natural to feel frustrated when you can't resolve the problems of those you care about, but don't let this frustration destroy you. Remember that the other person must also be willing to address their issues, and you can't do everything on your own.

Mantra 9: Trust Plays a Key Role in Lessening the Intensity of Worries

Trust eases worries by providing stability and calm. When we trust in ourselves, others, and life's flow, we let go of unnecessary anxiety and embrace peace. Trust reminds us that not everything is within our control, and that's okay. It helps us believe that, even in uncertainty, things will work out. Cultivating trust reduces worry and allows us to face challenges with a calmer, balanced mindset.

When you trust your abilities and judgment, you're less likely to be overwhelmed by worries. Self-trust empowers you to face challenges confidently, reducing fear of the unknown as you believe in your own resourcefulness and resilience.

Trusting in others, whether it's family, friends, or colleagues, helps alleviate the burden of feeling like you have to manage everything on your own. When you trust that others will support you, do their part, or offer help when needed, it reduces the worries that often come with uncertainty or responsibility.

Life is unpredictable, and many worries stem from our fear of the unknown. By trusting in the process, you accept that not everything is within your control, and that's okay. Trusting that things will unfold as they're meant to, even if the outcome isn't immediately clear, allows you to release unnecessary worries and focus on the present.

Sometimes, our worries arise from believing things must happen a certain way. Trusting the bigger picture means accepting that life works itself out, even if we can't see how. This perspective reduces worry by shifting focus from immediate concerns to a broader view of your life's journey.

In relationships, trust eases worries about misunderstandings, conflicts, or abandonment. Trusting your partner, friends, or family reduces anxiety about the relationship's stability and future. It fosters open communication, preventing minor concerns from becoming major issues.

Life often takes unexpected turns, leading to worries about being on the "right" path. Trusting your journey, knowing each step is part of your growth can reduce fears about the future and help you embrace change with confidence and calm.

The mantra is that trust acts as a powerful antidote to worry. Whether it's trust in yourself, others, the process, timing, the bigger picture, relationships, or your life path, cultivating trust helps you navigate life's uncertainties with greater ease and less anxiety. By fostering this trust, you can reduce the intensity of your worries and create a more peaceful, balanced state of mind

Mantra 10: Good Worries Should Be at the Top of Your List

Good worries should be at the top of your list because they reflect the aspects of your life that truly matter and require your attention. These worries often stem from your values, goals, and the desire to improve your circumstances or the well-being of those you care about. Prioritizing good worries helps you focus on what's most important, enabling you to make decisions and take actions that align with your long-term aspirations and personal growth.

For instance, worrying about your health can motivate you to adopt a healthier lifestyle, leading to better physical and mental well-being. Concerns about your financial stability can push you to plan, save, and invest wisely, securing your future. Worries about relationships might prompt you to nurture and strengthen your connections, fostering a supportive and loving environment.

By placing good worries at the top of your list, you can channel your energy into constructive actions that not only alleviate these concerns but also contribute to a more fulfilling and balanced life. This proactive approach ensures that you're addressing the most impactful areas of your life, helping you grow and thrive over time.

The mantra is to focus on the worries that align with your values and aspirations, for they guide you toward meaningful growth and a balanced, fulfilling life. Prioritize what truly matters, and let your actions reflect your deepest intentions.

CHAPTER 6

Regret: The Demon of Past Mistakes

R egret is one of the most pervasive and challenging demons faced by humanity, and it's rare to find someone who hasn't been touched by its influence. No matter how careful or perfect we strive to be, making mistakes is an inevitable part of being human. Sometimes, our errors are a direct result of our own actions, while at other times, external factors beyond our control lead us astray. Even when we believe we've done everything right, time may reveal flaws or imperfections we hadn't anticipated.

This demon haunts us by dragging us back to our past, reminding us of every mistake, every misstep, and everything that, in hindsight, seems less than perfect. The cruel reality of this demon is that it preys on the past, something we can never change or fix, no matter how much we might want to. Despite our best efforts to confront or resist it, regret has a way of resurfacing, often when we least expect it.

Regret creates an endless loop of self-torment, with our thoughts continually bouncing between the present and the past. Breaking free from this cycle is incredibly difficult because we're trapped by the unchangeable nature of our history. No amount of logic can fully counter the power of regret; it is an inescapable companion that resides within us, ever-present and persistent.

Throughout life, we encounter many forms of this demon, each one affecting us in different ways. If we start treating every regret with equal seriousness, we'll risk losing our peace of mind, as one regret after another will consume us. It's essential to discern which regrets warrant attention and which do not.

Some regrets, with minimal impact and little likelihood of recurrence, should be dismissed without much consideration. Others, with slightly greater potential for harm or recurrence, should be carefully examined so that we can learn from them and avoid repeating the same mistakes. But there are those regrets with profound, life-altering consequences and a high chance of recurring, and these must be taken seriously, analyzed deeply, and remembered as valuable lessons to prevent future errors.

Regret manifests in many forms, and understanding its various faces is key to confronting this demon. Let's explore some of these forms to gain a better understanding of how regret impacts our lives.

Regrets From Missed Opportunities in the Past

When we reflect on the past, we often find instances where we could have taken action but didn't, leading to a sense of regret later on. It's natural to feel this way, as we tend to believe that we should have seized those opportunities. However, this belief that we could have easily done things differently is often a misconception.

The notion that we could have acted differently in the past overlooks the reality of what was involved at the time. Some of those opportunities may have been far more challenging than they seem in hindsight, making it unclear whether our past selves were truly capable of handling them. Moreover, there were likely valid reasons why we chose not to pursue those paths at the time.

Even if we had taken those actions, there's no guarantee they would have led to positive outcomes. Doing so would have set off a completely different chain of events, the results of which are impossible to predict. Therefore, the assumption that everything would have been better had we acted differently is not necessarily valid.

It's also important to recognize that we often judge past decisions through the lens of our current self, which is almost like two different people with different perspectives. Who we are today is shaped by experiences and growth that our past self had not yet undergone.

In light of this, regrets about missed opportunities are not as justified as they may seem. Instead of letting them disturb our present, it's more productive to view them as learning opportunities. By doing so, we can prevent these regrets from clouding our present and use them as a guide for making better decisions in the future.

Regrets About Past Actions We Now Wish We Hadn't Taken

This form of regret covers the scenario that's a complete opposite of the previous one, where looking back in time we'll always find things we have done in the past which we now think we shouldn't have done, and we end up regretting them.

The most obvious reason for us to think this way comes from those bad examples where we did some things in our past and they didn't turn out good or as expected, forcing us to think that we shouldn't have done those things.

We forget one very important point in these regrets: that the results of something we did came only after we did that something, and the reason for results not coming out good could have been anything, and not necessarily just our actions. There's no way to see the results of doing something without actually doing that.

And just for the sake of discussion, even if somehow we are able to go back in time and stop those things from happening, the outcomes will change as a result of the new sequence of events, but there's no guarantee that things will be any better.

So, there is no weight in the assumption that things would have been much better if we wouldn't have done something that we think we shouldn't have done. There's no way we can predict the outcome of this.

Most of the points that we discussed in the previous point are relevant here as well so I'll not repeat them here, but we should make sure to not allow this form of regret to create disturbance in our present moments, just like the previous one.

Regrets Over Poor Choices and Decisions Made in the Past

Throughout the journey of our life, we are constantly faced with choices, and we make decisions based on what seems most appropriate at the time. As we move forward, some of these choices may prove to be mistakes, leading to regret. However, if we had known the outcomes in advance, we would have chosen differently.

Typically, our decisions are not made randomly, and they are the result of careful consideration of the available options, circumstances, and data at the time. We analyze the pros and cons, weigh the potential outcomes, and select the option that appears to be the best fit. Sometimes, multiple options may seem viable, but ultimately, we rely on our judgment to make the final decision.

Unfortunately, even decisions made with the best intentions and due diligence can later turn out to be wrong, leading to feelings of regret. However, if you could revisit the moment when you made those choices, you'd most likely find that they were the most logical options given the information you had at the time. The data or analysis may have been flawed, but you wouldn't have known that then, otherwise you would have made a different choice.

While regretting past decisions isn't inherently helpful, it can be valuable if used as a learning experience. Reflecting on past mistakes allows you to improve your judgment and avoid similar mistakes in the future.

In essence, the decisions and choices you made in the past were likely the best options available to you at the time, based on the knowledge and data you had. While that information may not have been entirely accurate or sufficient, and your analysis may have had flaws, you couldn't have known that in the moment. Rather than dwelling on regret, use these experiences to guide better decisions moving forward.

Regrets About Not Putting in More Effort in the Past

It's not very uncommon to hear people cribbing about not putting in more effort in the past, convinced that if they had only tried harder, they would be more successful and happier today. However, the truth is that there's no guarantee that their greater effort would have led to better outcomes. Success depends on numerous factors beyond just effort, so blaming past failures solely on not trying hard enough doesn't seem right.

Just for the sake of argument, let's assume that their more effort could have led to greater success, but why didn't that happen? The reality is that they didn't put in that extra effort, and there were reasons for that. Those reasons, rooted in who they were at the time, influenced their choices. Perhaps they lacked motivation, faced personal challenges, or simply had different priorities back then.

Moreover, effort is driven by many factors, including

interest level, motivation, and circumstances to name just a few. Even when we give our best, there's no way to know if that effort alone would have guaranteed success. Other elements, such as timing, resources, and luck, also play significant roles.

In reality, the feeling of not having put in enough effort will always be there because only after attempting something do we realize what was missing. However, it's important to remember that effort is just one piece of the puzzle here. Regretting past efforts without considering the broader context of success is unfair to yourself. Effort alone doesn't determine the outcome, and other factors beyond your control often influence the results.

Regrets About Not Using Time Wisely in the Past

Time is one of the most valuable assets we possess, yet we often fail to appreciate its true worth until it's too late. This is one of the most common regrets we hear all the time where people regret over not spending time wisely, and it affects people regardless of their financial status.

Wealthy individuals may find themselves regretting the years spent focusing solely on building and maintaining wealth, realizing too late that they neglected family and personal enjoyment in the process. They wish they had balanced their time better, spending more of it with loved ones and on life's simple pleasures, rather than being consumed by the pursuit of money.

On the other hand, those who struggle financially often regret not using their time more productively, believing they could have improved their circumstances if only they had been more mindful of how they spent their days. In doing so, they overlook the joy and fulfillment they gained from time spent with family and pursuing hobbies, because these experiences don't have a direct monetary value and are often forgotten as mere memories that fade over time.

Learning to manage time effectively is crucial. Without this skill, even if you have an abundance of time, you may not know how to use it wisely, leading to future regret over wasted opportunities. At times, you might think you're making the most of your time, only to discover later that there were better ways to spend it, sparking feelings of regret.

It'll be hard to find anyone who is completely satisfied with how they've used their time throughout their life. As we encounter new opportunities and experiences, it's natural to wish we had known about them sooner, allowing us to enjoy them for a longer period.

The irony is that life's time always seems too short for all the things we wish to do, making the regret of not using time wisely an almost inevitable part of the human experience.

Regrets About Not Prioritizing Ourselves Enough

Life as a human being is inherently complex, as it isn't just about us but also about those we love, care for, and feel responsible for. This complexity often leads to regret when people reflect on their lives and realize they never prioritized themselves, instead lived a life full of sacrifices for others.

Responsibilities arise at different times for different people. Some encounter them early in life, while others face them later. These responsibilities are often the primary reason why many of us struggle to focus on our own needs, as time is limited and must be allocated between caring for ourselves and fulfilling obligations to others.

When we feel responsible for someone or something, our personal needs often take a backseat. For example, older siblings may feel responsible for their younger ones, parents feel responsible for their children, and mothers, in particular, often bear the weight of the world's responsibilities, arguably more than anyone else.

People have their own desires, but the weight of responsibility often forces them to suppress these desires. The truth is, their desires are never truly extinguished, and they merely become dormant, waiting for the right time to resurface. When people don't receive the appreciation they hoped for after years of sacrifice, they may start to regret not prioritizing themselves. They may feel as though they've wasted their lives on thankless tasks, neglecting their own needs in the process.

Unfortunately, by the time their responsibilities have lessened or they finally have the chance to focus on themselves, it's often too late. The regret of not giving enough attention to oneself when the time was right can be a heavy burden to bear.

And this list of regrets can be endless. This demon doesn't stop there, and it relentlessly finds new ways to torment us, resurrecting past mistakes and painful memories, making us relive and regret them all over again.

The Good Side of Regret

Like many of the other demons discussed in this book, even regret has two sides: a good side and a bad one. We've already explored some of the negative aspects, so let's take a closer look at the positive side.

One of the most valuable aspects of regret is its potential to teach us lessons from the past. Regret often arises from actions we did or didn't take. While we can't change what's already happened, we can use those experiences to guide our current and future decisions. Without regret, we might overlook our past mistakes, missing valuable opportunities for growth and learning.

Additionally, sharing your regrets with others can serve as a powerful tool for guidance. By using your experiences as real-life examples, you can help those you care about avoid similar mistakes. They don't always have to learn the hard way when you can offer them the wisdom gained from your own regrets.

Similarly, you can benefit from others' regrets, learning from their experiences to steer clear of potential pitfalls.

Another positive aspect of regret is that it allows us to confront and resolve unresolved feelings that may be buried deep within us. By acknowledging and addressing these feelings, we can find closure and prevent them from haunting us in the future.

These positive qualities make this demon worthy of a presence in our system. However, like most challenges, regret has its downsides, and it's important to recognize that while it can be helpful, it can also be a source of significant distress.

Mantras for Dealing With the Regret Demon

Now, let's explore some mantras that can help us overcome the regret demon. By integrating these mantras into your daily life, you can start to dissolve the negative emotions that regret brings, allowing you to live more fully and with greater peace of mind.

Mantra 1: Every Decision Was the Best Choice at the Time It Was Made

Regret over past decisions is one of the most common ways by which this demon torments us. This mantra can serve as a powerful tool to combat our regrets.

If you think back to any decision you've made, you'll realize that it wasn't made impulsively or without any consideration. We typically weigh our options, analyze the information available, consider the pros and cons, run "what-if" scenarios, and carefully think through our choices before making a decision.

Yes, it's possible that the information we relied on wasn't entirely accurate or complete. However, if we had known that at the time, we would have made adjustments accordingly. The point is that our decisions are not made haphazardly; they are the result of careful thought and consideration.

Of course, there are moments when quick decisions are necessary, and even in those instances, we do our best given the circumstances, moving forward with hope and an understanding of the risks involved.

This means that every decision we make is the result of our best efforts and due diligence at that moment. The eventual outcome, whether good or bad, is influenced by numerous factors beyond our control.

When our decisions lead to positive outcomes, it's good to feel proud of our choices. But when things don't go as planned, it's crucial not to blame ourselves. Remember, your decisions were based on the best information and understanding you had at the time.

The mantra is to remind yourself that every decision you made was the best possible choice at that moment. The outcomes, whether favorable or not, are shaped by the data and knowledge available to you, along with other variables.

Instead of regretting your decisions, focus on learning from the outcomes and moving forward with greater wisdom.

Mantra 2: Learn From Other People's Regrets

Just as we gain wisdom from the experiences of others, we can also learn valuable lessons from their regrets.

When people share their regrets, they often reflect on the mistakes they've made in the past. Life is unpredictable, and there's a chance you might encounter similar situations. By listening to others' regret stories, you can learn from their experiences and potentially avoid making the same or similar mistakes.

However, there's a caveat to this approach. It's crucial not to rely solely on others' regrets when making your own decisions. Your circumstances may differ from those that led to someone else's regret, and if you base your decisions solely on their experiences, you might misjudge the situation and make a poor choice.

Instead, use the insights gained from others' regrets as additional data points in your decision-making process. Adapt what you've learned to fit your own unique circumstances, rather than blindly following someone else's path.

In some cases, your situation may closely resemble one that led to another person's regret. In these instances, it's wise to pay attention to their lessons and avoid repeating their mistakes.

The core of this mantra is recognizing that you don't have to learn everything the hard way through your own firsthand experience. You can gain valuable insights from the regrets of others, allowing you to make more informed decisions.

Likewise, sharing your own regrets with others can help them learn from your experiences, creating a cycle of shared wisdom and mutual growth.

Mantra 3: Remember That All Decisions Are Yours, Even When They're Unwanted

As we navigate through the journey of our life, we continuously make decisions, and while some lead to success, others may result in failure or even disaster.

Many of these choices are made solely by us, without any outside influence. When these decisions turn out poorly, we often regret them, but we can usually find some comfort in acknowledging them as our own mistakes, allowing us to move forward.

However, there are times when we make decisions under external pressure, influence, or obligation. When these decisions go wrong, we regret and blame others for their influence. But it's important to recognize that, ultimately, every decision you make is yours, whether it was made freely or under duress.

If you found yourself compelled to make a certain decision due to external forces, there were likely reasons why you chose not to resist those pressures. Perhaps you lacked the courage to oppose, wanted to preserve relationships, or had other priorities. Whatever the case, by accepting those forces, you made a decision, and therefore, it belongs to you.

The mantra here is to take ownership of all your decisions, even those made reluctantly or under external influence. Don't waste time regretting them or blaming others for forcing your hand. Instead, accept responsibility and learn from the outcomes, especially if they didn't turn out as expected.

Mantra 4: Each Cycle of Regret Gives You Another Opportunity to Look Back at Things

This demon often revisits us in cycles, bringing up painful memories from the past. However, this mantra encourages you to see each cycle not as a torment but as an opportunity to reassess your mistakes, gain new perspectives, and learn valuable lessons.

Though this idea may seem familiar, it's a crucial point we should never overlook, making this mantra deserving of its place here. Just as re-reading a book, watching a movie again, or revisiting a place can reveal something new each time, reflecting on past mistakes can also uncover fresh insights.

Regret gives you the chance to revisit experiences you're unhappy with, pushing you to confront and learn from your past. Without regret, you might never take the time to review your mistakes. So, when regrets bring these past mistakes to mind, even if they stir negative emotions, try to see them as opportunities to learn something new and grow.

By re-examining your past, you'll uncover more reasons behind your mistakes each time, which can help you feel more at peace with them. These insights not only strengthen your ability to confront regret but also provide valuable lessons to help you and others avoid similar errors in the future.

The mantra is to view each cycle of regret not as torment but as an opportunity to reassess your mistakes, gain new perspectives, and learn valuable lessons. Every time you revisit a past regret, you'll uncover new insights and reasons why things unfolded the way they did.

Mantra 5: Forgiveness is a Powerful Tool to Confront the Regret Demon

The regret demon is a pervasive and crippling emotion, trapping us in a relentless cycle of negativity. It keeps us stuck in a loop of self-blame, revisiting past events, and harboring resentment toward ourselves or others. Regardless of how this demon enters our systems, we often find ourselves entrapped by its grip.

Forgiveness is a powerful tool that can shatter this cycle, bringing closure to past regrets and enabling us to move forward.

Some regrets stem from our own actions, decisions, or mistakes, leaving us to hold ourselves accountable. In these instances, self-forgiveness is essential. Recognize and accept your mistakes without harsh judgment, understanding that mistakes are part of being human. Learn from your past, release the guilt, and let go of the negative emotions that hold you back.

Other regrets are tied to the actions or decisions of others, where we feel that their choices have led to our pain, and we blame them for our negative experiences. In these cases, forgiving others is key to overcoming these regrets. By empathizing with their perspective and releasing the blame, we free ourselves from the emotional burden.

Sometimes, we find ourselves the target of others' blame, becoming indirect victims of their regrets. Forgiving those who blame us, and accepting that their blame often comes from their own hurt, is crucial. Apologize and make amends where necessary, then forgive yourself.

The mantra here is that forgiveness is vital in dealing with the regret demon, no matter its source. By forgiving ourselves and others, we can break free from the cycle of regret, find closure, and cultivate peace of mind and healthier relationships.

Mantra 6: Even a Carefully Planned and Calculated Decision Can Occasionally Turn Out Wrong

Even with careful planning and thorough analysis, decisions can sometimes lead to unexpected outcomes. As we've discussed throughout this chapter, most of our decisions are based on a solid analysis of the available data, with the depth of that analysis varying depending on the significance of the decision.

However, no matter how meticulously we plan, every decision carries an element of uncertainty. There's always the possibility that the outcomes won't align with our expectations.

After making a well-calculated decision, it's natural to believe that we've chosen the best possible path and to expect positive results. But when things don't go as planned, we often find ourselves regretting the decision altogether.

The mantra is to accept that not all decisions will yield perfect outcomes due to the inherent unknowns involved. Even with the most thorough planning and calculations, there's always a chance that things may not turn out as expected. Understanding and accepting this reality can help us manage this demon and move forward with greater resilience.

Mantra 7: Avoid Regret by Comparing Yourself to Others

We often fall into the trap of comparing ourselves to others, especially those who seem to be in a better position. This habit can be a significant source of regret.

It's common to look at successful people and think, "If only I had done what they did, I would be more successful today." But this line of thinking is both unproductive and draining. Throughout your life, you've made choices based on your understanding and vision at the time. Each decision was made with the belief that it was the right one for you at that moment. Don't diminish those choices by comparing yourself to others.

There's no guarantee that replicating someone else's actions would have led to your success. Success is influenced by countless factors, and your actions are just one part of the equation.

The mantra here is to avoid comparing yourself to others in a way that leads to regret over your perceived failures. Instead, use those comparisons as a source of inspiration and motivation. Learn from the experiences of others and apply those lessons to your future endeavors. While you can't change the past, you can still shape the future.

Mantra 8: Don't Let Others Hold You Accountable for Their Regrets

Whether intentionally or not, you might become a source of

regret for others, leading them to blame you for the negative outcomes they experience.

There are times when people regret your involvement, blaming you for preventing them from pursuing something they wanted, or for agreeing with you on decisions that didn't turn out well. You might also encounter situations where people regret seeking your help, following your suggestions, or spending time with you, and then hold you responsible for their unfavorable outcomes. Additionally, some might accuse you of imposing your views on their decisions, which they later regret.

However, while they may blame you for their regrets, they often overlook the fact that the decision to involve you was ultimately theirs—whether by choice, influence, or perceived obligation. They had the option to exclude you from their decisions but chose not to.

By regretting these scenarios, they're essentially disagreeing with the decisions made by their own past selves, decisions they now regret. Whatever their reasons were for involving you—whether by choice, persuasion, or force—the fact remains that they chose to keep you involved.

The mantra here is to acknowledge that while it's okay to listen when others blame you for their regrets, don't take their criticisms to heart. Your current self is not responsible for their past decisions, just as your past self wasn't responsible for their choice to involve you.

Mantra 9: Changing Past Decisions Will Alter Everything, Even the Good You Have Now

When you reflect on your life at this moment, you'll notice that while it may not be perfect, there are still many good things and people in it. These positive aspects exist because of the unique path you've traveled, with each decision moving you from one point to another.

The good things and people in your life contribute to its quality in various ways—some offer support when you need it, others bring joy and laughter, and some provide emotional comfort simply by being there. These elements are the result of the specific trajectory your life has taken.

If you were to go back and alter decisions you now regret, the entire course of your life would change. Many of the good things and people you cherish today might never have become part of your life. While life might bring new opportunities and relationships, there's no guarantee they would match or exceed the value of what you currently have.

The saying "a bird in the hand is worth two in the bush" reminds us that what you have now is certain, whereas what you might gain by changing the past is uncertain. Consider how your experiences—books you've read, places you've visited, movies you've watched—have shaped your mind. Imagine how different you would be without those experiences.

Even though regrets might tempt you to make different choices, doing so would lead to a life vastly different from the one you know today. Regret focuses on specific moments, often overlooking the bigger picture that defines your life as a whole.

The mantra here is to recognize that changing past decisions often means losing what you've already gained. Every choice carries potential losses and gains, but there's no assurance that an altered path would lead to a better life than the one you have now.

Mantra 10: Give More Importance to Your Present

This may seem obvious and repetitive, but since it's such a crucial point we often overlook, this mantra deserves its place here.

Regret draws its strength from the past, allowing negative events to overshadow your present. The more you focus on the present moment and what you can do now, instead of dwelling on what could have been, the weaker this demon becomes, eventually losing its hold on you.

The key is to let the painful memories of the past stay in the past. However, the regret demon won't easily allow that and will continually try to keep those memories fresh in your mind. Instead of attempting to forget or avoid them, accept your past mistakes as lessons learned. And when you start sharing these lessons with others, you reinforce your acceptance of the past, demonstrating that it no longer disturbs your peace.

When you fully embrace your past and the lessons it offers, regret loses its power to haunt your present. It can no longer disrupt your current life, as you have accepted and moved on from those events.

The mantra here is to make your present your top priority. By doing so, you prevent past regrets from ruining your current life. To achieve this, you must accept and own your past, allowing it to serve as a source of growth rather than a source of pain.

CHAPTER 7

Relationships: The Demon of Connections

The best way to describe the value of relationships in our lives is that they are the angels in our lives, enriching our existence and adding vibrant colors to our world. Each relationship, with its unique blend of qualities, contributes to the overall tapestry of our lives, making them more fulfilling and meaningful. They are the primary sources of enrichment, enhancing our quality of life in countless ways.

However, the way we manage our relationships, by complicating them with unnecessary complexities, can sometimes turn these blessings into burdens. By introducing demons like comparison, unrealistic expectations, and unnecessary worries, we complicate relationships, transforming them into something that can feel more like a demon than a blessing.

From the moment we are born until the day we leave this world, we engage in numerous relationships—family, friends, colleagues, and even pets. Each relationship has its own lifespan and evolves differently over time. Some, like those with family, may last a lifetime, while others, such as those with colleagues, might be more transient.

A thought-provoking quote I once heard said, "If we want to keep the university of relationships running smoothly, the mathematics and politics departments must remain the weakest." While this may have held true in simpler times, modern complexities have necessitated some level of calculation and strategy in maintaining healthy relationships. However, if these elements become too dominant, they can have negative effects.

There's no denying that relationships are one of the greatest gifts in life, providing us with purpose and joy. Yet, like any good thing, they require effort and management. Without proper care, relationships can deteriorate, becoming fertile ground for several demons in our system.

Maintaining relationships is often challenging due to the numerous demands and competing priorities we face. It requires time, effort, and a genuine commitment to nurturing the bond. Relationships are essentially a balance of give and take, with each party contributing to its success.

Every relationship is unique and cannot be compared equally to another. For example, within a family, a father's relationship with each of his children will differ, influenced by various factors. Similarly, a mother's relationship with each family member will be distinct, as will the relationships among the children themselves. These dynamics evolve over time, reflecting changes in the family's growth and individual development.

While understanding significantly strengthens the bonds between family members, misunderstandings and unrealistic expectations can weaken these connections, potentially turning relationships into their demonic forms, resulting in conflict and distress.

The truth is, despite our best efforts, conflicts and misunderstandings will inevitably arise in relationships. It's impossible to meet everyone's expectations all the time. At times, we must prioritize certain relationships, which can lead to others feeling neglected.

This is where this demon thrives, exploiting the relationship conflicts, imperfections and unmet expectations within our bonds. No relationship is flawless, and these imperfections provide opportunities for discord to grow.

Most relationships begin on a positive note, as they wouldn't start otherwise, but over time, some may deteriorate, becoming sources of distress. However, there are exceptions where relationships might start with tension or animosity. While some of these relationships may improve over time, others might remain strained or even worsen. It's these troubled relationships that this demon often targets to create disturbances in our lives.

Relationships are intricate and multifaceted, and at any given moment, you'll find yourself navigating through a complex web of connections. By understanding these complexities and staying mindful of potential pitfalls, you can strive to maintain healthier, more fulfilling relationships while effectively managing any negative experiences that may arise.

The ROI of Relationships

ROI, or return on investment, is a term typically associated with finance, but it is surprisingly relevant in the context of our relationships as well. At first, the idea of applying ROI to relationships might seem odd, but it will soon become evident to you why this analogy fits so well in this context.

It's not uncommon to hear people express frustration over how much they've done for someone—a friend, a relative— only to feel that they received little or nothing in return. You've likely experienced similar feelings yourself at some point, sharing your disappointment with others.

To me, this scenario resembles an investment, where one person expects a return based on the time, energy, and effort they've invested in another person. Whether we realize it or not, this dynamic often functions like an investment, with potential returns that can be either positive or negative, much like financial investments.

This demon preys on our negative experiences in relationships where the returns fall short of our expectations or are nonexistent. These disappointments stem from the implicit expectations we naturally develop in the relationships we maintain.

To strengthen any relationship, you must invest time, energy, and sometimes sacrifice. However, the challenge arises from the expectations that accompany these investments. After investing so much, it's natural to anticipate timely and appropriate returns.

The irony is that even when returns do materialize, if they aren't as timely or substantial as expected, we often feel let down, giving this demon an opening to torment us. This internal conflict can leave us torn: one part of us may want to withdraw from the relationship because the returns don't seem to justify the effort, while another part wants to continue because of the value we place on the relationship and other compelling reasons.

The Justification of ROI in Relationships

Whether or not it's justified, the reality is that the concept of ROI—return on investment—is deeply embedded in our relationships. There are many types of relationships where this expectation is perfectly reasonable. In these cases, the relationships exist specifically because the parties involved have clear, mutual expectations of returns from one another.

A great example where ROI is justified is in business partnerships, where the relationship is fundamentally based on the exchange of value and the expectations surrounding that exchange. The ROI here is clear and central to the relationship's existence.

It might sound extreme, but it's true to an extent that even our personal friendships are ROI-driven, as many of them begin with some expectation of return on the effort we invest. It's important to clarify that in this context, the ROI isn't monetary. It could be anything from emotional support to companionship. The saying "a friend in need is a friend indeed" highlights the implicit ROI involved in friendships.

Typically, we form friendships with like-minded individuals who bring joy during good times and offer support during tough times. While a friendship might start quickly, it takes time to develop to a point where the give-and-take aspect fades into the background. Most friendships begin with a balanced exchange—you give and receive equally. As these friendships mature, the expectations often lessen, and the relationship becomes more unconditional.

However, there are other personal relationships where the concept of ROI should be viewed differently. In these relationships, the ROI is of a different nature—it's an instant, invisible return felt by the person at the giving end.

A perfect example is the relationship between parents and their children. When parents make sacrifices for their kids, the joy they feel from knowing their actions contribute to their children's happiness and well-being is an immediate return on their investment. While the world may view these actions as sacrifices, in reality, they are investments with instant returns.

The problem arises when, even after receiving these immediate returns, we still desire more from certain relationships.

So, while there is always some form of ROI associated with relationships—whether visible or invisible—the real challenge lies in managing our expectations. This demon is ever-watchful, ready to pounce when our investments don't yield the returns we hope for. Ultimately, it's up to us to decide whether the returns or the relationship itself holds greater value.

Challenging Relationships

While most relationships in our lives begin on a positive note, there are exceptions that start off on shaky ground, perhaps due to initial conflict, rivalry, or tension. Over time, many relationships that were once strong can deteriorate for various reasons, leading to challenging dynamics. These difficulties can arise from issues on one side or both, depending on the underlying problems.

Every challenging relationship comes with a history, offering valuable insights into what went wrong. By exploring these troubled connections, we can better understand the complexities involved.

At any stage in our lives, we manage a complex network of relationships, each with its own set of expectations and demands. It's nearly impossible to maintain all of them in perfect harmony, so some inevitably become strained. Each difficult relationship presents its own unique challenges.

The important thing to remember about any challenging relationship is that it remains a relationship. Despite the difficulties, we often hold onto it for a reason, rather than letting it go entirely.

During the good times of any relationship that has since gone bad, none of the involved parties could have imagined that it would one day deteriorate. The idea that something so positive could take a negative turn is often unimaginable when everything seems to be going well. These relationships are particularly painful because they remind us of the good times we once shared, making us yearn for those moments again.

This demon keeps the memory of these troubled relationships and their happier times alive in our system. However, if we shift our perspective, we can get motivation to keep these relationships going, with the hope that they might one day return to a positive state.

Throughout life, you'll constantly be balancing relationships that fluctuate between good and bad. It's not a matter of choice but a necessity to learn how to manage them as best as you can. Simply getting upset over challenging relationships won't resolve anything.

Appreciate the warmth of your positive relationships and cherish the good memories from the difficult ones, while continuing to work on improving them. Always remember, even though a relationship has become challenging, there's a reason it's still part of your life and it's not dead yet.

A Very Special Kind of Relationship: Family and Friends

The one thing that makes us feel truly special and at home in this world is our family. It consists of those who have been with us from the day we were born and others who come into our lives later, such as a spouse, children, and close relatives.

Though family is one of the greatest treasures we have, no family is perfect. Every family experiences its share of issues and discord among its members, yet despite these differences, our love for our families remains strong. Family is that sweet and sour relationship we're born into and carry with us throughout the journey of our lives until the end of our days.

The importance of family in our lives is paramount, and there's no doubt that our entire existence revolves around our families. We live and die for them.

Next in importance are our friends. Just as we are nothing without our families, we are also nothing without our friends. They play a vital role in our lives.

The key difference between family and friends is that while family is given to us, friends are chosen by us. We select friends based on our own interests and values, gravitating towards like-minded people whose company we enjoy. You might find yourself liking your friends more than your family at times, as friends are chosen, reflecting your personal preferences, whereas family is a relationship you're born into.

However, with family, there is an implicit connection and bond that offers warmth and a sense of belonging, keeping you connected to them in a unique way.

So, it's no overstatement to say that family and friends are the lifeblood of our existence in this world, and without them, we would be incomplete.

Self-Relationship

We humans are inherently complex beings, navigating a variety of relationships throughout our lives, in all of our worlds. Among these, one relationship stands out, straddling the line between our personal and internal worlds—our relationship with ourselves, or what can be termed as a "self-relationship."

This self-relationship is unique in its longevity, accompanying us from the moment of our birth until the day we leave this world. Though it might seem unusual, our relationship with ourselves is remarkably similar to our relationships with others, except that in this case, we are on both sides of the interaction.

Just as we strive to make others happy, we also engage in activities that bring us personal joy. Similarly, as we sometimes find faults in others, we also encounter aspects of ourselves that we dislike. We can be just as self-critical as we are of those around us.

Interestingly, despite believing we know ourselves

completely, the reality is that we do not. Although we understand ourselves better than we understand others, there are still aspects of our character that remain unknown. As life unfolds, we continue to discover more about who we are.

The journey of life is, in many ways, a journey of self-discovery. We often surprise ourselves by achieving things we once thought impossible, challenging our own preconceived notions of our abilities. Along the way, we also refine our understanding of our likes, dislikes, strengths, and weaknesses.

The self-relationship requires careful management, much like any other relationship, to ensure it remains healthy. Moreover, maintaining a delicate balance is crucial. For example, self-trust is vital for building confidence, but blind trust without validation can lead to overconfidence and potential failure. On the other hand, excessive self-doubt can impede success, though a certain degree of doubt can be beneficial by motivating us to validate our strengths and capabilities. However, not every doubt can be fully resolved, and at times, taking a leap of faith becomes necessary.

High expectations of ourselves can also be challenging to meet, potentially leading to low self-esteem and disappointment. Comparing ourselves to others who seem to be in a better position can breed feelings of inadequacy and low self-worth.

If we fail to manage our self-relationship well, it can become a breeding ground for various demons in our system such as overconfidence, inferiority or superiority complexes, self-pity, and low self-esteem, among others. Therefore, nurturing a balanced and healthy relationship with ourselves is essential for our overall well-being and personal growth.

Relationships and Responsibilities

Responsibilities are a core element of any relationship,

shaping how it functions and grows. However, when responsibilities become overwhelming, they can strain relationships and transform them into demons causing stress rather than support.

In many relationships, particularly in parenting, the weight of responsibilities is significant. Parents are tasked with providing not just the basic necessities like food and shelter, but also nurturing their children into educated, responsible, and ethical individuals. This involves a continuous effort to make sure they are socially aware and financially responsible, preparing them for the complexities of adult life.

These responsibilities can become overwhelming, leading to stress and potential conflict. Similarly, in romantic or professional relationships, an imbalance in responsibilities can create tension, resentment, and a breakdown in communication.

To prevent responsibilities from transforming into their demonic selves, open communication and healthy sharing of duties are essential. In personal relationships, this might mean supporting one another, while in professional settings, it involves clear communication and fair division of tasks.

Ultimately, while responsibilities are an inevitable part of relationships, managing them thoughtfully ensures that relationships remain strong, supportive, and fulfilling.

Key Factors for a Healthy Relationship

Relationships are intricate and multifaceted, demanding time, energy, and various other resources to keep them healthy and thriving. Like a complex structure, they require a solid foundation supported by multiple pillars. While different relationships have unique needs and requirements, there are certain fundamental elements that are essential across the board. Though we may not always be able to meet every demand placed on us by our relationships, focusing on these core factors can help ensure they survive and thrive.

Some of the key factors that are crucial to any relationship include need, respect, trust, communication, understanding, and love.

Need is a foundational element in any relationship, as both parties typically seek something from each other. This need can be physical, mental, or emotional, and it varies from person to person. Needs can be mutual or one-sided, but they form the basis of the connection between individuals.

Respect is another critical component for sustaining a relationship. While one-sided respect is not uncommon, mutual respect significantly strengthens the bond between individuals. When all parties involved respect each other, the relationship is likely to endure.

Trust is essential for deepening and maintaining relationships. Building and preserving trust takes time and effort and may require sacrifices along the way. Trust is fragile and can easily be damaged if not carefully nurtured, making it a crucial aspect to manage.

Communication serves as the heart and soul of any relationship. While most relationships rely heavily on communication, there are exceptions where the connection remains strong even with infrequent interaction. Regardless, effective communication is vital for understanding and connection.

Understanding plays a major role in navigating the misconceptions and imperfections inherent in all relationships. Not everything can be perfectly communicated, and even when communication occurs, it may not always be clear. Understanding helps bridge these gaps and manage expectations.

Love is perhaps the most powerful force in any relationship. It often serves as the foundation upon which all other factors rest. Love alone can sustain a relationship, and even one-sided love can keep a relationship alive.

In addition to these core factors, many other elements contribute to the health and longevity of relationships. However, focusing on these key factors provides a strong foundation upon which any relationship can be built and maintained.

The Art of Living in a Complex Ecosystem of Relationships

In today's intricate social landscape, we are all involved in multiple relationships, each at various stages of harmony or discord. We exist in a vast web of connections—an ecosystem of relationships—where each of us plays a small, yet significant, role. Navigating and maintaining these relationships requires considerable effort, as each one comes with its own set of demands and expectations. Surviving and thriving in this complex ecosystem is a challenging task, and mastering it is an art that not everyone perfects.

When relationships are mismanaged, they often give rise to numerous demons within us. Managing multiple relationships, each with its competing demands, can create a multitude of such dark forces at any given time. As discussed earlier, it's nearly impossible to handle all relationships flawlessly, so it's almost certain that some issues will always be present in your life.

It might seem easier to sever ties with difficult or poorly managed relationships, but in reality, this is often not possible. Various compelling reasons may force you to maintain these connections, even when they are a source of stress. Therefore, learning the art of managing multiple relationships and the challenges they bring is not just a choice but a necessity if you wish to preserve your mental well-being while navigating this relational ecosystem.

Another critical aspect of relationships is their inherent

fragility. Relationships are difficult to build, even harder to maintain, and yet, they can break with surprising ease. The strength of a relationship often depends on the tolerance levels of those involved. Relationships with low tolerance levels are particularly delicate and require constant attention, as they are more prone to breaking under pressure. Unfortunately, many of the relationships you encounter will fall into this category, burdened with high expectations that make them fragile and demanding.

It's important to remember that even the strongest relationships can be fragile and susceptible to breaking, so none should be taken for granted. The key challenge here is that while you can control your own actions and reactions, you have no control over how others think or behave.

Although mastering the art of managing a complex web of relationships is a deep and intricate skill, the mantras I'm about to share can offer some guidance to help you navigate this intricate web of connections more effectively. Let's explore a few key insights that may help you better understand and manage your relationships.

Mantras for Dealing With the Relationships Demon

And now, let's explore some mantras that can help us confront and manage the relationship demon. By following these mantras and internalizing their messages, you can build stronger, healthier relationships that are more resistant to the challenges and stress that this demon brings.

Mantra 1: Every Relationship Has Its Own Unique Balance of Giving and Receiving

Relationships fundamentally revolve around the concept of giving and receiving. Everyone involved in a relationship has obligations to contribute and expectations of what they hope to receive in return. In essence, each party in a relationship has certain expectations of the others.

However, not all relationships are perfectly balanced, and the ratio of give and take varies depending on the needs of the people involved. A person may have different expectations of different individuals, influenced by factors such as the type of relationship, age, circumstances, behavior, history, and more.

The reality is that no relationship can maintain an exact equilibrium of giving and receiving; there will always be some degree of imbalance. It's important for everyone involved to recognize this truth and manage their expectations accordingly. Sometimes you may give more, and at other times, you may receive more in return.

If you fail to acknowledge that each relationship has its own distinct ratio of give and take and instead start comparing them, the outcomes can be disappointing. Expecting someone to treat you exactly as they treat others is unrealistic. There will always be differences, however subtle, and it's crucial to accept this with an open mind.

A good example is the relationship between parents and their children. Each child is unique, and so are their relationships with their parents. If all children expect identical treatment from their parents, it's simply not feasible.

Comparisons can harm relationships, so it's important to recognize that each one is unique, with its own dynamics of giving and receiving, and avoid comparing them to others.

On the flip side, you won't be able to behave the same way in every relationship you have. If this thought crosses your mind or is brought up by others as a complaint, you shouldn't feel guilty about it.

The mantra is to understand that each relationship has its own unique balance of give and take, and therefore, comparisons between relationships are neither valid nor productive. Accepting this reality will lead to healthier and more fulfilling relationships.

Mantra 2: The Strength of a Relationship Will Evolve Over Time

Relationships are not static, and their strength will inevitably change as time passes. Some relationships grow stronger, while others may weaken, and in some cases, they might not withstand the test of time and could even end.

It is unrealistic to expect any relationship to remain unchanged in form and strength forever, as countless factors influence a relationship's strength, and these factors are constantly in flux.

As people evolve, so do their priorities and circumstances, and these shifts inevitably impact the strength of their relationships. This change is natural and unavoidable.

Moreover, relationships depend on various factors beyond just the involvement and interest of the people involved. A shift in any of these factors can lead to a corresponding change in the relationship itself.

Another important point to consider is that relationships involving rigid individuals are often closely tied to specific conditions, making them vulnerable to breaking if those conditions change. Conversely, relationships with flexible individuals can adapt to changes more easily due to their elasticity. However, even the most flexible relationships have a threshold, and beyond that point, they may begin to weaken and could eventually break.

The mantra is to avoid expecting relationships—and the people in them—to stay the same forever. Instead, acknowledge and accept the changes that occur, and continuously adjust your expectations to align with the evolving dynamics. By embracing relationships in their new forms with an open mind, you can help them grow stronger and last longer.

Mantra 3: If You Consider Relationships as Investments, Understand Their True ROI

This mantra builds on the earlier discussion about ROI in relationships, emphasizing its importance further.

In the context of professional and business relationships, it's common to view them as investments—established with the expectation of receiving some form of return. However, when it comes to personal relationships, thinking of them as investments can seem unusual, even selfish.

Yet, there are instances where people do have high expectations of returns in their personal relationships, treating them similarly to investments. In business relationships or certain friendships, the returns on investment might take time to materialize, while in personal relationships, the returns are often immediate. For example, when you do something for someone you care about, their happiness is the return on your investment. Expecting more in return from them, however, is akin to asking for bonus returns, which can strain the relationship.

The value of returns in personal relationships is very subjective and can only be truly assessed by people involved in them. These returns are often intangible and implicit, felt rather than measured. Sometimes, from an investment perspective, a relationship may not make sense, yet those involved may find happiness in it. It's important to accept that not all relationships need to be analyzed through the lens of investment. After all, we are humans, and not everything operates like a business.

The mantra is that while business relationships and certain friendships might be assessed based on expected returns, personal relationships, even if seen as investments, should not carry explicit or tangible expectations of ROI. The real return is the satisfaction you feel from the positive impact your actions have on those you care about.

Mantra 4: Relationships Never Truly Die, Even After They Break

In many ways, relationships are like commodities—they experience fluctuations, rising and falling in strength over time. At any given moment, you'll find yourself in a variety of relationships, some strong, some weak, and others that seem broken.

However, it's important to recognize that even relationships in a broken state aren't truly dead. They still contain a spark of life, a potential for revival.

A hard truth is that not all our relationships can remain strong throughout our lives. Inevitably, some will weaken, and many may even seem to break. But even when we refer to them as broken, they are not entirely gone—they are simply faded versions of their former selves. The memories created in those relationships can never be erased, only buried deep within us.

Broken relationships still hold value, primarily because of the good times we once shared. These memories, though sometimes painful, can be cherished and serve as a reminder of why we might want to rekindle those connections.

The mantra here is that since relationships never truly die, you should never completely give up on the possibility of restoring a lost or broken one. The spark is already there; it just needs more fuel. However, it's crucial to understand that while you can control your own efforts in a relationship, its success depends on both sides working together to strengthen it. If the other party isn't willing to engage, the relationship may remain in its weakened state.

Mantra 5: Anger Fuels the Flames That Can Destroy

Relationships

Anger is a destructive force, and when it intertwines with the challenges of a relationship, the combination can be lethal. Simply put, anger and healthy relationships cannot coexist.

Every relationship experiences ups and downs, and rough patches are inevitable. It's natural to feel angry during these difficult times, but letting that anger take control can be dangerous.

Relationships naturally gather a collection of memories—good, bad, and ugly. Unresolved feelings and past hurts often linger within us like emotional baggage that's hard to let go of. Anger, in particular, has a tendency to unearth these buried emotions, especially the negative and painful ones, often at the worst possible moments and in ways that are counterproductive.

Rather than resolving issues, anger tends to spew out harsh words and blame, further damaging the relationship. It can escalate an already tense situation, pushing things from bad to worse, and even creating new wounds that may never fully heal.

Ironically, our frustration at not being able to mend a troubled relationship often leads us to direct anger at the very people we want to reconnect with.

The mantra is that, while it may be difficult, controlling your anger is essential if you want your relationships to endure tough times. Anger never mends a relationship; instead, it deepens the divide.

Mantra 6: Force in Relationships Acts Like a Slow Poison

When things aren't going smoothly, our instinct is often to use force to make them happen. Similarly, when a relationship hits a rough patch, the natural reaction is to apply force to try to fix it. While this approach might seem reasonable in some rare situations, it's generally harmful. For instance, in parenting, being strict can be necessary at times, and when balanced with love, care, and freedom, it can be effective. However, this is a delicate balance and should not be confused with exerting force.

The real issue arises when people consistently use force to control their relationships, shaping them according to their own desires. While force might seem effective initially, it soon backfires as the other person begins to push back. The initial compliance in such relationships often stems from fear, lack of courage, or some vested interest. Over time, however, as these factors change or as the person gains confidence, resistance grows, and the relationship starts to crumble under the weight of this force.

In some cases, you might use force out of anger or a need to feel in control, but this approach is unsustainable in both personal and professional relationships. If you impose your will on employees, they will eventually leave. Likewise, if you exert undue pressure on family or friends, they might tolerate it for a while, but they'll eventually distance themselves.

The mantra is to avoid using force in your relationships unless it is the absolute last resort. While force may provide temporary results, it cannot sustain a healthy, lasting relationship.

Mantra 7: Master the Art of Acceptance to Strengthen Your Relationships

If you aim to maintain long-lasting and healthy relationships, understanding and practicing acceptance is essential. Expectations can place a heavy burden on relationships, often leading to dissatisfaction and even causing them to break down.

A major issue with expectations is that many of them are unspoken, leaving those involved unaware of their existence.

As a result, these unmet expectations create frustration, not because the other person didn't want to meet them, but because they didn't know they existed.

Additionally, it's unrealistic to expect anyone to fulfill all of your expectations. Various factors can prevent this from happening, so if your happiness depends on every expectation being met, disappointment is inevitable.

While it may be difficult to eliminate expectations entirely, you can learn to accept outcomes that don't match your ideals. There are countless reasons why your expectations might not be met or may deviate from the standards you've set, and until you embrace the art of acceptance, you will likely continue to struggle with dissatisfaction.

Acceptance doesn't mean lowering your expectations; it means increasing your flexibility in dealing with the outcomes. This approach allows you to look at things from others' perspectives and understand their limitations in meeting your expectations.

People have their own ways of doing things, and when you start accepting their approaches instead of imposing your own, they will naturally feel more comfortable around you. This comfort, born from acceptance, can bring you closer to them and strengthen your relationships.

The mantra is to cultivate acceptance in your relationships. However, it's important to remember that accepting outcomes doesn't mean you start expecting others to do the same in return. Be careful not to let new, implicit expectations arise as a result of your acceptance.

Mantra 8: Keep Relationships Separate to Prevent Potential Conflicts

At any point in life, you'll have a variety of relationships with different people, each distinct in its nature and demands.

Some people may overlap across these relationship groups, acting as unintended conduits for information to leak from one group to another.

Each relationship has its own unique dynamics and challenges, and managing them within their own context is usually straightforward. However, when you bring people from different relationships together, things can become complicated. While mixing these groups may go smoothly most of the time, there are moments when conflicts can arise, putting you in a difficult position where maintaining neutrality becomes nearly impossible, and you might feel pressured to take sides.

In the realm of multiple relationships, honesty isn't always the best policy. Managing multiple relationships often involves navigating potential conflicts, and being entirely truthful in every situation can sometimes lead to more harm than good. You can be honest, but it might come at the cost of damaging your relationships or creating tensions between others.

Sometimes, you'll find yourself in situations where you're asked to discuss people from one relationship with those in another. In these cases, you'll need to tread carefully, balancing on a fine line between truth and diplomacy. There's always the risk that someone will spread what you say, leading to complications and putting you in a difficult position.

The mantra is to be mindful when mixing people from different relationships. If you foresee potential conflicts, it's best to keep these groups separate whenever possible.

Mantra 9: Old Relationships Will Fade, and New Ones Will Form

The saying "nothing lasts forever" holds true for relationships as well, as they are unlikely to remain unchanged over time. Our network of relationships will inevitably shift, sometimes due to deliberate choices and other times because of factors beyond our control.

As we journey through life, we'll lose some old relationships and form new ones. Various events in our lives—such as moving to a new place, changing jobs, getting married, or meeting new like-minded people—trigger these shifts.

When we relocate, we might maintain contact with a few close connections from our previous location, but many relationships will naturally fade away. Simultaneously, we'll forge new bonds in our new surroundings.

Similarly, changes in our relationship matrix occur as we transition through different life stages. However, not all changes are initiated by us; some come from others as they move away, following their own paths, while new people enter our lives without any action on our part.

While many changes in our relationships are positive, there are times when we need to let go of toxic relationships that no longer serve us. In such painful moments, accepting these changes is crucial, or we risk getting trapped in the past. It's important to remember that we are merely participants in the game that destiny is playing with us.

The mantra is to accept the reality that relationships will evolve over time. While we may feel the pain of losing some, new relationships will come into our lives, bringing joy and new opportunities for connection.

Mantra 10: Cherish the Good Moments From Past Relationships for Your Own Happiness

While we may wish to maintain all our relationships in perfect condition, the reality is that this is impossible. The complex nature of relationships, with their constant challenges and competing priorities, makes it difficult to keep them all thriving.

The reality is that not all of your relationships will last

forever. Some may become toxic, bringing more pain than joy, and will eventually break. Every relationship faces its own set of issues that require effort to resolve, but sometimes these issues grow too large, or the people involved lose interest, leading to the relationship's end.

When a relationship breaks down, it often leaves behind a trail of painful memories, especially during its final stages. However, as time passes, those broken relationships often become a mix of both good and bad memories.

You have a choice in how you remember these past relationships—either by focusing on the bad times or by cherishing the good. Dwelling on the negative aspects will only prolong your pain, forcing you to relive those moments in your mind. On the other hand, recalling the good times can bring you comfort and remind you of the joy you once shared.

These positive memories can even be the reason you might consider rekindling a relationship in the future.

The mantra is to focus on the good moments from your past relationships, using the bad experiences as lessons on what to avoid in the future. This mindset will help you handle broken relationships in a positive way, and possibly even revive them one day, perhaps in a different form or intensity. Remember, relationships never truly die; they just fade away, and there's always a chance to bring them back to life.

CHAPTER 8

Over Encouragement: The Demon of Excess Motivation

There are many actions we take with the belief that we are helping others, often leaving us with a sense of self-satisfaction for giving back to those we care about. However, the reality can be quite different from our assumptions. While we think we're offering support, we may unintentionally be doing more harm than good.

It's not very uncommon to assume we know what's best for someone without fully understanding their unique circumstances or needs. This chapter explores one such unintended consequence of our well-meaning actions, illustrated by the phrase "You can do it!"—a perfect example of how we can inadvertently introduce pressure rather than support in someone's system.

When embarking on something new or unfamiliar, it's natural to have doubts and fears of failure. No matter how well-prepared we are, there are always uncertainties and risks. In such moments, we often hope for encouragement from those we trust—friends, family, and loved ones. Words like "You can do it" are intended to boost our confidence and push us forward, often serving as a powerful motivator.

This phrase has become so common and widely used that it feels like an official source of encouragement, something we know well and use frequently in our lives.

But let's try to look at it from a different angle.

While encouragement generally motivates us, there are times when it can become a burden. Excessive encouragement can push us to take on more than we can handle, leading to failure. When this happens, it often leaves us with a sense of guilt, as we feel we've let down those who encouraged us. The irony is that the encouragement, meant to empower us, can instead become an obligation to succeed—not for our own sake, but to meet the expectations of others. It can feel as though we are striving to fulfill someone else's dreams, rather than our own.

The Hidden Pitfalls of Over-Encouragement: Balancing Support and Pressure

To better understand this concept, let's consider a scenario involving a young boy in your neighborhood who is attempting something for the very first time. Based on what you know about his abilities, you have a strong sense that he is likely to fail in this endeavor. While in this case, you have some insight into the boy's capabilities, there will be other situations where you may not have a clear understanding of someone's skills or circumstances, leaving you to make guesses based on superficial knowledge about them.

Returning to the scenario, despite your doubts, you decide to encourage the boy to give it a try. You believe it's better for him to attempt and possibly fail than to avoid trying altogether—a classic mindset. Naturally, you might use the familiar phrase, "You can do it," to offer support.

At first glance, this approach seems harmless. After all, you're just offering encouragement to help boost the boy's confidence. However, while your words may uplift his spirits, they might not alter the reality—he could still fail. Of course, there's value in learning from failure, and that's not the point of contention here.

Now, let's shift perspectives and view this situation from the boy's point of view. As he prepares to try something new, he likely has his own doubts about succeeding, and is looking for encouragement to build the courage to take that leap.

When you and others express strong confidence in your encouragement, you unintentionally leave little room for the possibility of failure. This over-encouragement gives the boy not only a boost in confidence but also a heavy burden to succeed. Yet, because he's trying something new and may not have the necessary skills, he fails. This failure doesn't just disappoint him; it makes him feel ashamed and guilty for letting down those who believed in him. He starts to feel responsible for meeting others' expectations, rather than simply learning from the experience.

Clearly, this outcome wasn't what you or others intended when offering encouragement. Your goal was to build his confidence, not to create an overwhelming pressure to succeed.

So, where does the problem lie? The issue isn't with the act of encouraging; it's in how that encouragement is delivered.

The Proper Approach to Encouraging Others: Avoiding the Pitfalls of Over-Encouragement

Just because phrases like "You can do it" have become so common, doesn't mean we should use them thoughtlessly or undermine their significance. In the example above, by over-encouraging the boy, you may have unintentionally planted a seed of anxiety—a demon that pressures him to succeed and punishes him if he fails.

It's important to remember that with the power to

encourage comes the responsibility to do so thoughtfully and effectively, without causing unintended harm. Before offering encouragement, take a moment to assess the person's abilities and the likelihood of success or failure in the situation. Tailor your encouragement based on this assessment.

If you're unable to fully evaluate the situation, you can still offer support, but it's crucial to include words that acknowledge all possible outcomes. For example, instead of simply saying, "You can do it," a more balanced approach might be: "You can do it if you give it your best effort. Don't worry about failing, especially since it's your first time trying—what matters is that you tried."

This approach delivers two key messages. The first encourages the person to try despite their doubts, while the second prepares them to handle a possible failure with grace. The best part is that this balanced encouragement doesn't create undue pressure; instead, it leaves room for the possibility of failure and equips the person to cope with it.

Some might argue that this method dilutes the confidence of the person being encouraged, suggesting that acknowledging the potential for failure could make them more likely to accept it lightly. However, it's important to remember that you chose to include the possibility of failure precisely because you had concerns about their abilities and anticipated the likelihood of failure.

By offering balanced encouragement, you empower others to try new things while also protecting them from the undue stress of unrealistic expectations. This way, you help them grow without introducing unnecessary demons of pressure and guilt.

When You're on the Receiving End of Over-Encouragement

We've just explored a scenario where you might have unintentionally introduced anxiety and pressure into someone else's system through over-encouragement, and how to avoid doing so. Now, let's consider the opposite situation —when you become the recipient of this kind of excessive encouragement.

Imagine you're in a situation where others express strong confidence in your success, even though you're almost certain of your failure. Under the influence of their encouragement, you take on more than you can handle and ultimately fail. This can feel like trusting others' opinions over your own instincts, leading to disappointment.

However, there's an interesting silver lining: sometimes others might see potential in you that you can't see yourself. In such cases, trusting their belief in you could be the right choice—but only after you've done your own due diligence to understand what they see in you.

The key thing to remember when you're on the receiving end of over-encouragement is not to blindly accept others' confidence in your success. Instead, assess the authenticity of their belief in you. They might be using encouraging words simply to motivate you, without a solid basis, which could set you up for failure.

While it's great to feel supported by those around you, it's crucial that their confidence in you doesn't turn into a source of pressure. Your motivation to succeed should come from within, not from others' expectations. And if you do fail, don't let guilt over disappointing others weigh you down.

Remember, success or failure is influenced by many factors, and your efforts and abilities are just part of the equation. It's okay to fall short of others' expectations as long as you know you gave it your best or did as much as you wanted to, even if you could have done more. There's a difference between having abilities and using them to their fullest potential—true success lies in the latter.

This also means that while it's wonderful to share your

successes with others, you don't owe anyone an explanation for your failures. You should be the primary judge of your own failures, unless you seek feedback to learn from them.

When We Are Both the Giver and Receiver of Over-Encouragement

As we continue to delve into the demon of over-encouragement, let's examine a scenario where we fall victim to this demon by over-encouraging ourselves, especially when we are experiencing self-doubt or a lack of confidence. In this case, we become both the source and the target of over-encouragement within our own minds—a phenomenon I'll refer to as self-over-encouragement. While self-encouragement is generally positive, it can sometimes lead us astray.

There are moments when we have a desire to pursue something, but our self-assessment convinces us that failure is likely because we either lack the necessary skills or the circumstances are unfavorable. We find ourselves torn between the heart's desire and the mind's resistance.

In such times, we often step in to boost our own confidence, convincing our mind to align with our heart's wishes. If successful, we enter the "I can do it" mindset. However, this self-over-encouragement can sometimes lead to overconfidence. Ignoring our doubts, we may become overly convinced of our success without properly reassessing our abilities, and as a result, we might take on challenges that exceed our capacity, leading to failure.

In these instances, our mind's initial caution proves to be justified, and we are left to wrestle with regret. If we had been more pragmatic, we might have heeded our mind's warnings and avoided failure. Instead, the over-encouragement demon managed to sway us into taking a risk we were ill-prepared for.

To avoid this pitfall, it's important to strike a balance.

While we should listen to our heart to understand our true desires, we must not completely disregard our mind's practical concerns. Conversely, relying solely on the mind can prevent us from taking any risks at all.

Self-over-encouragement should be used as a tool for motivation only when there is a healthy balance between what the heart desires and what the mind realistically supports.

Not Everything is Everyone's Cup of Tea

At first glance, this phrase might seem like just a random collection of words, but it captures a fundamental truth: not everyone can do everything. Often, people fail when they attempt something outside their area of interest or expertise. The likelihood of failure increases when passion and skill are lacking.

While I don't entirely agree with the idea that certain things are simply beyond our reach, there is some truth to it. I believe that with hard work, determination, and perseverance, we can achieve almost anything. However, the reality is that there are areas where we may struggle despite our best efforts. Success often requires more than just effort—it demands genuine interest and an alignment with our natural abilities.

Considering the vast number of things in the world, it's unrealistic to expect anyone to excel at everything. Each of us have unique interests, abilities, strengths, and limitations, making us more suited to certain activities over others. Our chances of success are highest when we focus on areas that align with our natural inclinations.

Moreover, many endeavors require teamwork, where individuals complement each other's strengths and weaknesses. Collaboration and mutual support are key to collective success, with one person's limitations being offset by another's strengths.

Understanding that it's okay not to be able to do everything can relieve a lot of pressure. Instead of trying to master everything, it's crucial to focus on what we do well and where we can make meaningful contributions. This shift in focus helps prevent feelings of inadequacy and fosters a sense of purpose.

Finding your "cup of tea" is essential. Sometimes, you may already know what it is, while other times, you'll discover it through trial and error. As the saying goes, sometimes you find your passion, and sometimes it finds you.

Furthermore, when you find yourself under pressure to do something that you feel is not your "cup of tea," it's important to muster the courage to say no to those who have expectations of you. At the very least, communicate that you will make an effort but might not succeed—don't just fail without a word.

Finally, when encouraging others, it's important to recognize their strengths. Encouraging people in areas where they excel leads to genuine motivation, while pushing them toward things that don't align with their abilities can result in over-encouragement, which may have the opposite effect. Encouragement should be empowering, not overwhelming.

The Good in Over-Encouragement

While encouragement is generally seen as a positive force, over-encouragement can sometimes be perceived as a double-edged sword. However, despite its potential downsides, when used wisely, over-encouragement can have its benefits.

Encouragement naturally boosts confidence, and over-encouragement can lead to overconfidence. Though overconfidence often gets a bad reputation, there are moments when it is exactly what's needed to overcome challenges or seize opportunities.

One of the greatest strengths of encouragement is its ability to lift people out of a state of self-doubt. It provides the necessary motivation to push past insecurities and take action.

At times, others may see potential in you that you haven't yet recognized in yourself. When they express this through encouragement, especially with specific examples, it offers you the chance to discover strengths and talents you were previously unaware of.

Parenting is a prime example of how encouragement can be transformative. It helps nurture confident and successful children who aren't afraid to try new things or face the possibility of failure. They learn that it's better to attempt and fail than to avoid opportunities out of fear.

Sometimes, all it takes is a little encouragement for someone to realize they're ready to take the next step towards success. It gives them the confidence to take the plunge when they might otherwise hesitate.

In the battle against worry and self-doubt, encouragement is a powerful tool.

Mantras for Dealing With the Over-Encouragement Demon

Now, let's explore a few mantras that we can adopt to tackle this demon effectively. These mantras will help you keep the over-encouragement demon in check, allowing you to stay focused on genuine growth and self-improvement.

Mantra 1: Don't Assume a Request for Help or Advice is a Request for Encouragement

When people reach out to you for help or advice, it's usually because they value your expertise, experience, or insights in a particular area. They may seek your guidance for various reasons, but it's important to remember that not every request for help also implies a need for encouragement.

It's human nature that often leads us to misinterpret situations and make assumptions that may not align with reality. It's not uncommon to assume that when someone asks for your advice, they also need encouragement. This can lead to offering more than what was actually asked for, possibly overwhelming the person or going beyond what is helpful.

It's important to understand that your advice provides the information and perspective someone needs to further analyze their situation. They might still be in the early stages of contemplation, where they are gathering facts and considering their options. In such cases, while your advice is valuable, any additional encouragement might be premature or misplaced.

If you offer encouragement when it's not yet needed, it may not have the intended effect. Later, when the person truly needs that boost of encouragement, you might assume you've already provided it, missing the opportunity to support them when it really counts.

Therefore, when someone asks for help or advice, focus on delivering exactly that—help or advice. Hold back on encouragement unless you detect a clear need for it.

The mantra is to give advice when asked, and save encouragement for when it's truly needed. Unsolicited encouragement often lacks impact and can waste your effort if offered at the wrong time. By providing encouragement prematurely, you may miss the opportunity to truly support someone when they genuinely need it.

Mantra 2: Your expertise Doesn't Entitle You to Over-Encourage Others

Being an expert in a particular field may make your insights valuable to others, and people might even enjoy hearing your knowledgeable perspectives. However, possessing deep knowledge can sometimes lead to an unconscious assumption that you have the authority to encourage others freely, believing your expertise grants you that right.

The reality is that, even as an expert or genius in a subject, you might unintentionally over-encourage someone who isn't as proficient in that area. In doing so, you could set them up for failure by pushing them beyond their current capabilities. What comes easily to you might be a monumental challenge for someone else.

The key is to remember that, regardless of your level of expertise, it's essential to assess the other person's abilities before offering encouragement. Your expertise should primarily be used to help and guide those in need, and you should reserve encouragement for moments when it's genuinely needed and appropriate.

The mantra is to understand that your expertise doesn't entitle you to over-encourage others at every opportunity. Instead, use your knowledge to guide, and offer encouragement only when it's truly needed.

Mantra 3: Sift Through the Encouragements You Receive to Uncover Valuable Insights

You will encounter encouragement from various sources, each with different intentions, and it's up to you to discern the valuable ones from the rest.

Encouragement—or even over-encouragement—can come from well-wishers, manipulators, and those who are indifferent to your outcomes.

Some of your well-wishers may offer encouragement simply because they want to see you succeed, regardless of your capabilities. Their intentions are good, but their encouragement may not always be grounded in reality. On the other hand, some well-wishers see genuine potential in you and may over-encourage you to push harder and realize that potential.

Manipulators, however, may encourage you with ulterior motives, seeking to serve their own agendas. Recognizing these individuals is crucial to avoid becoming a pawn in their plans, where they benefit at your expense.

Then there are the neutral encouragers—those who encourage you out of habit or a sense of obligation, without any real concern for whether you succeed or fail. Their encouragement is often superficial and lacks any genuine interest in your outcome.

It's essential to acknowledge all forms of encouragement but not to accept them blindly. Filter them carefully, understanding that not all encouragement is in your best interest.

The mantra is to understand that not all encouragement is equal. It's important to recognize the intentions behind it, whether from well-wishers, manipulators, or indifferent individuals. By understanding the motivations, you can make sure you're acting on advice that truly supports your interests. Accept encouragement thoughtfully, not blindly.

Mantra 4: View Encouragement as a Supplementary Insight, Not the Final Verdict

Encouragement can be immensely beneficial when it's relevant and applied thoughtfully, but it also has its downsides, particularly when it manifests as over-encouragement. Whether it's external validation or self-motivation, encouragement has its place—it helps you validate your assumptions and dispel doubts, pushing you forward when you're uncertain.

However, if encouragement isn't aligned with your

true abilities, it can become over-encouragement, setting unrealistic expectations and leading to potential failure. Therefore, it's crucial not to rely solely on encouragement but rather to treat it as an additional data point in your overall analysis.

In essence, don't begin or end your decision-making process with encouragement alone. Starting with it might indicate a lack of internal drive, while ending with it implies you're placing blind trust in the encouragement without critical examination. Instead, incorporate it as one step in a more comprehensive process.

Encouragement can be valuable, particularly when it comes from people you respect or consider experts. However, it's important to remember that while they may offer insightful advice, they don't fully understand your unique capabilities and circumstances. Ultimately, you are the best judge of your actions.

Never accept encouragement as the final word without conducting your own thorough analysis, regardless of its source.

The mantra is to treat encouragement as a supportive tool, not the deciding factor. Use it to enhance your self-assessment, but always trust your own judgment above all.

Mantra 5: Cultivate Self-Motivation Rather Than Relying on Others' Encouragement

We've all experienced those moments when our confidence was low, and a word of encouragement from someone else gave us the boost we needed. It's natural to seek reassurance when facing uncertainty, and sometimes external encouragement can be just the push we need to take action. However, depending entirely on others for confidence can make us reliant and limit our ability to self-motivate.

External encouragement, especially from someone with relevant experience or expertise, can be valuable. It can help validate our efforts and provide insight that we might not have considered. But the most enduring and reliable source of confidence comes from within. True confidence is built on self-recognition of your strengths, abilities, and accomplishments, and believing in yourself even when external encouragement is absent.

The key to sustainable confidence lies in self-awareness, self-acceptance, and self-belief. You can develop this internal strength by cultivating a positive self-image, setting realistic and achievable goals, and celebrating your personal achievements—regardless of whether others acknowledge them or not.

While supportive feedback from others can be helpful, it's crucial to strike a balance between external encouragement and your internal sense of self-worth. Over-reliance on encouragement from those who don't truly know you can lead to overconfidence or misguided efforts, potentially pushing you toward failure.

The mantra here is not to depend solely on others' encouragement for motivation and confidence. Instead, use external validation to complement and reinforce the self-assurance you've already developed within yourself. Let it serve as an additional layer of support, but always remember that your primary source of motivation and confidence should come from within.

Mantra 6: Recognize the Uniqueness of Everyone's Need for Encouragement

Throughout this chapter, we've emphasized that while encouragement can be beneficial, over-encouragement can have negative effects. Since each person is unique, what serves as encouragement for one individual may be excessive for another.

The effectiveness of encouragement depends largely on who you're encouraging and the context. For example, encouraging a mathematical genius to excel in math exams is appropriate and meaningful. However, offering the same level of encouragement to someone who struggles with math could overwhelm them, leading to unintended negative consequences.

There's a fine line between encouragement and over-encouragement, and it's crucial to adjust the intensity of your encouragement based on the individual's needs and abilities. The content of your encouragement is important, but so is the tone with which you deliver it.

Everyone has unique needs when it comes to encouragement, and what motivates or inspires one person might not have the same effect on another. To provide meaningful and effective encouragement, it's essential to understand and respect these individual differences.

Some people thrive on external praise and recognition, finding it a powerful motivator that boosts their confidence. Others may be more self-motivated, drawing strength from within and requiring less external encouragement to feel confident and fulfilled. Then, there are those who might dislike external encouragement altogether, finding it unnecessary or even counterproductive.

The mantra is to recognize that people have varying needs for encouragement to act with confidence. By understanding and honoring these differences, you can tailor your approach to make your encouragement more effective and meaningful, ensuring it aligns with each individual's preferences and needs.

Mantra 7: Ensure That Your Encouragement Doesn't Unintentionally Become a Lecture

Encouragement is a powerful tool for boosting confidence, offering support, reassurance, and positive reinforcement in a way that motivates and uplifts without judgment or criticism. It helps individuals recognize their strengths, acknowledge their efforts, and believe in their abilities.

In contrast, a lecture is typically a one-way communication from an expert to an audience, delivering information, advice, or instructions. While informative, lectures often lack consideration for the recipient's perspective or feelings unless specifically designed as an interactive discussion.

Both encouragement and lectures have their own significance, but they serve different purposes. People generally respond more positively to encouragement because it aligns with their personal goals and motivates them in a supportive manner. Lectures, on the other hand, can feel more imposed, especially if unsolicited, and often include repetitive or less engaging content.

The challenge arises when, in the flow of offering encouragement, we unintentionally slip into a lecturing mode. When encouragement is overdone with repetitive points or excessive examples, it can lose its uplifting nature and morph into a lecture—something that the recipient might not appreciate, especially if they don't see you as an expert on the subject.

To avoid this, it's essential to approach encouragement with empathy, active listening, and respect for the other person's viewpoint. Focus on providing constructive feedback and engaging in a genuine dialogue to understand their thoughts and feelings.

While using examples in encouragement can be helpful, overloading your message with too many examples can shift the tone toward a lecture.

The mantra is to be mindful of the fine line between encouragement and lecturing, making sure that your well-meaning support doesn't unintentionally become a lecture. By keeping this in mind, you can ensure your words remain uplifting and well-received, rather than turning into something the recipient may not want to hear.

Mantra 8: Be Cautious of Hidden Motives Behind Over-Encouragement

We all appreciate encouragement from others, especially for the positive reasons we've discussed so far. However, there are times when people may offer over-encouragement without considering whether it's genuinely beneficial for you, often because they are more focused on their own interests.

Sometimes, encouragement from others may seem to come from genuine care and support, but hidden motives can lie beneath the surface. In some cases, people may encourage you with the intent of manipulating or influencing you for their own gain. For instance, a colleague might seem supportive by offering encouragement, but their true motive could be to sway you into doing something that benefits them more than it benefits you.

Similarly, someone might encourage you to pursue a path where you're likely to fail, not out of concern for your success, but because they want to see you stumble. In other situations, people may push you to complete tasks that are lower on your priority list but are critical for their own work, even if those tasks offer little benefit to you.

It's also common for friends, particularly teenagers, to encourage risky or dangerous behavior for the sake of entertainment, downplaying the potential dangers while urging you to act for their amusement.

In our complex world, there are countless examples where encouragement is given with ulterior motives, often disregarding your well-being. Being aware of these potential hidden agendas can protect you from falling victim to manipulative schemes.

However, it's important not to become overly cynical or distrustful of all encouragement. If you do, you might miss out on genuine support from those who truly care about you.

The mantra here is to be cautious when receiving excessive encouragement, especially from those who aren't known to be your well-wishers. There's a chance their intentions may not align with your best interests and could be driven by their self-interest. Yet, it's equally important to remain open to sincere encouragement from those who genuinely want to see you succeed.

Mantra 9: Encouragement Can Work Wonders, When Offered Correctly

While over-encouragement can lead to unintended negative effects, offering encouragement is still a powerful and positive act—when done correctly, it can work wonders. The key is to be mindful and deliberate in your approach, providing encouragement at the right moment to maximize its impact.

Sometimes, a small dose of encouragement is all someone needs to push through that final stretch. Often, people give up just before reaching their goal, feeling that their efforts aren't paying off. This is precisely when your encouragement can make a difference, helping them to persevere and achieve success, especially when you see potential in what they're doing.

There are also times when you might recognize potential in someone that they haven't yet realized. In such cases, your ongoing encouragement can help them tap into that potential. Parenting offers a prime example of this, where parents often encourage their children to realize their capabilities—though it's important not to overestimate or push too hard, which can lead to over-encouragement.

One crucial aspect to remember is the importance of active listening before offering encouragement. Understanding the other person's perspective allows you to tailor your support to their specific needs and concerns, making your encouragement more relevant and impactful.

Genuine encouragement helps people feel that you truly believe in them and their abilities, fostering a sense of confidence and motivation. When delivered thoughtfully, it can inspire action, empower individuals to pursue their goals, and make them feel valued and capable.

The mantra here is to recognize that well-intentioned encouragement, when delivered with care and sincerity, can truly work wonders. It has the power to uplift, inspire, and empower others to reach their full potential. Just be sure to listen and understand their perspective before offering your words of support.

Mantra 10: Sometimes, Withholding Encouragement is the Right Choice

While encouraging others is generally a great idea, there are situations where withholding encouragement may be the more appropriate response.

By choosing not to encourage, you can help individuals develop independence and self-reliance. When people constantly rely on external validation, they may struggle to build their own confidence and decision-making abilities. Withholding encouragement can prompt them to engage in critical self-evaluation, leading to a more honest assessment of their performance and a clearer understanding of areas that need improvement.

In situations where you recognize a lack of ability or a high likelihood of failure, offering encouragement can create false assurance, potentially setting someone up for disappointment. Similarly, encouragement might set unrealistic expectations, preventing people from maintaining a realistic and grounded perspective in this competitive and challenging world.

Facing challenges without constant encouragement can also help individuals build resilience, as it forces them to navigate adversity and setbacks on their own, strengthening their ability to handle future obstacles.

There are also times when withholding encouragement is better because the person may be overwhelmed by receiving it from multiple sources. For instance, if someone narrowly misses winning a race, they might be inundated with encouragement to "try a bit harder next time," when what they really need is space to process their emotions.

The mantra is that, while encouragement is generally beneficial, there are moments when holding back is more effective. This approach can better support someone's growth and development, helping them become more self-reliant and confident in their own abilities.

CHAPTER 9

Needs, Wants and Greed: The Demons of Survival, Yearning and Insatiable Desires

When you reflect on needs, wants, and greed, you'll notice their presence in every aspect of your daily life and across all areas of your existence. They are intricately woven into the fabric of our lives, influencing our thoughts, decisions, and actions.

On closer examination, you'll see that they represent three distinct levels of the same underlying drive—the motivation to acquire resources or achieve goals. This progression begins with a need, evolves into a want, and ultimately escalates into greed.

A need represents the bare essentials required for survival, well-being, and functionality. Without meeting these needs, our health, security, and ability to function effectively are at risk. Wants go beyond these essentials, representing desires for things that are beneficial but not crucial for survival. Greed, on the other hand, is an excessive craving for far more than what is necessary, driven by an insatiable desire that surpasses what is needed or even deserved.

Among these three, only needs are non-negotiable—they must be met for us to lead a healthy life. Wants begin to set us apart from other species, playing a significant role in shaping our materialistic world. Greed, while often seen negatively, has also contributed to this evolution, though with more complicated consequences.

You might wonder why I'm discussing these three in the context of demons within us. The reason I've dedicated a full chapter to them is that each, in its own way, acts as a demon, haunting us throughout our lives. These forces are intertwined with every moment we live, shaping our experiences and influencing our choices.

Let's delve deeper into the nature of these demons, exploring how they manifest in our lives and the ways in which they consume us.

The Needs Demon

Need isn't a single concept but an umbrella that encompasses various forms, such as physical needs, mental needs, social needs, safety needs, financial needs, and more.

For instance, physical needs like food, water, and air are fundamental for survival; we need a certain minimum amount of each to stay alive, and without them, life is impossible. Financial needs, like money, are crucial in our world as nearly everything requires financial resources. Social needs, like having people we trust and share our lives with, are essential for a fulfilling social life.

Technically, needs shouldn't be seen as a demon since they are vital for our survival and guide us toward what is essential in this materialistic world. However, needs can become haunting when we cannot meet them, transforming into a demon that torments us.

By definition, a need is the bare minimum required for

survival, but in reality, needs often expand over time. This growth can result from natural progression or from the gradual inclusion of wants and greed into our list of essential needs.

The good news is that this demon can be tamed. We can control it by reducing our needs to a manageable level, making it easier to satisfy them. Through self-control, we can gradually reduce our needs to the minimum necessary for survival.

In some extreme cases, some individuals have managed to lower their needs to incredibly minimal levels and still survive. There are stories of saints who have survived on almost no food, water, or even oxygen.

Another positive aspect of this demon is that once a need is satisfied, it remains dormant until the next cycle begins. For instance, hunger subsides after eating and only returns when the next hunger cycle starts. This creates intervals of relief while managing the need demon.

In terms of its demonic nature, no matter how minimal your needs may be, this demon will persistently haunt you if they go unmet. However, this haunting has a purpose—it's a crucial warning that you must address your needs in order to survive.

Primary and Secondary Needs

The need demon can be divided into two major categories: primary and secondary needs.

Primary needs are the bare essentials required for survival, such as food, water, shelter, clothing, healthcare, and security. These needs are universally recognized as fundamental for maintaining life and health.

Secondary needs arise when we seek to enhance our quality of life beyond mere survival. These needs often emerge from personal aspirations, cultural influences, and societal norms. Examples include education, comfort, convenience, social status, entertainment, and leisure. Essentially, anything that starts as a want or greed but has crossed the line into the territory of becoming a need.

The conflict between primary and secondary needs often arises because secondary needs are seen as less essential by others. They might view you as spoiled by materialistic influences if your needs go beyond the basics.

While primary needs are essential for survival, secondary needs play a significant role in shaping our quality of life and personal fulfillment. Balancing these needs is crucial to managing the demons within us.

For the sake of discussion, it's worth noting that these needs and their associated "demons" have evolved alongside us, from our days as cave dwellers to the modern society we live in today. As humans have progressed, so too have the complexities of our needs and the ways in which they manifest, reflecting our ongoing evolution.

The Wants Demon

Wants are desires that go beyond what is essential for survival or basic well-being. By their very nature, they can be seen as a demon, something that exists outside our list of must-haves for survival, and they can haunt us if left unfulfilled. While we can survive without satisfying our wants, doing so may come at the cost of some of our happiness, as much of our contentment is tied to these desires in our materialistic world.

The origin of this demon lies within us—it's born from our own yearning for things beyond our basic needs. Therefore, we must be prepared to face the troubles this demon brings if we're unable to satisfy our wants. In essence, this monster is a direct creation of our own cravings.

For clarity and simplicity, I'll use "wants" and "desires" interchangeably in this discussion, even though they have subtle differences. They represent the same demon in this context.

A quite relevant explanation of desire I once heard is that when your need for food is fulfilled and your hunger vanishes, the urge to eat something extra and tasty, like dessert, is desire.

Since our wants are self-created, theoretically, we should be able to reduce them to a level that is easily satisfied, leaving us completely content with no unfulfilled wants. However, in reality, our wants tend to grow in both number and intensity, so even after reducing some and eliminating others, there will always be a list of unfulfilled desires in our system.

Another important point is that when we think we've killed a want, we've often only suppressed it into dormancy, not eliminated it entirely. The notion of killing a want is often just an illusion; the desire still lingers, lying dormant and waiting to resurface when triggered.

To illustrate this, let's walk through a situation where you need a car to commute to work. An affordable economy car would suffice for that need. But you might want to buy a more expensive, luxurious car that, while it does everything the economy car does, offers additional features and a sense of pride in ownership.

You might suppress this desire by convincing yourself that it's not worth spending extra money on a premium car when the economy car serves the same purpose. You may even end up buying the economy car. However, every time you see that premium car you once desired, the buried want resurfaces, as the desire for that car never truly disappeared.

So, while it is possible to control our wants or desires, it may come at the cost of some happiness, as these wants, though unnecessary, do contribute to our sense of joy.

The Greed Demon

Greed is the most dangerous of the trio, holding the strongest grip on us. Like want, greed is born from our desires, but it's far more excessive and, by its very nature, insatiable. Your desires morph into greed when you crave something far beyond what you actually need or deserve—usually in the realms of material wealth, power, or indulgence. Greed often disregards ethical considerations and the well-being of others, making it an inherently selfish force.

Greed is a demon with an unquenchable appetite, relentlessly haunting you no matter how hard you try to satisfy it. The more you attempt to appease this demon, the more it grows. The most sinister aspect of greed is that, in your effort to satisfy its demands, you might go so far as to deprive others of their basic needs, always prioritizing your own greed over the well-being of others.

In today's world, where materialistic pursuits are abundant, it's easy to find justifications for our greedy desires. We live in a society where possessions are highly valued, and often, our greed is rationalized, even glorified.

There's no denying that greed has played a significant role in human history, particularly in our evolution. Many wars have been fought over wealth and power, driven by greed, resulting in the deaths of billions. This raises an intriguing question: where would the descendants of those billions of people live in today's overcrowded and resource-depleted world? Perhaps, in some twisted way, these acts of greed have contributed to maintaining a balance in nature.

Although greed is a creation of our own making, controlling it is incredibly difficult because it's such a powerful force. The hunger of this demon cannot be sated, no matter how much you acquire, and it's often condemned for its inherently destructive nature.

Greed vs Ambition

Greed and ambition are often used to describe strong desires, but they occupy very different ends of the desire spectrum.

Greed refers to an intense and selfish desire, particularly for wealth, power, or material possessions. It often implies an excessive or insatiable craving that can lead to unethical behavior or harm to others. Greed is generally seen in a negative light because it suggests a disregard for the well-being of others in pursuit of personal gain.

Ambition, on the other hand, is a strong desire to achieve something, typically involving a drive for success, growth, or improvement. Ambition is usually viewed positively, as it can lead to personal and professional development, goal achievement, and contributing positively to society.

While ambition is generally seen as a motivating force that drives individuals to strive for better, it can become problematic and cross into the realm of greed if it turns into an obsession or begins to harm others.

In essence, greed is often seen as a negative, self-centered force, while ambition is considered a positive, goal-oriented drive.

Rethinking Needs, Wants, and Greed in Modern Life

From a young age, we've been taught that to become better and more content human beings, we should focus solely on our basic needs and guard against falling into the traps of wants and greed. Even many philosophers have echoed the same idea, presenting it as a foundation for a happy and content life.

This philosophy suggests that by sticking to our needs and avoiding the lure of wants and greed, we can protect ourselves from a cycle of endless desires. It's widely believed that once we begin chasing after wants and greed, we risk getting caught in a never-ending spiral, making it nearly impossible to break free.

While I don't entirely disagree with this perspective, I also don't fully agree with it. I hold a slightly different view. Nevertheless, I think it's a useful principle to keep in mind, especially when we find ourselves tempted by the allure of wants and greed.

When it comes to these so-called "demons," I believe that everyone is different, and so are their needs, wants, and levels of greed. It's important to recognize that what one person sees as a need might be viewed as a want or even greed by someone else. This largely depends on individual perceptions and the thresholds people set for when a want or greed becomes a need.

For instance, consider air conditioning. To an average person, air conditioning might seem like a luxury—a nice-to-have rather than a necessity. However, if someone feels uncomfortable or has difficulty sleeping without air conditioning, then for them, it becomes a need, regardless of what others might think. Others might label this person as spoiled, but I would argue that they simply have different needs.

That said, I would categorize air conditioning as a secondary need because there will inevitably be times when it's unavailable due to various circumstances, and in those moments, adaptation is necessary.

My intention here isn't to justify indulgence, but rather to acknowledge and adapt to the evolving needs in our increasingly materialistic world, even when some of these needs might be classified by others as wants or greed.

When it comes to wants and greed, it's true that they aren't essential for survival. However, life isn't solely about survival

—it's about so much more. The reality is that many of our wants contribute significantly to our happiness, and when those wants go unmet, our happiness is directly affected. We might continue to survive, but at the expense of our joy.

Similarly, while greed is generally viewed as negative, there are times when it brings us happiness, and it's okay to savor those moments, provided that satisfying our greed doesn't come at the expense of someone else's needs or compromise our ethical standards.

The Good in Needs, Wants and Greed

Though often viewed negatively, each of these "demons"—needs, wants, and greed—plays a crucial role in our lives, making it impossible to completely eliminate them from our system.

The Role of Needs

Needs are fundamental to our existence, requiring no justification for their presence. They sustain life by demanding the essential minimum for our survival. Unfortunately, in some cases, even meeting these basic demands can be a challenge, particularly in situations of poverty, where access to the essentials becomes difficult.

Needs establish the basic requirements we must fulfill to live. Our bodies have evolved a system of alarms to ensure these needs are met—hunger signals our need for food, thirst reminds us to hydrate, sleepiness prompts rest, and tiredness urges us to take a break. Alongside these natural alarms, there are also artificial systems that help us address other forms of need.

The presence of needs is therefore intrinsic to our survival, unquestionable in its importance. To add a touch of humor—the needs are indeed needed.

The Role of Wants

Our wants differentiate us from other species. While animals focus primarily on fulfilling their needs for survival, humans aspire to more. Wants drive us beyond the satisfaction of basic needs, propelling us toward achievements that go far beyond mere survival.

Wants can be seen as a double-edged sword. On one hand, this demon prevents us from feeling content with what we have. On the other hand, they push us out of our comfort zones, driving us to seek and attain more than what our needs alone could provide. Without wants, we might fall into complacency, never striving for a better life or greater accomplishments.

This might seem to contradict with the concept of a contented life, but the world is full of opportunities and material pleasures that beckon us. Wants motivate us to reach for these, adding richness and satisfaction to our lives. Although materialistic, these desires often contribute to our happiness.

While our evolution may have been rooted in fulfilling needs, wants have played a significant role in shaping our progress. Throughout history, our ancestors could have stopped evolving once their basic needs were met. However, their desire for more—both for themselves and future generations—kept them moving forward. This relentless pursuit of more has brought us to where we are today and continues to drive us towards the future.

Wants also bring color and purpose to our lives, offering reasons to enjoy life beyond mere survival. In our professional lives, for example, it's often our wants that align with our passions, guiding us toward the work that fulfills us. Socially, our desires lead us to seek out like-minded friends and experiences. On a personal level, wants inspire us to pursue a life that's not just adequate but truly fulfilling.

Wants are pervasive, playing a vital role in our lives. They are a worthy presence in our system, provided they don't overpower us or lead us down the wrong paths.

The Role of Greed

Greed, by its very nature, is often seen as an evil—a sin and a demon to be avoided, to prevent it from consuming us. Greed represents an overwhelming urge to acquire something, often far beyond what we need or deserve. Because of its insatiable nature, greed is never fully satisfied.

However, like a coin with two sides, greed has a positive aspect when viewed as an excessive form of want. Since greed is more intense than want, it can drive us to achieve things beyond our wildest imagination. It can push us far beyond our perceived limits, but we have to be careful, as this force can propel us in either the right or the wrong direction.

At times, a mere desire or want isn't enough to push us beyond certain thresholds, even when we have untapped potential. It's in these moments that greed can act as a catalyst, compelling us to tap into hidden reserves of energy and determination to achieve what we deeply desire.

While greed is largely seen as negative, it can occasionally serve a purpose by pushing us to surpass our own limitations. However, it is a force that must be carefully managed, a demon to be kept under control.

Mantras for Dealing With the Needs, Wants and Greed Demon

Here are a few mantras to help manage the influence of needs, wants, and greed—the "demons" in our lives. By following these mantras, you can navigate the complex interplay between needs, wants, and greed, ensuring that each serves its rightful purpose in your life.

Mantra 1: Identify Your Needs and Ensure You Can Meet Them Even in Your Worst-Case Scenario

I've mentioned this mantra before in the context of dealing with worry, but it's crucial enough to deserve its own focus here, especially when it comes to ensuring your needs are covered during challenging times.

One of our biggest worries is the fear of not being able to meet our needs in tough situations. This concern is valid and should be addressed as part of better planning for our future. Regularly evaluating your needs is a good practice to ensure they are up-to-date and can be met even during bad times.

Start by identifying all your needs, including both essential primary needs and secondary needs that are desirable but not critical. Then, envision the worst possible scenario and assess whether you could still meet these needs under such circumstances. If you can, you're well-prepared for difficult times.

If you find that some secondary needs cannot be met in a worst-case scenario, consider reducing their importance in your life. Keep them as long as you can fulfill them, but be prepared to let them go if necessary.

If any primary needs appear to be unmet in your worst-case scenario, this is a significant issue that needs immediate attention. You must be able to fulfill all your primary needs, regardless of the situation.

In general, aim to stay within your primary needs and reduce the number of secondary needs where possible. This approach will help you build resilience and ensure survival.

The essence of this mantra is to clearly identify your needs and plan how to meet them even in the worst situations. By prioritizing primary needs and adjusting secondary ones, you can maintain well-being during challenging times. This preparation not only equips you for emergencies but also encourages a mindful and balanced lifestyle.

Mantra 2: Pursue Your Wants for a Happier Life Without Becoming Enslaved by Them

Meeting your needs allows you to survive, but fulfilling your wants enables you to live a life shaped by your desires. Living entirely free of wants is a challenge—almost impossible unless you've reached a state of sainthood, which is particularly difficult in today's world overflowing with material pleasures. It's natural to have desires that bring us happiness. While this happiness might be superficial, for many, it's enough to satisfy the conscious mind.

While wise advice often encourages us to live with just our basic needs, minimize our wants, and completely abandon greed, this can be hard to achieve in a conscious state of mind. Philosophically, it may sound ideal, but in practice, it can feel like a compromise on your happiness. The days of cave dwellers, who only needed to satisfy their basic needs, are long gone.

In today's world, it's perfectly okay to have wants, as long as you can fulfill them without stretching yourself beyond your comfort zone. In fact, pursuing your wants can help maintain your sanity, especially since so much of our time and energy goes into meeting basic needs. Without the pleasure and happiness that come from fulfilling our desires, life could feel quite monotonous.

The key is to remember that there will be times when you cannot satisfy every want, and it's important to accept this without losing your peace of mind. These are the moments when self-control is essential, and you must acknowledge that not everything can always go the way you wish.

Balancing the fulfillment of your wants with the need to

maintain control over your desires is crucial for a happier and more fulfilling life.

The mantra here is to clearly identify your wants, stay realistic, and strike a balance between enjoyment and restraint. This approach allows you to satisfy your desires without becoming captive to them, leading to a life where your wants enhance, rather than control, your experience.

Mantra 3: Recognize the Positive Aspects of Greed, but Keep It Under Control

Greed is often viewed as pure evil, and we are advised to banish this demon from our lives. While this is true in many cases, as discussed earlier, even a demon like greed has some positive aspects. When properly managed, greed can lead to motivation, ambition, and the drive to achieve more.

Despite its negative reputation, greed can be harnessed for good if controlled wisely. You can channel the drive and ambition that greed brings, using it to push yourself toward new heights and achieving your most challenging goals—without letting it consume you.

Greed has a unique quality that can push you beyond your limits, and this is what you must exploit. Use it as a source of motivation to reach your hardest dreams. However, be cautious—greed can easily turn against you, growing rapidly and potentially devouring you if left unchecked. What starts as a tool for ambition can quickly become a force that controls you instead.

To prevent this, it's crucial to monitor the growth of your greed. Without resistance, greed will continue to grow, making you increasingly vulnerable to its negative effects. Keep a close watch on your ambitions to ensure they remain within ethical boundaries.

To keep greed under control, it's important to value what

you already have. Stay grounded in the present, appreciating your current achievements, possessions, and successes, even as you work toward future goals. Challenge the mindset that convinces you that you must have something at all costs.

The mantra here is that even a demon like greed, when controlled and positively directed, can be a powerful motivator for success and growth. The key is to remain vigilant, setting ethical boundaries around your ambitions and keeping greed in check. By doing so, you can harness its positive qualities while avoiding its destructive potential.

Mantra 4: Everyone is Unique, and So Are Their Needs, Wants, and Greed

It's essential to recognize and remember that everyone is different, and so too are their needs, wants, and levels of greed. Without this understanding, it's difficult to truly grasp the motivations and desires of others, which can lead to misunderstandings, unrealistic comparisons, and friction in relationships.

What might seem unnecessary to you could be a critical need for someone else, and you might not always receive a logical explanation for it. Accepting this without judgment is crucial. The saying, "one man's trash is another man's treasure," perfectly captures this idea.

Acknowledging and understanding that each person is unique, with their own distinct needs, wants, and greed, is fundamental to understanding human behavior. It's also key to fostering smoother relationships and reducing judgment.

While basic needs are somewhat universal, more specific needs can vary greatly based on personal circumstances and cultural backgrounds. Wants, on the other hand, are highly subjective, driven by personal preferences, aspirations, and external influences. Similarly, the intensity and focus of greed differ from person to person, making each of us "greedy" in our own way.

It's not uncommon to feel better about ourselves when we perceive our own needs to be fewer or simpler than those of others. However, rather than questioning or judging others for their needs, wants, and greed, it's important to accept them as they are, for the sake of maintaining healthy relationships.

For example, consider the need for sleep—everyone requires different amounts, and this shouldn't be questioned unless it's causing issues. Similarly, someone's desire for a luxury car, when an economy model would suffice, shouldn't be challenged unless it represents a financial decision far beyond their means.

But there are exceptions, such as in parenting, where guiding children to balance their needs, wants, and greed is necessary. If they struggle to find this balance, it's important to step in and help them get back on track.

The mantra is to recognize that everyone has unique needs, wants, and greed. Understanding and respecting these differences is key to building harmonious relationships. By accepting these variations without judgment, we can achieve deeper understanding and greater harmony with one another.

Mantra 5: You Have Only One Life, So Focus on Truly Living, Not Just Surviving

One of life's harshest truths is that we only have one chance to live, and while everyone is aware of this fact, only a few truly grasp its essence and lead a rich, fulfilling life that goes beyond mere survival.

For a content life, it's often suggested to minimize our needs to the bare essentials required for survival, thus avoiding the struggles associated with fulfilling them. However, there's a significant difference between simply surviving and truly living. When you prioritize living, your list of needs expands to include secondary needs, wants, and even some elements of greed, all of which contribute to a happier and more meaningful life.

Prioritizing living over mere survival means embracing life fully, going beyond basic existence to enjoy meaningful and joyful experiences. As we progress through life, our needs naturally evolve and expand. While many of these will be genuine needs, others may stem from wants and greed that have morphed into perceived needs. These might not qualify as true needs, but if they bring you happiness and are within your means, they deserve a place in your life.

The challenge arises when our needs outgrow our capacity to satisfy them. In such cases, it's important to reevaluate and adjust your needs to better align with your ability to fulfill them, while also learning to reduce the impact of unmet needs on your well-being.

The mantra here is to recognize that since we have only one life, we should prioritize truly living over simply surviving. This may involve a bit more effort to satisfy a blend of needs, wants, and greed, but the reward is a richer, more fulfilling life. While minimizing needs can lead to contentment, it's also worth spending some of that time and energy enjoying life, even if it means embracing a bit of struggle along the way.

Mantra 6: Know Your Needs, Savor Your Wants, and Channel Your Greed

After recognizing the presence of these internal demons—needs, wants, and greed—and accepting their role in our lives, the next step is learning to manage them wisely. While these elements are interconnected, each one is distinct and requires a unique approach to harness their potential benefits.

Balancing your needs, wants, and greed in a way that enriches your life without harming yourself or others can lead to a truly rewarding and meaningful existence.

Needs are straightforward—they are essential for basic survival and should be prioritized accordingly. These are the non-negotiables of life, the foundation upon which everything else is built. However, it's important to regularly reassess your needs, both primary and secondary, to ensure they remain under control and do not escalate unnecessarily.

Wants, on the other hand, are about enhancing your happiness. While it's impossible to satisfy all your desires, identifying your most important wants and pursuing them can bring joy and satisfaction. It's also crucial to acknowledge and let go of those wants that are unattainable, preventing unnecessary frustration.

Greed, often viewed negatively, is an inevitable part of human nature. Instead of attempting to eliminate it entirely, a more effective approach is to channel greed into a force for good. Greed, when managed carefully, can drive you to achieve higher goals and greater success. The key is to stay vigilant, recognizing when greed is leading you astray, and having the discipline to control it when necessary.

The essence of this mantra lies in understanding and balancing these three aspects of life: meeting your essential needs, mindfully enjoying your wants, and leveraging your greed in a positive and ethical way. By doing so, you can cultivate a life that is both fulfilling and balanced.

Mantra 7: Monitor Your Growing Wants to Prevent Them from Becoming Needs

Each of us has a unique mix of needs, wants, and greed, which we often perceive as necessary for our survival, happiness, and growth. While it's obvious that we need to keep our greed in check, there's another subtle shift that requires our attention: the transformation of our wants into perceived needs.

It's essential to be aware of how our desires can gradually

evolve into something we feel we cannot live without, leading to a cycle of constant craving and potential dissatisfaction. By monitoring this transformation, we can maintain a healthy balance and ensure our wants do not overpower our true needs.

While allowing some wants to become needs can enhance our happiness, it's crucial to keep track of this process. If maintaining these new needs becomes difficult, you'll know where to make adjustments.

Most of us start with basic, essential needs, but as time goes on, these needs tend to expand. Some of these additions are genuine and justified, but others begin as mere wants and eventually become so ingrained that we mistake them for necessities.

To manage this, we should prioritize our wants based on their importance and impact on our lives. By focusing our time, energy, and resources on the most significant wants, we can enhance our lives without compromising our essential needs.

Additionally, it's important to set clear boundaries on how much we indulge in our wants and to cultivate self-discipline to resist unnecessary indulgences.

The mantra here is to keep a close watch on your growing wants, as they can subtly transform into perceived needs, potentially leading to dissatisfaction and making it harder to meet your basic needs. By taking a holistic view of your life and maintaining a balance between fulfilling your needs and enjoying your wants, you can indulge in your desires without letting them overshadow what's truly essential. This balance is key to leading a more fulfilling and contented life.

Mantra 8: You Needs, Wants and Greed Will Evolve With Time, Circumstances and Experiences

Ideally, we might wish for our needs, wants, and greed to remain minimal and constant, freeing us from the ongoing effort to satisfy them. However, just as everything in life changes over time, so too will these aspects of our desires. Their evolution is inevitable.

Your needs, wants, and greed are not fixed; they will shift and change as you progress through the various stages of life. Recognizing and accepting the dynamic nature of these demons is crucial for maintaining balance and well-being.

As you transition through different life stages—starting a job, getting married, becoming a parent, relocating, or retiring —your priorities will naturally shift. It's essential to adjust your goals and plans to align with these new stages and transitions.

Circumstances such as changes in your financial situation, living conditions, environment, health, and relationships also play a significant role in shaping your needs, wants, and greed. These shifts are a normal part of life.

Additionally, exposure to new experiences—traveling, meeting new people, trying new things, learning about different perspectives and cultures, adopting new hobbies, reading, and watching films—will inevitably introduce changes in your desires. New areas of interest will open up, leading to an evolution in what you need, want, and perhaps even what you greedily pursue.

These changes are a natural part of life in our materialistic world. The key is to accept these evolving desires and strive to satisfy them as long as they are within your reach, rather than worrying about why they are changing.

Moreover, it's equally important to extend this understanding and acceptance to others. When you notice changes in their needs, wants, and greed, approach these shifts with empathy rather than questioning or complaining about them.

The mantra here is to understand and accept that your needs, wants, and greed will change over time, influenced by circumstances and exposure to new experiences. This understanding is vital for maintaining a balanced and fulfilling life. By regularly reassessing and recalibrating your priorities, and staying flexible and adaptable, you can navigate these changes with grace and purpose.

Mantra 9: Make Sure Your Desires Are Truly Your Own, Whether Internal or Externally Influenced

In the materialistic world we live in, it's challenging to identify desires that originate purely from within. Many of our wants are, in fact, the result of external influences. As we discussed in the previous mantra, our desires evolve as we gain more exposure to new things and perspectives, meaning external factors heavily shape what we think we want.

It's important to recognize that not all of our desires are entirely self-generated. Often, we're influenced by what we see in others, adding those desires to our list at varying levels of intensity. While some of our wants are genuinely ours, rooted in our core values and capable of bringing us true happiness, others may simply reflect external influences, lacking clear reasons for being on our list.

These externally driven desires often exist because we think we should want them, but fulfilling them may not bring true satisfaction. In fact, we might not even feel a sense of loss if we choose to discard them. Therefore, it's crucial to evaluate our desires, saving ourselves the unnecessary effort of pursuing wants that don't truly resonate with us. Although it can be challenging to distinguish between genuine desires and those shaped by external pressures, it is an effort worth making.

That said, there are exceptions where it's acceptable to have some externally influenced desires, particularly when it helps us navigate societal norms, as long as these wants don't cause harm or lead us astray.

Our desires can be categorized into two types: intrinsic and extrinsic. Intrinsic desires originate from within and offer deep personal satisfaction, such as those related to personal growth, creativity, and self-expression. While they might be slightly influenced by external factors, the driving force is internal. Extrinsic desires, on the other hand, are driven by external motivations, such as status or material gain, and should be carefully evaluated for their actual contribution to our happiness.

Peer pressure plays a significant role in shaping our desires, with influences coming from friends, family, and societal expectations. It's essential to ask yourself if you would still want the same things without these external pressures.

Take time to reflect on whether a desire truly adds meaningful value to your life. Prioritize those that align with your personal passions and curiosity, rather than those that simply follow trends or popular opinion.

The essence of this mantra is to ensure that your desires are genuinely your own. Achieve this through self-reflection, evaluating the impact of external influences, aligning your wants with your core values, and regularly reassessing your goals. By doing so, you cultivate a more authentic and fulfilling life, driven by what truly brings you happiness and satisfaction, free from external pressures.

Mantra 10: Recognize and Understand the Needs, Wants, and Greed of Others

While our lives primarily revolve around our own journeys, we are deeply interconnected with the people around us—family, friends, colleagues, and acquaintances. The people in our lives are important to us, so their needs, wants, and ambitions should be significant and deserve our attention.

Understanding others' needs, wants, and ambitions is crucial for fostering empathy, improving communication, and building strong, healthy relationships. Since everyone is unique, it's important to recognize that people have different basic needs shaped by their circumstances and backgrounds.

Beyond basic needs, people have various desires and aspirations. Acknowledge that others also have ambitions and a drive for more, and seek to understand the motivations behind these desires to connect with them on a deeper level.

When it comes to greed, it's important to remember that what may appear as greed on the surface could have a deeper story behind it. Perhaps someone has had a particularly challenging past that shaped their personality, leading them to develop a strong desire for security, success, or material wealth. This perspective aligns with the saying, "Don't judge a book by its cover," reminding us not to make quick judgments about others without understanding their full story.

Cultural norms and values play a significant role in shaping a person's needs and wants. Gaining insight into these cultural influences can help you navigate relationships with people from diverse backgrounds more effectively.

Developing patience, tolerance, and a non-judgmental attitude is key. Avoid making assumptions or quick judgments about others' needs and desires. Sometimes, you may need to put logic aside and accept that others' needs, wants, and ambitions may not always have a clear explanation.

The mantra is to understand and appreciate the needs, wants, and ambitions of others. This requires empathy, effective communication, and a willingness to see things from their perspective. By embracing this approach, you can build stronger, more meaningful relationships and connect with others more authentically.

CHAPTER 10

Guilt: The Demon of Perceived Wrongdoing

Guilt is one of the most insidious emotions, a silent demon that eats us from within. It thrives on our feelings of helplessness and shame, often stemming from the belief that we've done something wrong, failed to act when we should have, or ignored our true desires. This belief leads to self-condemnation, making us feel terrible about ourselves and our actions.

This demon has the power to inflict deep emotional distress, triggering feelings of shame, regret, and anxiety. It distorts our perception of situations, often making them seem worse than they are, and traps us in a cycle of self-blame. This internalized blame can be a heavy burden, taking a toll on our mental health and overall well-being.

The concept of guilt is deeply rooted in the moral framework that governs our behavior as civilized human beings. When we step outside these boundaries, guilt haunts us, reminding us of our perceived transgressions.

Guilt can arise from various sources. Sometimes, it originates externally, where others blame us for something, and we internalize that blame. Other times, guilt is self-imposed, where we become our harshest critics, holding ourselves accountable for perceived wrongdoings, failures, or inactions.

Regardless of its source, guilt only takes hold when we accept responsibility for the perceived wrongdoing. As humans, we have an innate mechanism that triggers emotional reactions to our actions. When our actions or inactions result in harm or wrongdoing, guilt emerges as a natural response. Often, we may ignore these feelings until someone else brings them to our attention.

It's also important to recognize that guilt can be self-generated based on our own beliefs about right and wrong, even if others don't share the same perspective. Sometimes, our guilt is rooted in false assumptions, and if we had all the facts, we might realize it's baseless. Unfortunately, we often suffer from guilt based on these misconceptions without ever knowing the full truth.

No one is immune to guilt; it touches everyone in one way or another. In our complex social structures, it's nearly impossible to avoid feeling guilty about something. From the moment we wake up until we go to bed, we're likely to encounter situations that provoke guilt.

Guilt varies greatly from person to person, both in its intensity and duration. For some, it's a short-lived discomfort, while for others, it can be paralyzing. Some people move past their guilt quickly, while others carry it with them for years. In some cases, guilt is a constant companion, lingering in our thoughts.

Whatever roles we play—son, daughter, parent, spouse, friend, colleague—there's a unique version of guilt associated with each. Since we all play multiple roles, we often find ourselves dealing with many forms of guilt simultaneously. How we manage these feelings is up to us.

For instance, as a father, you might feel guilty for not

providing enough for your family. If you focus on earning more, you may feel guilty for not spending enough time with them, and if you spend more time with them, you might feel guilty for not providing financially.

As a mother, guilt can stem from not feeding your children well enough, not maintaining the house, or neglecting your professional life. Even after dedicating all your time to your family, you might still feel guilty for not taking care of yourself.

As children, we often feel guilty for not meeting our parents' expectations or not helping them as much as we should, especially as they age.

In our professional lives, struggling or failing can lead to guilt for not being attentive enough, while success can bring guilt for neglecting personal relationships.

As students, guilt arises from spending time on leisure activities instead of focusing on studies, feeling like we're letting down the parents who sacrificed so much for us.

Guilt can be triggered by the simplest things, like sleeping in and missing an important meeting, and it can linger throughout the day in various forms.

While this list of guilt triggers is endless, it illustrates how deeply ingrained this demon is in our lives. The guilt demon haunts us in countless ways, and while I can't cover them all here, it's important to recognize the pervasive influence it has on our everyday existence.

Guilty for Not Feeling Guilty

This is a unique and paradoxical form of guilt where you feel guilty for not experiencing guilt over a perceived wrongdoing. It occurs when you believe you've done something wrong but don't feel the expected remorse because you have strong justifications for your actions.

However, in the back of your mind, there's a lingering discomfort because you think you should feel guilty, based on a moral standard or societal expectation. This creates a conflict within you, where you feel guilty for not feeling guilty, leaving you torn between whether or not you should experience guilt.

The positive aspect of this internal conflict is that it offers you a second chance to reassess your actions. If, upon reflection, you conclude that you should feel guilty, it gives you the opportunity to correct your mistake. Without this self-questioning, you might never revisit actions you initially dismissed as guilt-free.

On the flip side, just because you have a nagging feeling that you should feel guilty doesn't necessarily mean you are guilty. Your justifications for your actions may still be valid. It's also important to remember that excessive overthinking can lead to self-doubt, causing you to second-guess yourself under the pressure of this guilt, and potentially convince yourself of wrongdoing even when none exists.

While it's wise to reconsider your actions and the associated feelings, it's equally important not to automatically trust these counter feelings. Evaluate them, but do so with a balanced perspective, ensuring that you don't unjustly label yourself as guilty.

Inappropriate Guilt: Feeling Guilty When You Shouldn't

Throughout our lives, we often find ourselves feeling guilty for certain actions or inactions, typically blaming ourselves for these feelings. This guilt can originate from within or be influenced by external accusations. As we go through life, we inevitably make mistakes, and unfortunately, some of these lead to feelings of guilt.

When you're convinced of your guilt due to a perceived wrongdoing, it's easy to overlook the possibility that the situation may have arisen for reasons beyond your control. It's also possible that what happened, even if it seems wrong, was actually the best possible outcome given the circumstances. Thus, while you may feel certain of your guilt, the reality may be that you're not guilty at all.

Another perspective to consider is that a mistake might be a direct result of your actions, or it could be an unforeseen consequence that you couldn't have anticipated. If you reflect on past mistakes, you might realize that some were inevitable, with no alternative outcomes. Guilt stemming from such mistakes is inappropriate—while it's important to learn from them, you shouldn't hold yourself responsible in a way that burdens you with unnecessary guilt.

In essence, there are times when you may feel guilty for perceived wrongdoings, but in reality, you shouldn't. Understanding this can help you distinguish between appropriate and inappropriate guilt, allowing you to move forward without the weight of undeserved blame.

Survivor's Guilt

Survivor's guilt is a profound and complex emotional response experienced by those who survive a traumatic event while others around them do not, sometimes leaving them as the sole survivor. Although they may feel fortunate to have survived, this relief is often accompanied by a deep sense of guilt for those who did not.

This type of guilt is commonly seen in the aftermath of natural disasters, accidents, wars, or terrorist attacks. The intensity of these emotions can be particularly strong if the survivor believes they could have done something to prevent the others' loss or if they are the only one who survived.

Survivor's guilt often brings with it feelings of anger and sorrow. While it's natural and justified to feel sadness for those who didn't make it, it's important to remember that life is fragile, and some events are simply beyond our control.

In some cases, survivors pull through due to their courage, quick thinking, or presence of mind—qualities that others may not have been able to exercise in the moment. In these instances, sharing their experiences and survival stories can be valuable, offering lessons that others can learn from.

Luck also plays a significant role in such situations, where some survive while others do not, with no logical explanation other than the randomness of fate or the workings of destiny.

Survivor's guilt is a challenging and painful emotion, but with the right support and coping strategies, it's possible to work through the guilt and find a path to healing. Over time, survivors can find meaning and purpose, honor those who were lost, and rediscover the joy of living.

Lack of Guilt

There are situations where people experience a lack of guilt, which can be a complex issue influenced by psychological, social, and moral factors.

On the positive side, not feeling guilty can be entirely appropriate when someone hasn't done anything wrong or isn't responsible for any wrongdoing. In such cases, the absence of guilt is justified.

Ignorance can also play a role in this. Sometimes, people may not feel guilty simply because they are unaware that their actions have caused harm. This is often seen when harm is an unintended consequence of well-intentioned actions. Since the intentions were good, people may not recognize the negative impact of their actions and therefore feel no guilt.

In other cases, people may lack guilt because they have valid justifications for their actions. They may acknowledge their involvement in a situation but feel they have a legitimate reason that absolves them from guilt.

On the negative side, a lack of guilt can be a major

characteristic of psychopathy, a personality disorder where individuals have no sense of remorse for the harm they cause others. Psychopaths often have justifications for their actions and tend to blame others rather than taking responsibility. Unlike those who unintentionally cause harm, psychopaths will never admit to their mistakes, regardless of the evidence.

Similarly, individuals with narcissistic traits may also lack guilt due to their inflated sense of self-importance and entitlement. These individuals never blame themselves for anything and are driven by their desires without regard for the harm they may cause others. Their lack of guilt makes them immune to the influence of this powerful demon, leaving them guilt-free by design.

The absence of guilt in such individuals can make them dangerous, as they will go to any lengths to satisfy their needs without considering the consequences for others. This lack of guilt can strain relationships, as others may feel hurt or wronged without any acknowledgment or apology. Over time, a consistent failure to express guilt or remorse can damage a person's reputation and social standing, leading to isolation and distrust from others.

Understanding the reasons behind a lack of guilt and addressing it can help improve relationships, personal well-being, and social harmony.

Guilt From Actions and Inactions

Guilt can stem from both what we do—our "actions"—and what we fail to do—our "inactions." Understanding these two sources of guilt is crucial for managing and controlling this powerful demon.

Guilt from actions arises when we regret something we've done that has caused harm or violated our moral or ethical standards. This type of guilt is a direct or indirect result of our actions and lingers as a constant reminder of our mistakes.

It tortures us by keeping these mistakes fresh in our minds, making us wish we could undo what we've done.

Examples of actions that can lead to guilt include using hurtful words that offend or harm someone, engaging in unethical behavior, or causing physical or emotional harm, whether intentional or not. This guilt makes us ashamed of our actions, repentant for our wrongdoings, and desperate for a way to undo them.

To address guilt for actions, we can apologize to those affected and take steps to make amends, learn from our mistakes to prevent them from happening again, and seek forgiveness from others and ourselves.

Guilt from inactions occurs when we regret not taking an action that could have prevented harm, helped someone, or improved a situation. This form of guilt haunts us for our inactions, reminding us of the damage that could have been avoided if only we had acted.

Examples of inactions that can lead to guilt include failing to help someone in need, missing out on great opportunities, or not speaking up against injustice or wrongdoing. This guilt makes us feel powerless, regretful of missed opportunities, and overly critical of ourselves for not taking the steps we should have.

To address guilt for inactions, we can acknowledge and accept our inactions, strive to be more proactive in similar situations in the future, and forgive ourselves, recognizing that sometimes we simply fail to act.

Understanding and addressing guilt from both actions and inactions allows us to manage this demon more effectively and helps us to learn and grow from our experiences.

Collective Guilt

In this form, the guilt demon doesn't target a single

individual but instead afflicts a group of people involved in some wrongdoing that caused harm to others. The resulting damage leads the entire group to share a sense of guilt.

While the group collectively bears responsibility for the wrongdoing, it's likely that not everyone was equally at fault. Some members may have played a more aggressive role, leading the others. Additionally, there may be members who were not directly responsible for the wrongdoing but still carry guilt simply because they were part of the group.

Similarly, some individuals may have had no active role in the wrongdoing but feel guilty for not stopping others from committing it. Members of such a group might not dwell on their actions individually, but when they come together, the guilt resurfaces, bringing the incident back to the forefront of their minds.

It's not uncommon for the more vulnerable members of the group to break down and confess, which can bring the entire group under scrutiny and expose everyone involved to consequences.

The Guilt Trap

A guilt trap is a situation where someone becomes ensnared in a cycle of persistent and often irrational guilt, leading to constant self-blame and emotional distress. This cycle can push individuals into actions that further harm their well-being.

While a guilt trap can originate from within, fueled by our own self-blame, it is often set by external sources with vested interests. These external forces manipulate you into doing something that serves their selfish goals, regardless of the harm it may cause you.

In such cases, the root of this guilt is manipulation by others who exploit your sense of responsibility and empathy. Their primary aim is to control or influence your behavior, actions, or decisions by making you feel guilty.

To set a guilt trap, these manipulators blame their targets for various issues or mistakes, regardless of actual responsibility, and cast themselves as victims to elicit sympathy and guilt. They also set unreasonable expectations, causing their targets to feel guilty for failing to meet them.

As a result, the targets—those caught in the trap—experience overwhelming guilt, heightened anxiety, and stress due to the relentless pressure to meet impossible demands. This leads to a loss of self-confidence and an increase in self-doubt.

Often, these targets are so distressed that they turn to the very manipulators who set the trap, mistaking their guidance as genuine help. This only deepens the trap, causing them to make even more mistakes.

A guilt trap is a serious and inappropriate situation, deliberately created to manipulate you into serving someone else's interests. It is crucial to recognize and eliminate such traps to protect your well-being.

The Good Side of Guilt

Though guilt is often seen as a parasite that eats away at our happiness, it surprisingly has a bright side that justifies its place in our system. Despite its negative impact and the discomfort it causes, guilt plays a vital role in maintaining the checks and balances in our lives.

When properly managed, this demon can serve as a moral compass, motivating us to make amends, avoid harmful behavior, and strengthen our relationships. It pushes us to acknowledge our mistakes, take responsibility for our actions, and become more empathetic and responsible individuals.

This demon heightens our awareness of how our actions

impact others, encouraging us to understand their feelings and perspectives. It fosters a sense of responsibility and maturity, driving us to apologize and repair the damage we've caused, to the extent possible, as not all harm is reversible.

Guilt also offers valuable learning opportunities, teaching us to avoid repeating mistakes and to consider the consequences before we act. Without the feeling of guilt after serious missteps, we might be more prone to repeat them in the future.

This is one reason why guilt is often used as a teaching tool with children when they make significant mistakes. By helping them feel guilt, we guide them toward learning from their mistakes, becoming more accountable, and avoiding similar mistakes in the future. Of course, there's a right and wrong way to deliver such lessons, but that's a discussion for another time.

Additionally, guilt plays an indirect yet vital role in preserving relationships by making us aware of and taking responsibility for actions or inactions that harm our connections with others.

In essence, guilt is a necessary presence in our lives. It has the potential to make us better people, which is why it holds a place of importance in our system.

Mantras for Dealing With the Guilt Demon

Let's explore some key mantras that can help you manage and overcome the burden of guilt. By applying these mantras, you can confront guilt in a healthy and constructive way, allowing it to serve as a tool for growth rather than a burden on your well-being.

Mantra 1: Own Your Actions or Inactions That Cause Guilt

Living in this complex world, it's nearly impossible to go through life without experiencing guilt. As a human, you're bound to make mistakes, whether intentional or not, that may lead to feelings of guilt. This demon lingers within you, using your conscience as its weapon, tormenting you until you confront it.

You might try to ignore or escape your guilt, but it's futile; guilt resides within you, and it will follow you wherever you go. The past is unchangeable, etched in stone, and it's not going anywhere.

The first step to confronting this guilt demon is to acknowledge its presence and take responsibility for the actions or inactions that led to your guilt. This means recognizing the role you played, understanding the impact of your behavior, and taking steps to make amends.

Begin by revisiting the situation, reflecting on your role, and reviewing the actions or inactions that brought about your guilt. Honestly assess your behavior and its consequences, resisting the urge to justify your actions.

Next, try to understand the impact you caused by empathizing with those affected by your choices. Take ownership by accepting responsibility without shifting the blame onto others.

Then, make amends—offer a sincere apology to those affected, take steps to correct the situation where possible, and learn from the experience to avoid repeating similar mistakes in the future.

Finally, forgive yourself. Everyone makes mistakes; it's an inherent part of being human.

The mantra is to accept responsibility for your actions or inactions that led to guilt. It's a powerful step toward freeing yourself from its burden. This involves honest introspection, analyzing the situation, understanding the impact of your behavior, making amends, and learning from the experience to prevent future mistakes.

Mantra 2: Eliminate Inappropriate Guilt From Your System

As discussed earlier, not all guilt you carry is appropriate. Holding onto inappropriate guilt is senseless, as it means you're punishing yourself for mistakes you haven't actually made.

Inappropriate guilt arises when your feelings of guilt are disproportionate to the situation. This type of guilt often stems from wrong assumptions, unrealistic self-expectations, or external influences rather than genuine wrongdoing. There are several ways this inappropriate guilt can find its way into your system.

Sometimes, inappropriate guilt is the result of disproportionate reactions—blaming yourself excessively for minor mistakes or for situations beyond your control, or feeling guilt far more intense than the circumstances justify.

At other times, it stems from unrealistic self-expectations— feeling guilty for not achieving perfection, setting impossibly high standards for yourself, or engaging in relentless self-criticism over perceived shortcomings.

In many cases, inappropriate guilt originates from personal assumptions, which may be based on your own perceptions. If your perception deviates from reality, these assumptions become invalid, making the guilt that arises from them inappropriate.

Another possibility is feeling guilty over a decision or action that was actually the best choice under the circumstances, even if it appears as a mistake on the surface. Such guilt is inappropriate because the so-called "mistake" was justified given the situation, though it might not be apparent to others who only see it superficially.

External influences can also lead to inappropriate guilt—feeling guilty due to others' expectations or judgments, even when you've done nothing wrong, or experiencing guilt for defying social or cultural norms.

In some cases, you might be caught in a "guilt trap" set by someone else, where guilt is induced to manipulate you. This type of guilt is inherently inappropriate, as it arises from someone else's unrealistic expectations or external pressures.

The mantra here is to recognize that inappropriate guilt, regardless of how it entered your system, does not deserve to linger. You don't deserve the suffering it causes, so you should actively seek to identify and eliminate inappropriate guilt from your system.

Mantra 3: Don't Hold Yourself Fully Responsible for What's Causing Your Guilt

When you've accepted responsibility for a mistake that's causing you guilt, it's natural to start placing all the blame on yourself. However, when dealing with guilt, we often take on more responsibility than is fair or accurate.

The reality is that many factors contribute to any situation, and your role is just one part of a larger whole. This means you are only partially responsible for the success or failure of any outcome, including your mistakes.

Many situations involve multiple elements and people, so blaming yourself entirely overlooks the broader context. Often, responsibility is shared among various parties, and it's important to recognize that others may also have played a role.

While it's crucial to take responsibility for your part in any mistake, hold yourself accountable, and work towards repairing any damage caused, it's equally important not to blame yourself entirely. Even if you had done everything perfectly, there's no guarantee that the mistake wouldn't have occurred due to factors beyond your control.

Remember, there are always elements beyond your understanding or influence, and some of these unknown factors may have contributed to the mistake for which you're taking sole responsibility.

This mantra is essential because, in moments of deep guilt, when you're convinced of your role in a wrongdoing, it can help you see that you are just one of the many reasons the event occurred. You shouldn't bear the full weight of the blame.

The mantra is to understand the broader context of your actions that are causing guilt, and to recognize the influence of external factors and other people involved. This will help you avoid unnecessary and disproportionate self-blame.

Mantra 4: It's Impossible to Be Entirely Free of Guilt

While the idea of living a guilt-free life is appealing, it's more of a fantasy than a reality. In the complex world we inhabit, countless situations arise daily that give birth to feelings of guilt.

It's important to accept that you won't be able to completely eliminate every feeling of guilt. Some guilt may linger due to the complexity of human emotions, the nature of the relationships involved, or the severity of the actions that caused it. Certain mistakes are simply irreversible, and the guilt they generate may never fully disappear. Embracing this reality allows you to live with guilt without letting it control your life.

The truth is, perfection is unattainable. Everyone makes mistakes during moments of imperfection, which inevitably lead to the emergence of guilt.

Another reason mistakes—and the resulting guilt—are unavoidable is that you can't predict every outcome of your actions. Even if you try to foresee every possible consequence, the actual outcome may differ from your expectations.

While a significant portion of our guilt stems from our own actions or inactions, other sources of guilt include misplaced self-blame or external influences. Sometimes, guilt is imposed on us by others, either to make us recognize our mistakes or due to their own hidden agendas.

There's also guilt born from empathy, where we feel remorseful after hurting someone else. Defying social or cultural norms can lead to guilt for not adhering to societal expectations. We might feel guilty for overeating or for not eating enough. The list of reasons for guilt in our lives is endless.

The mantra is to understand that it's impossible to be entirely free of guilt, as there will always be triggers for it. Moreover, guilt is an inherent part of the human experience—it helps us learn, grow, and take responsibility. By accepting, understanding, and managing guilt effectively, you can keep it from overwhelming you and stealing your happiness.

Mantra 5: Forgiveness is Essential for Overcoming Guilt

Forgiveness plays a crucial role in overcoming the guilt that can weigh heavily on us. This includes not only forgiving others but also extending forgiveness to yourself.

If your actions have hurt others, seek their forgiveness by offering a sincere apology, acknowledging the harm caused, expressing genuine remorse, and taking concrete steps to make amends and repair any damage done.

Equally important is forgiving yourself. Treat yourself with the same kindness and understanding you would offer to others. Self-forgiveness helps you release the emotional burden of guilt and find peace of mind by overcoming demons like anger and resentment, which often stem from guilt.

By forgiving yourself, you recognize that making mistakes is a natural part of being human. This self-acceptance helps rebuild your self-esteem and self-worth, allowing you to embrace your imperfections without harsh self-judgment.

While forgiving yourself is generally a positive step, there is a potential downside: once you forgive yourself, you might no longer feel the same level of guilt, and the mistakes that once troubled you could seem less significant. This could make you more prone to repeating those mistakes without the deterrent of guilt. In other words, forgiving yourself too easily might compromise the conscience that once kept you accountable for your actions.

On the other hand, refusing to forgive yourself and continuing to punish yourself for past mistakes is equally unproductive. This approach neither improves how you feel nor resolves the issues caused by those mistakes.

As for forgiving others—when you forgive those whose mistakes have caused you harm, and now make them feel guilty, it can help mend strained relationships and relieve them of their burden of guilt. At the same time, it will bring you peace of mind and a satisfaction of doing the right thing.

The mantra is that forgiveness is essential for dealing with guilt. By acknowledging your guilt, taking responsibility, making amends, and finally forgiving yourself, you can effectively release its burden. This process should include forgiving others, seeking forgiveness from others as well as offering it to yourself.

Mantra 6: Be Mindful That You Can Be a Source of Guilt in Others

So far, we've focused on the guilt that haunts you personally, but this mantra addresses another perspective—how we can become the source of guilt in others. Sometimes, we do this intentionally, and other times unknowingly, without realizing the impact of our actions. In some cases, others may feel guilty because they've wronged us.

Guilt is a powerful demon, and it's essential to recognize that our words and actions can sometimes cause others to feel guilty. Being mindful of this can help us avoid unnecessarily introducing guilt into someone else's system.

Often, people aren't aware of the mistakes they've made or the harm they've caused until someone points it out to them, which can introduce the guilt demon into their system. While it's important to make others aware of their mistakes—giving them a chance to feel guilt and make amends—the way this guilt is introduced can significantly affect them.

Everyone has different levels of emotional sensitivity, and what might seem minor to you could deeply affect someone else. Words have power, and thoughtless comments, criticisms, or actions that convey blame or disappointment can easily induce guilt in others without you realizing it. Even jokes that seem harmless to you might leave a lasting scar on someone else.

To avoid unintentionally causing guilt in others, it's important to be thoughtful in how you communicate. Frame your words carefully, offer constructive feedback instead of blame, and show empathy to reduce the likelihood of causing unnecessary guilt.

Avoid making comparisons, as everyone has unique strengths and weaknesses, and comparisons can lead to feelings of inadequacy and guilt. It's also crucial to set realistic and attainable expectations for others, as unrealistic expectations can lead to feelings of failure and guilt.

As for others feeling guilty due to their own mistakes—if you see that someone is burdened by guilt because of a mistake they made that harmed you, offering forgiveness can help relieve them of that burden.

The mantra is to be mindful of how your words and actions can induce guilt in others. This awareness is crucial for avoiding the introduction of this demon into their lives. If you must introduce guilt to help someone recognize their mistakes and encourage improvement, ensure your feedback is constructive, delivered kindly, and free from blame or comparisons to achieve the desired effect. Moreover, forgive them for their guilt stemming from mistakes that harmed you to help alleviate them of its burden.

Mantra 7: Harness Your Guilt as an Opportunity for Improvement

This mantra builds on the ideas we've explored throughout this chapter. While guilt is often seen as a negative force, it can actually serve as a powerful catalyst for personal growth and improvement when approached constructively.

Guilt provides a valuable opportunity to reflect on your mistakes, learn from them, and avoid repeating them in the future. It can also make you more aware of similar pitfalls, helping you to navigate life with greater care and consideration.

Furthermore, once you fully grasp your mistakes, you can share your insights with others, allowing them to learn from your experiences. Without guilt, you might miss the chance to offer this valuable help.

To turn guilt into an opportunity for improvement, start by analyzing your actions and inactions that led to these feelings. Understand the impact of your behavior on yourself and others. Identify what went wrong, consider what you could have done differently, and use these lessons to improve your responses in similar situations in the future.

If your actions have hurt someone, offering a sincere apology and taking steps to make amends shows that you're already on the path to personal growth. Additionally, it's not uncommon to use guilt as a tool to encourage improvement in others, by making them aware of their mistakes and helping them realize the need for change.

The mantra is that guilt, when approached constructively, can be a powerful opportunity for personal improvement. By acknowledging your guilt, learning from your mistakes, making amends, and forgiving yourself, you can transform this challenging emotion into a motivation for positive change, helping you become a better version of yourself.

Mantra 8: Support Others in Overcoming Their Guilt

In this complex world, almost everyone has faced the burden of guilt at some point. When you see people in your close circle struggling under the weight of this guilt, it's important to offer them support, regardless of whether you had any role in causing it.

If you've intentionally invoked guilt in someone to help them recognize their mistakes, it's crucial to guide them in taking responsibility. Encourage them to make amends and repair any damage their actions may have caused. Once they've made improvements, help them forgive themselves so they can release their guilt and move forward.

If you find yourself the victim of unjust blame, which in turn makes others feel guilty for wrongfully accusing you, strive to forgive them and help them release their guilt. Your direct intervention might surprise them, but it can be incredibly effective in alleviating their guilt.

Even when you have no direct role in someone's guilt, you can still play a significant part by helping them address and overcome it.

There may be situations where you've unintentionally caused guilt in others without even realizing it. Stay mindful of this possibility so you can recognize and prevent such occurrences in the future.

To help others deal with their guilt—create a warm, supportive environment where they feel safe to express their feelings without fear of judgment. Show empathy and acknowledge the context of their guilt.

Before you offer help, it's important to validate whether their guilt is justified. Their feelings may arise from real mistakes, or they could stem from unrealistic expectations, external pressures, or false assumptions.

Avoid rushing to alleviate their guilt by simply telling them not to feel guilty. Instead, help them explore the underlying reasons for their guilt and work through those issues. Encourage them to analyze what specific actions or inactions triggered their guilt, and help them understand the impact of these actions on themselves and others.

Remind them that making mistakes is a natural part of being human, and that they can learn valuable lessons from these experiences.

You can also share your own experiences with guilt to offer perspective, helping them learn from your mistakes and avoid similar pitfalls in their own lives.

The mantra is to help others navigate their guilt by fostering a warm, supportive environment, offering guidance, and encouraging self-forgiveness. By actively engaging, showing understanding, validating their feelings, and promoting positive actions, you can help transform their guilt into a catalyst for personal growth.

Mantra 9: Evaluate if You Are Caught in a Guilt Trap Created by Someone Else

Earlier in this chapter, we explored the concept of a guilt trap—a manipulative and harmful situation designed to coerce you into serving someone else's interests. Recognizing and eliminating these traps is crucial because your guilt, in this case, is being used to fuel someone else's agenda.

While it's possible to fall into a guilt trap on your own, these traps are often set by external influences driven by others' selfish motives. These individuals manipulate you by pushing you into a guilt trap, which they then use as leverage for their benefit.

One of the most telling signs that you're in a guilt trap is a persistent sense of guilt with no apparent way out. Instead of finding resolution, you may feel increasingly entangled in your guilt, often accompanied by the influence of external forces.

To detect whether you're caught in a guilt trap, it's essential to examine the nature of your guilt. Start by validating whether the guilt you feel is genuinely yours—stemming from your own mistakes—or if it has been planted by someone else to manipulate you.

It's important to distinguish between well-meaning individuals who introduce guilt to help you recognize and correct your mistakes and those who manipulate you for their gain. The former are not setting a guilt trap; instead, they are watching out for you, offering guidance, and helping you overcome your guilt in a constructive way.

However, others may not have your best interests at heart and may induce guilt solely to manipulate you. If, upon reflection, you realize that your guilt has been orchestrated by someone else for their selfish purposes, you should make every effort to break free from that trap.

Spotting the difference between manipulators and well-wishers can be challenging, as manipulators often go to great lengths to present themselves as acting in your best interest. However, if someone seems to be pushing guilt on you without justifiable cause, that can serve as a clue that they may not have your well-being in mind.

The mantra is to validate the source of your guilt. If you discover you're ensnared in a guilt trap set by someone else, take decisive action to free yourself from that manipulation.

Mantra 10: Give More Importance to Your Present and Future

This timeless mantra is universally applicable, making it a valuable inclusion in this chapter.

When we reflect on our guilt, it often stems from past actions or inactions that give rise to an inner turmoil, disrupting our present and hindering our progress toward a better future.

As long as you remain fixated on your guilt, you'll be trapped in the past, with this demon continually haunting you. However, when you start prioritizing your present and future, you'll find the motivation and inner drive to confront your guilt and begin living freely in the present.

It's important to remember that while giving more importance to your present and future is a crucial first step toward freeing yourself from the grip of guilt, this alone isn't enough. You must still acknowledge your guilt, take responsibility for your mistakes, make amends, and forgive yourself.

While you should forgive yourself, don't forget the lessons learned from your mistakes, as these will help you avoid repeating them in the future.

The essence of this mantra is to prioritize your present and future by adopting the mindset that the past is behind you, and you've done all you can. It's time to move forward, enjoy the present, and prepare for a brighter future. By embracing this mindset, you'll prevent past guilt from haunting you and ruining both your present and your future.

CHAPTER 11

Envy and Jealousy: The Demons of Desire and Fear of Loss

W hen discussing the demons that plague us, we cannot overlook the destructive duo of envy and jealousy. These two demons act as weapons of self-destruction, forged by our own thoughts, making us both the creators and victims of these inner demons.

We are the ones who choose to be envious and jealous, so we bear responsibility for allowing these demons into our lives, leading us down a path of self-destruction.

Though often mistaken for the same emotion and sometimes used interchangeably, envy and jealousy are distinct demons, each with its own triggers and impacts. They both stem from our insecurities, comparative nature, and desires—often fueled by external influences—and they relentlessly consume our peace of mind.

The Envy Demon

Envy arises when you long for something you lack but see in others—whether it's a possession, quality, achievement, or anything else that ignites a desire in you. The nature of envy is such that satisfaction only comes when you acquire what sparked your envy or surpass the person who possesses it. However, this satisfaction is short lived, as new reasons for envy will quickly arise.

Envy can originate internally from your own unfulfilled desires or be triggered externally by observing others. The "comparison demon" plays a significant role in this process. Internal envy emerges when you want something but can't have it, and you see someone else with it. External envy, on the other hand, is sparked when you see someone with something you didn't previously desire, but suddenly, you want it desperately.

Envy is a natural human emotion, and it's almost impossible to be entirely free from it. No matter how content you are, there will always be something that someone else has that you wish to possess.

The Jealousy Demon

Talking about jealousy, while this demon may seem just like envy, it's a different emotion—covering the different part of the spectrum—where you have a fear of losing someone or something valuable to you—like a possession or a relationship —to someone else. Your insecurities play a major role in your jealousy, as it often stems from your insecurity about the stability of what you possess.

Jealousy can severely impact relationships, leading to trust issues, resentment, and conflict. It often brings with it feelings of insecurity, anxiety, and sadness, making you feel inadequate or unworthy. Constant worry about losing someone or something can create significant stress and anxiety.

Jealousy can also lead to destructive behaviors, such as excessive suspicion, paranoia, possessiveness, and, in extreme cases, aggression. Common scenarios include feeling jealous when your partner spends time with someone else or when a close friend grows closer to another person, causing you to fear they might abandon you.

The Reach of Envy and Jealousy

This deadly duo—envy and jealousy—haunts us in all of our worlds.

In our personal lives, envy and jealousy can arise between siblings, creating a bittersweet dynamic where one might feel happy for their sibling's success yet simultaneously troubled by these demons.

In our social lives, there is no shortage of reasons to fall prey to envy and jealousy. We may envy others for their better lives, wealth, status, appearance, or other materialistic attributes. Similarly, it's common to feel jealous of losing friends to others, as our social fabric provides fertile ground for these demons to thrive.

In the professional world, where competition and challenges are in abundance, these demons find plenty of opportunities to torment us. We may envy a colleague's success or recognition, feeling a sense of injustice when others achieve more. Jealousy may emerge as we worry about losing our projects, work, or recognition to others.

And no matter which aspect of our lives these demons originate from, they are ever-present in our inner world, constantly haunting us.

How Envy and Jealousy Lead to Social Isolation

Both of these demons have the potential to lead to social isolation. When individuals are consumed by these feelings, they might withdraw from others or push them away, either due to insecurities or a fear of being judged.

Jealousy, for instance, can cause individuals to fear

abandonment, leading to controlling behaviors where they try to monitor or restrict others. This controlling nature can suffocate relationships, causing others to distance themselves.

Envy, on the other hand, can make individuals feel inadequate or unlucky, diminishing their self-esteem. This lack of confidence can make social situations uncomfortable, leading them to avoid gatherings and interactions.

Furthermore, when envy and jealousy drive people to speak negatively about others, it creates a toxic environment. Those around them may not want to be associated with such negativity, further isolating the person at the center of it.

Over time, these demons can create a barrier between individuals and their social circles, resulting in feelings of loneliness and disconnection. Therefore, it is crucial to address and manage envy and jealousy to maintain healthy and fulfilling social relationships.

The Influence of Envy and Jealousy in Human History

Throughout history, envy and jealousy have been powerful and pervasive forces, influencing a wide array of events, relationships, and society's developments. These demons, though often linked and sometimes used interchangeably, have distinct impacts on human behavior, leading to both constructive and destructive outcomes.

Politics and Power

In the realm of politics, envy and jealousy have driven individuals and groups to engage in power struggles, where the desire to surpass rivals or the fear of losing influence leads to manipulation, betrayal, conflict and even dirty crimes. These demons can fuel ambitions and push leaders to extreme actions, often with far-reaching consequences for entire nations.

Royal and Family Rivalries

Throughout our history, in royal courts and among families, envy and jealousy have been central to many rivalries, where the desire for power, recognition, or love has led to deep-seated animosities. These demons can drive individuals to act against their kin or peers, leading to divisions, conspiracies, and sometimes tragic outcomes. These demons have shaped the fates of families and influenced the succession of power throughout history.

Art and Literary

Even the creative world is not left from their influence, where these demons have often been catalysts for both innovation and discord. Artists and writers, driven by a desire to outshine their peers or by fear of being overshadowed, have pushed the boundaries of their work, leading to remarkable achievements. However, these same emotions can also lead to bitter rivalries, where personal and professional conflicts overshadow the creative process.

Scientific and Intellectual Rivalries

In the pursuit of knowledge, envy and jealousy have led to competition among scientists and intellectuals. While this competition can lead to groundbreaking discoveries and advancements, it can also create environments of rivalry and tension, where personal grudges and the fear of being outdone hinder collaboration and progress.

Social and Class Dynamics

On a broader societal level, envy and jealousy have played significant roles in shaping social hierarchies and class dynamics. The desire to attain what others have or the fear of losing one's status can lead to social unrest, revolutions, and shifts in power structures. These demons can drive movements for change, but they can also perpetuate cycles of inequality and resentment.

Religious and Ideological Conflicts

Envy and jealousy have also been significant in the realm of religion and ideology. These demons can drive conflicts between different groups, where the fear of losing influence or the desire to maintain dominance leads to clashes. Such tensions have often resulted in divisions within societies, as well as long-lasting conflicts that shape the course of history.

Cultural and National Ambitions

Envy and jealousy have also influenced the ambitions of cultures and nations. The desire to surpass other nations or the fear of losing cultural dominance has driven expansions, colonization, competitive rivalries, and even wars. These demons have shaped the interactions between different societies and the course of global history.

Personal Relationship Issues

On a more personal level, envy and jealousy are central to many conflicts within relationships, whether between friends, partners, or family members. These emotions can lead to mistrust, insecurity, and ultimately the breakdown of relationships. The fear of losing someone's affection or the desire to possess what another has can drive individuals to actions that harm both themselves and others.

Summing Up

In summary, envy and jealousy have been deeply embedded in human history, driving both positive and negative outcomes. While they can motivate individuals and groups to achieve great things, they can also lead to conflict, division, and destruction. Understanding their influence offers valuable insight into the complexities of human behavior and the forces that shape our world.

The Good in Envy and Jealousy

It may seem counterintuitive to think that demons as destructive as envy and jealousy could have a positive side, but surprisingly, there is a silver lining to their presence.

While envy and jealousy are often viewed as negative forces, they also possess certain qualities that can be beneficial if harnessed correctly. Instead of striving to eliminate these demons entirely—which is nearly impossible—we can learn to channel them in ways that motivate, inspire, and provide insight into our insecurities.

Envy, for instance, stirs a powerful desire within us, driving us to pursue our goals with renewed vigor. This intense motivation can increase our chances of success, as envy highlights the areas in our lives where we feel deficient and pushes us to improve. It encourages self-reflection, helping us to clearly identify our desires, values, and aspirations. When managed well, envy can even enhance relationships by prompting us to celebrate the successes of others, fostering mutual respect and admiration.

Similarly, jealousy, though often seen as purely negative, can have positive effects when properly controlled. It can underscore the importance of a relationship or possession, drawing our attention to areas that need nurturing. Jealousy can also provide valuable insights into our insecurities and unmet needs, encouraging us to be more attentive and considerate towards those we care about. This awareness can deepen our connections and strengthen our commitments.

In some cases, jealousy can spark a healthy sense of

competition, motivating us to better ourselves in areas where we feel insecure. It also promotes better communication, as it prompts us to engage in open and honest conversations about our needs and desires with those around us.

In conclusion, while envy and jealousy are typically seen as harmful, their presence can be surprisingly beneficial if we learn to harness their energy in positive ways.

Mantras for Dealing With the Envy and Jealousy Demons

Now, let's explore the mantras that can help you effectively deal with these destructive demons. By incorporating these mantras into your daily life, you can manage and transform the emotions of envy and jealousy into positive forces that contribute to your personal growth and overall well-being.

Mantra 1: Recognize the Hidden Struggles Behind Success

There are moments when you might feel envious of someone else's success, especially when it appears that they haven't put in as much effort as you have. However, the reality may be very different from your perception of their hard work. You may believe they haven't worked hard enough to deserve their success, but this view is based on your limited perspective of how they should have worked and what you've observed. It's possible they've faced challenges and put in effort in ways that aren't visible to you, or that the work required for their success was different from what you imagine.

It's important to understand that everyone has their own unique struggles on their life journey, and what you see on the surface doesn't always reflect the full story. There may be hidden struggles behind someone's success that you're unaware of, and all you see is the end result.

Additionally, success can be influenced by many factors

beyond hard work, such as recognizing and seizing the right opportunity at the right time. Success often involves knowing exactly what needs to be done and patiently waiting for the right moment to act.

The mantra here is to avoid envy by acknowledging that others' success, which might seem effortlessly attained, could be the result of unseen struggles or their ability to strategically navigate opportunities.

Mantra 2: Comparisons Can Be a Major Source of Envy

As humans, we have a natural tendency to compare ourselves to others, especially those who seem to be more successful or have what we desire. This habit can easily lead to feelings of envy, negatively impacting our mental and emotional well-being. In extreme cases, these comparisons can even lead us to feel overwhelmed and believe that we are particularly unlucky compared to others.

When you look around, it's common to notice others who appear more successful or possess things that you long for but have yet to attain. Feeling envious in these situations is normal, and it's not uncommon for such envy to spiral into a sense of being unlucky or less fortunate.

The root cause here is comparison—this powerful demon thrives when you measure yourself against others, especially those you perceive as being better off. Envy born from comparison distracts you from your own journey, causing you to focus more on others' successes rather than your own progress.

When you compare yourself to others, your entire attention is on the differences between your life and theirs. If their circumstances seem significantly better, you may start feeling inferior or inadequate, giving envy an entry in your system. This desire to have what others have, combined with resentment for not having it, can deeply affect your self-esteem and self-worth.

However, it's important to remember that you're only seeing the visible successes or possessions of others, without knowing the full story of how they got there. Everyone's journey is unique, and you may be comparing your beginning to someone else's middle or end, which is inherently unfair.

Additionally, everyone has their own set of challenges and struggles, many of which are not visible to others. You might be unaware of the difficulties they've faced, making your comparison incomplete and inaccurate.

While comparisons are a natural part of life and are bound to happen, it's crucial to shift your perspective. Instead of letting comparisons lead to envy, use them as opportunities to learn and grow. View others' successes as inspiration for your own journey, and focus on appreciating what you already have.

The mantra here is to recognize that while comparison is a natural human instinct, it can lead to envy if left unchecked, harming your mental and emotional health. By understanding the uniqueness of everyone's journey, minimizing comparisons, and using them as learning opportunities, you can reduce the impact of envy and concentrate on your own growth.

Mantra 3: Recognize That You Can Be a Source of Envy for Others

So far we've primarily focused on managing the envy you feel, it's equally important to recognize that you might also be a source of envy for others. Everyone possesses something that others may lack, and if what you have is something others desire, it can trigger envy in them.

Often, the reasons for others' envy are apparent, but there are situations where their envy might seem illogical— sometimes even your seemingly insignificant possessions or qualities might become objects of envy due to someone else's desires.

Even if you feel like you're at the bottom of the ladder, with nothing worth envying, it's likely that something you have—be it peace of mind, contentment, or a particular skill—might be enviable to others. For instance, a wealthy person might envy a poor man's peace of mind, something that wealth alone cannot buy.

It's important to be aware of how your successes and achievements might be perceived by those around you. This doesn't mean you should downplay your accomplishments, but rather, share them with humility and thoughtfulness, avoiding any form of boasting. Being considerate of others' feelings and sensitive to their situations can help mitigate any negative impact your success might have on them.

Instead of unintentionally fostering feelings of inadequacy, use your achievements as a source of inspiration and motivation for others. Understand the emotions and challenges of those who may feel envious of you, and offer support where you can. Encourage them to focus on their own journeys rather than comparing themselves to you or others.

Create an environment where everyone feels valued and included, regardless of their level of success.

The mantra here is to recognize that you, too, might be a source of envy for others. Understanding this can help you maintain healthy relationships by being mindful of your actions and words, sharing successes modestly, offering encouragement, and fostering an inclusive environment that values everyone's unique journey.

Mantra 4: Shift Your Focus From What Triggers Your Envy to Center on Yourself

Envy is a powerful demon, and escaping its grip can be

challenging. When you're under its influence, it's easy to become fixated on what others have, losing sight of your own well-being and growth in the process. This fixation can lead to a state of constant dissatisfaction and unhappiness.

When your attention is locked onto the possessions and successes of others, you end up neglecting your own potential and accomplishments. Envy diverts you from your own path of happiness and success. Redirecting your focus from what triggers your envy to your personal growth and well-being is a crucial step in overcoming this demon, and there are compelling reasons to make this shift.

First, remember that your time is limited. You can either spend it envying others' achievements or use it to work toward your own. Focusing on yourself gives you the opportunity to identify what's missing in your efforts, allowing you to address those gaps and achieve your own goals.

Another reason to shift your focus is that by obsessing over others, you might overlook what you already have, putting your own possessions and accomplishments at risk. Everything you value requires time, energy, and attention, including the things you already possess.

Moreover, envy can blind you to your own achievements. While you're busy envying others, you might fail to recognize and celebrate the progress you've made in your own life.

Regardless of what or who triggers your envy, remember that the true victim of envy is always you. It is you who suffers the most when you constantly compare yourself to others and feel inadequate.

The mantra is to redirect your focus from what causes you envy to your own growth and well-being. By concentrating on self-improvement, gratitude for what you already have, limiting comparisons, and celebrating others' successes, you can diminish feelings of envy and create a more positive and fulfilling life for yourself.

Mantra 5: Recognize That You Can Be a Source of Jealousy for Others

There'll hardly be anyone who hasn't faced the jealousy demon at some point, as it's a complex and natural emotion. Just as you may feel jealous of others, it's important to recognize that you, too, can be a source of jealousy for those around you. Understanding this can help you manage your relationships with greater empathy and awareness.

There are several ways you might unintentionally trigger jealousy in others. For example, forming new relationships can stir jealousy in those who were previously close to you. When someone new becomes important in your life, others might fear losing their special place, leading to tension and jealousy among friends or colleagues, which can disrupt the harmony of your relationships.

Recognizing this is the first step toward addressing jealousy that others might feel because of you.

Another common trigger is a shift in attention. For instance, if you're close to someone (Person A) and begin to focus more on someone else (Person B), Person A might feel neglected or replaced. This shift can lead to jealousy and insecurity as they perceive a loss of your attention and affection.

To mitigate this, try to engage in group activities that include both Person A and Person B. This can foster mutual understanding and reduce feelings of exclusion. If you sense that someone is feeling jealous, address it openly but sensitively. Acknowledge their feelings and reassure them of their importance in your life.

Strive to balance your time and attention among your friends or loved ones so that no one feels left out or undervalued. Try to see the situation from the jealous person's perspective, as understanding their emotions can help you respond more thoughtfully. Continually reassure them of their significance in your life.

The mantra is to recognize that you can indeed be a source of jealousy for others. Understanding this is key to maintaining healthy, balanced relationships. By communicating openly, balancing your attention, fostering inclusivity, and considering others' perspectives, you can navigate jealousy gracefully and maintain strong, positive connections with those around you.

Mantra 6: Don't Let Your Insecurities Transform Into Jealousy

The insecurities within you can easily overpower your behavior and morph into jealousy if not managed properly, and this transition has a potential to strain your relationships and harm your emotional well-being.

Your insecurities may originate internally within yourself or by some external influence, but regardless of their source, they need to be controlled before they start creating havoc in your system.

The first step to deal with this situation is to acknowledge your insecurities and understand their roots, as knowing their origins can help you address them more effectively. That involves understanding what specifically makes you feel insecure, as your insecurities may be triggered from countless sources such as looks, professional success, relationships, or social status.

Also some of your past experiences may have a role in contributing to your insecurities.

Communicate openly and honestly with friends and loved ones about your feelings and insecurities, so they have an opportunity to address any misunderstandings leading to your insecurities.

The mantra is that insecurities have a potential to lead to jealousy, influencing your behavior negatively. By acknowledging your insecurities, understanding their roots, and openly communicating with friends and loved ones, you can manage them effectively and reduce the likelihood of them transforming into jealousy.

Mantra 7: Communication is Key to Addressing Jealousy

Effective communication is crucial in managing and resolving jealousy within any relationship. Open dialogue is essential, whether you are experiencing jealousy or if someone else is feeling jealous towards you.

Misunderstandings are common in relationships and often give rise to feelings of jealousy. Clear, honest, and thoughtful communication can help to clarify these misunderstandings, build trust, and strengthen your connection.

The first step in open communication is to acknowledge and express your feelings and insecurities that may be fueling jealousy, doing so without placing blame or making accusations. Once you've shared your concerns, it's important to listen to the other person's perspective, validate their feelings, and demonstrate that you understand their viewpoint.

When others are jealous of you, engage in open-ended conversations to uncover the root cause of their feelings. Clarify any actions or behaviors that may have been misinterpreted and emphasize your commitment to the relationship to build a sense of security and trust.

The core of this mantra is recognizing that communication is key to managing jealousy, especially in relationships. By openly expressing feelings, demonstrating trust, seeking mutual understanding, and consistently reassuring your commitment, you can effectively address jealousy issues and cultivate more trusting and supportive relationships.

Mantra 8: Don't Anchor Your Happiness to Achieving What Stirs Your Envy

Envy can be a negative force, making you feel sad about something you desire but don't yet have. However, if you shift your perspective, you'll see that envy is also revealing what truly matters to you. It's a signal, affirming your desires and showing you what you value. Not everything you see around you will spark such strong emotions, but when envy does, it's pointing you toward something important.

The next step is to take action towards achieving that goal. But here's the reality: despite your best efforts, not every goal will be achieved exactly as you envisioned. The real issue arises when you tie your entire happiness to the success of a single goal. If you fail, you might be left with sadness and frustration, feeling like all your time and energy was wasted. In truth, that's not entirely accurate, and even in failure, there are valuable lessons to be learned.

Another possibility is that what you desired under the influence of envy might not bring you true happiness once achieved. Sometimes, what you were chasing turns out to be just an illusion of your desire, leaving you unfulfilled despite reaching your goal.

I once heard a wise saying: "Happiness is not a destination, it is a way of life." Embracing this mindset means finding joy in the journey, not just in reaching the end. Don't base your happiness solely on achieving what triggers your envy. Instead, focus on enjoying the process of pursuing your desires. Pay attention to the steps you're taking, the lessons you're learning, and the progress you're making along the way.

Celebrate the small victories and the effort you put in each day. By finding fulfillment in the journey itself, you'll discover that true happiness comes from within, not from external achievements or comparisons.

The mantra is to recognize that while envy might initially bring sadness, it also reveals what you truly desire. Rather than anchoring your happiness to achieving what triggers your envy, shift your focus to enjoying the journey toward your goals. This way, you can find joy and fulfillment in the process itself.

Mantra 9: Recognize the Role of the Past in Fueling Jealousy

The past can often cast a shadow over the present, even when it comes to feelings of jealousy—whether it's your past experiences or your partner's. For instance, when your partner spends a lot of time with a new friend, it might trigger jealousy because it reminds you of a previous relationship where similar behavior led to betrayal. It feels like history is repeating itself, and your insecurities begin to take over.

Similarly, seeing your partner interact with a past partner, even in a friendly manner, can stir up feelings of insecurity and jealousy. The same applies to your partner when they are haunted by their own past or by yours.

These insecurities create a fertile ground for jealousy to grow within your relationship. The past can also become a source of jealousy in other ways. After a breakup or divorce, some people maintain friendly relationships with their ex-partners, especially when there are shared responsibilities, like co-parenting. In these situations, they might constantly worry that their current partner feels jealous, even if that's not the case. However, this concern isn't unfounded, as it's not uncommon for current partners to feel insecure, fearing that their partner might return to their ex.

Sometimes, it's not your past or your partner's past that triggers jealousy, but the experiences of someone close to you. For example, witnessing the breakdown of your parents' or friends' relationships can plant seeds of jealousy in your own relationships when you observe similar patterns, even if there's no real connection between the two.

Jealousy-driven doubt is like a slow poison, and it's crucial to address it before it deeply affects your relationship. If you trust your partner but have doubts because of past experiences, work together to find ways to improve the situation.

The mantra is to recognize how the past can fuel jealousy in your relationships and to take action before it lingers too long. Like a slow poison, unresolved jealousy needs to be addressed promptly to protect the health of your relationship.

Mantra 10: Over-Possessiveness Can Be a Major Cause of Jealousy

There are many reasons why someone might feel jealous, and over-possessiveness is a significant culprit. Being overly possessive creates an environment where jealousy can easily thrive. Possessiveness is a natural human trait, often driven by insecurity and a desire to control or "own" someone or something. When you're overly possessive, you fear losing that person or thing and want them at your disposal whenever you wish.

For example, you might have a friend or partner who is always there for you, but they demand your full attention and time whenever they feel the need. If they see you spending time with someone else, they may become jealous, fearing that you prefer the other person over them.

Over-possessiveness is often mistaken for love and care, but it is more accurately a sign of fear and a sense of entitlement. While it might bring a temporary sense of security, it can quickly become a serious issue, leading to jealousy in relationships.

When you're overly possessive of someone, and you see them growing close to someone else, even if it's just a casual friendship, jealousy naturally arises. The same holds true for others: when someone is overly possessive of you and you begin forming new friendships, they may start showing signs of jealousy.

These individuals may not intend to harm you, but you might feel trapped by their controlling behavior, with your freedom restricted as they become jealous at the slightest provocation.

It's wise to be aware of over-possessiveness in your relationships, as this awareness can help you navigate those demanding dynamics more carefully and prevent jealousy from taking root. You may need to be extra clear and explicit in your communication to reassure those who are overly possessive. Remember, you chose to be in these relationships, so managing them effectively is key to maintaining their health.

The mantra is to recognize that over-possessiveness, whether it's yours or your partner's, might be the underlying cause of jealousy in your relationship. Being mindful of over-possessiveness can help you better manage these demanding relationships and prevent jealousy from taking hold.

CHAPTER 12

Anger: The Demon of Rage

Anger is a powerful and pervasive emotion, and few, if any, can escape its grasp. It is a relentless demon that spares no one, affecting everyone who crosses its path. In the daily life of an ordinary person, it's almost impossible to go through a day without encountering this formidable force. The reasons for anger are abundant, and even when none are apparent, we often create them—it's simply human nature.

Anger is among the most common demons, lurking everywhere, all the time. People are perpetually angry about something or someone. This demon grips us with a force akin to a drug, altering our personalities and leading us to behave in ways we often regret later. Often, by the time you realize the consequences of your actions performed under its spell, it's already too late..

The most troubling aspect of anger is how effortlessly it takes hold of us. Triggers are everywhere, waiting to ignite this volatile emotion. But not all anger is the same; it manifests in various forms, with varying intensity and duration, making its influence deeply subjective. Each individual experiences and expresses anger differently, even the same person may react differently in separate episodes of anger.

When it comes to intensity, some people experience only mild irritation, while others are consumed by violent rage. As for duration, anger can be short lived for some, linger for others, and, in extreme cases, last indefinitely. Sometimes, it lies dormant for long periods, only to explode unexpectedly like a volcano when triggered.

In severe cases, this demon can overpower its host, causing a dramatic transformation in both mental and physical states. Under its influence, one can lose all control, leading to actions and words that are out of character and often regrettable.

The irony of anger is that we succumb to it despite knowing that it rarely, if ever, leads to positive outcomes. Even when anger seems justified, there are always gentler, more effective alternatives. We understand that anger solves nothing, yet we repeatedly become puppets in the hands of this demon.

Anger drives us to say and do things we would never consider in a calm state, often with devastating consequences for our relationships and those we care about. Actions taken in anger rarely benefit anyone involved and usually lead to harm.

This demon is an ugly manifestation of our frustrations. Interestingly, during moments of anger, happiness is notably absent—these two emotions are mutually exclusive. When anger takes hold, it fills the void left by happiness, pushing it out of our emotional landscape.

One distinguishing trait of anger, compared to other demons, is its visibility. It's usually easy to spot that in people, except in cases of passive anger, where this demon is masked under a facade of calm.

Among all the demons we face, anger is perhaps the most frequent visitor in our lives. Not only do we battle with our own anger, but we also encounter it in others on a regular basis.

Let us explore this demon further to understand it better

and discover ways to manage its influence.

The Interconnections Between Anger and Other Demons

Many of the demons within us are closely linked to others, but anger stands out as one of the few that is connected to nearly every other demon in our system. Often, anger fuels these other demons, but there are times when it is the other demons that give rise to anger. Let's explore a few of these connections to better understand the profound impact anger has on our lives.

When examining the connection between anger and our relationships, it becomes clear that anger can have a deeply negative effect. In fact, this demon has the power to fracture even the strongest bonds. Anger can push people away, creating discomfort and anxiety in those who once felt close to us.

We often find ourselves getting angry with those closest to us for a variety of reasons, but the truth is, anger's damage can be severe, regardless of the relationship's strength. While those who care about us may tolerate our anger for a time, even their patience has its limits. Eventually, even the closest bonds can snap under the strain caused by anger.

Anger and comparison are distinct demons, yet comparison is a significant source of anger. When we compare ourselves to others who seem to be in a better position, especially when we are grappling with our own failures, anger is often born from this comparison.

Similarly, anger and ego are closely intertwined. Those with inflated egos frequently use anger as a weapon when their pride is wounded or challenged. Moreover, their anger flares up easily when their ego is unsatisfied.

Envy also plays a significant role in fueling our anger. When we become envious of someone else's possessions or achievements and fail to attain them despite our efforts, anger is an almost inevitable response. The same connection exists between anger and jealousy, where the fear of losing someone can ignite feelings of anger.

Anger, regret, and guilt are often inseparable companions. We may say or do harmful things in a fit of anger, only to realize the consequences too late, leading to deep feelings of regret and guilt over our actions.

Worry is another demon that often walks hand in hand with anger. We constantly worry about various aspects of our lives, and the realization that some things are beyond our control can leave us feeling helpless, giving rise to anger.

Anger and unmet expectations are also closely related. When our expectations are unmet, the first emotion that often surfaces is anger.

As for over-encouragement, even well-meaning encouragement can lead to anger when it creates undue pressure or sets unrealistic expectations.

When it comes to anger's connection with needs, wants, and greed, our ongoing struggles to satisfy these desires keep anger simmering within us.

The relationship between anger and past, present and future is profound: when the pain of the past intrudes upon our present or threatens our future, anger often arises as a natural reaction.

In these ways and more, anger is deeply connected to most of the other demons we carry within us.

The Misconception of Respect Rooted in Fear of Anger

I want to explore the correlation between anger and respect, as it has become far too common for the fear of anger to be mistaken for respect. This misconception is widespread, and it's essential to understand its implications.

There are situations where you may find yourself enduring the pain of dealing with someone who has anger issues, often someone close to you, and frequently someone older. You may struggle with whether to confront them or continue suffering in silence, often remaining trapped in this uncomfortable state.

It's not uncommon to feel intimidated by someone's anger, and that intimidation can sometimes be mistaken for respect. However, the reality is that your fear of their anger has little to do with actual respect. You might still respect them for their age or position, but in this context, it's the fear masquerading as respect. The positive aspect is that this type of fear has a breaking point and will eventually snap. However, the time spent under its influence is often painful and damaging.

Understanding this distinction is vital. If you believe you respect someone when, in truth, it's merely fear of their anger, it's essential to work on freeing yourself from that fear. Eventually, you'll come to this realization, but the time spent in that toxic state is detrimental to your well-being.

On the flip side, if you are the person whose anger others fear, mistaking that fear for respect, it's important to address your anger issues. By doing so, you may transform that fear into genuine respect.

While this dynamic is generally unhealthy, there is one scenario where it might serve a positive purpose: when children avoid bad behavior out of fear of their parents' anger. However, the downside is that this fear can create emotional distance, preventing children from experiencing warmth in the relationship and from sharing their true feelings and thoughts with their parents.

Understanding the Two Primary Forms of Anger: Passive and Aggressive

The anger demon is multifaceted, manifesting in various

shapes and forms. Here, I'll focus on two of the most prevalent types, keeping it concise since there's already extensive literature on the subject. Recognizing and understanding these forms of anger within yourself is crucial, as dealing with anger effectively requires a clear understanding of its nature.

The first form is passive anger, where individuals hide their anger, pretending everything is fine without showing clear signs. Instead, their anger surfaces indirectly through behaviors like sarcasm, procrastination, resistance, or stubbornness. The primary motivation behind this is to avoid confrontation. However, the danger of passive anger lies in how it becomes ingrained in the person's personality, leading to a constant state of stress due to suppressed emotions. Passive anger is like a dormant volcano, capable of erupting unexpectedly when triggered by certain situations.

The second form is open aggressive anger, where individuals express their anger through physical or verbal aggression. This can involve shouting, fighting, accusing, or bullying. It's a volatile and explicit form of anger, making it clear to everyone when someone is angry. This type can be explosive and unpredictable. The primary drive behind this behavior is the desire to maintain control. The major downside of open aggressive anger is that actions taken in the heat of the moment are often impulsive and poorly thought out, leading to regret and guilt afterward. Moreover, these actions can leave lasting emotional scars on those who are on the receiving end.

In reality, most of us experience a combination of these two forms, with varying degrees of intensity at different times.

The Rise and Impact of Collective Anger in Modern Society

Collective anger is a unique form of this emotion, where this demon targets a group of people rather than just an individual. It's particularly interesting because it involves a collective expression of anger, often triggered by a common cause or external influence.

In many cases, a core influencer emerges within a group of angry individuals, planting the seeds of anger and fueling it by provoking others to act out against a particular target. Sometimes, however, the group members are already angry, and they come together to amplify their collective strength against a perceived injustice or adversary.

Historically, mobilizing large groups and coordinating their reactions was challenging, leading to fewer displays of collective anger. However, in today's society, collective anger has become increasingly common. The rise of television, newspapers, mass media, social media, and other information-sharing platforms has made it easier than ever to spread an agenda quickly to a wide audience.

This ease of communication not only facilitates the dissemination of anger but also simplifies the process for ordinary people to join in and voice their collective frustrations, particularly through social media. As a result, collective anger has become a more frequent and impactful phenomenon in modern society.

Sources of Anger

Anger is typically a reaction to a specific trigger, whether it be a person, event, or circumstance. In other words, anger is a response to an external action. This demon enters our system through various channels, and the following are some of the most common sources.

When the Source of Our Anger is External

In our daily lives, numerous situations arise where other people or circumstances become triggers for our anger. These sources can include anyone from our close friends and family to strangers, public figures, or even the situations we find ourselves in.

Commonly, we become angry with others when they fail to meet our expectations, cause some inconvenience—either mentally or physically—or engage in actions we disapprove of. There is no shortage of people and situations that frequently trigger anger in our day-to-day interactions.

When our anger is directed toward people who aren't directly connected to us, such as a public figure, it typically has no immediate impact on them, though it might influence our decisions or actions in the future. For example, if a governor does something that angers us, we might choose not to vote for them in the next election.

However, the situation is different when our anger is directed at those close to us. In these cases, our anger not only affects us but also deeply impacts the people we care about. When we're angry with loved ones, our behavior often becomes harsh—yelling, shouting, or even throwing things in displays of aggression.

Even if the harsh words or actions are just heated reactions, they can leave lasting scars on the minds of those we love. Once spoken, words cannot be taken back, and they have the power to create permanent damage in relationships.

Additionally, our circumstances also play a significant role in fueling our anger. When we encounter unfavorable situations that lead to failure, it's common to direct our anger at the circumstances themselves.

When We Are the Source of Anger Within Ourselves

There are times when we become both the source and the victim of our own anger, introducing this destructive demon into our system ourselves. Throughout life, we make countless mistakes, and there's no shortage of situations where we find ourselves unhappy with our own actions or inactions that led to undesirable outcomes.

When things don't go as planned, especially due to our own mistakes, actions, or inactions, we often direct our anger inward. For example, when we fail because we didn't prepare adequately, we become angry at ourselves for not putting in the necessary effort. Similarly, when we're unable to achieve what our heart desires, it's common to feel frustration and anger toward ourselves for our perceived shortcomings.

One of the most prevalent reasons people become angry with themselves is dissatisfaction with their lives. When life doesn't seem to fulfill their expectations, they become angry, feeling they haven't accomplished enough or are far from where they want to be. In such moments, we often blame our past decisions, forgetting that we couldn't have predicted the outcomes when making those choices.

New Year's resolutions are a classic example of this self-directed anger. We make numerous promises to ourselves, but when we fail to keep them, it leads to frustration and anger. Similarly, we get angry when we make financial investments that result in losses, regretting our decisions and wishing we had chosen differently.

In all these situations, while we may be angry with ourselves, it's crucial to remember that no one else is involved. This means that in order to manage our anger, we only need to focus on controlling ourselves.

When We Are the Source of Anger in Others

Just as others can trigger anger within us, we too can become the source of anger in others. It's essential to recognize this because when someone gets angry with you due to your actions, the intensity of their anger directly impacts you, as you are the cause of that demon in them.

We navigate a complex world filled with challenges, and it's impossible to be perfect all the time. Inevitably, there will be moments when our actions—or lack thereof—provoke anger in others. This is especially true when it comes to meeting others' expectations; no matter how hard we try, we will occasionally fall short. While some people may brush off these disappointments, others might react with anger, making us the source of their frustration.

Acknowledging this reality is more practical than striving to meet everyone's expectations flawlessly, which is an unrealistic goal. Sometimes, well-meaning people, such as your parents, might see potential in you that they feel you're not fully realizing. If you choose to put in less effort than they believe you should, it can lead to their anger.

Sometimes, people intentionally provoke anger in others to incite an aggressive response. This can be done with various motives—occasionally with good intentions, aiming to push someone into action, but often for selfish reasons, where they manipulate you by exploiting your anger to serve their own interests.

There will be times when you unintentionally say something that upsets others, or when your actions don't sit well with certain people. No matter what you do, there will always be those who disapprove and respond with anger.

For public figures or celebrities, this is even more common. With a large audience scrutinizing every move, it's inevitable that some actions will anger some people, regardless of intent.

Ultimately, as human beings, we are bound to make mistakes, and some of these mistakes will upset others. However, it's not just errors that provoke anger; even actions done with the best intentions can anger those who perceive them differently or are negatively affected.

It's important to reflect on your actions or inactions that may be causing anger in others. If you can address and correct these issues, that's ideal. But if you can't, it may be necessary to manage the expectations others have of you to reduce the likelihood of becoming a source of anger for them.

Additional Triggers for Anger

While this may echo some of the points already discussed, it's crucial to underscore the importance of recognizing the triggers of anger, even at the risk of a bit of repetition. The reality is, our lives are filled with numerous triggers that can fuel and strengthen the anger within us. Some of the most common ones include pain, frustration, fear, helplessness, loss of control, and feeling overwhelmed.

In everyday life, we all experience various types of pain, both mental and physical. When these pains become unbearable or uncontrollable, one of the emotional responses that often emerges is anger. Similarly, throughout life, we encounter various fears—such as the fear of losing something valuable or the fear for the safety of a loved one. When these fears are beyond our control, anger is a natural response.

Frustration is another common emotion we encounter, often stemming from the realization that we cannot succeed in everything we do or control many aspects of our lives. This feeling of helplessness can easily give rise to anger.

Life, as we all know, is far from easy. It is filled with daily challenges that can make us anxious, worried, or exhausted. Even those who appear privileged or seem to lead an easier life from the outside face their own unique challenges. When life becomes overwhelming, it can feel like we're barely keeping our heads above water, and in such moments, anger often arises as a side effect of this intense pressure.

This list of anger triggers is extensive and could go on indefinitely. Recognizing and understanding these triggers is vital to managing and mitigating the anger that they can produce.

The Anger Deadlock

A common scenario in today's society is what I would call an "anger deadlock." This occurs when two people, both angry with each other, refuse to communicate, each waiting for the other to apologize first. This standoff results in a stalemate where both parties suffer, waiting for the other to break the silence.

In this double-edged situation, both individuals feel hurt and wronged, leading to a breakdown in communication. Each person believes they are justified in their anger and expects the other to make the first move. Such deadlocks can spawn other demons and have the potential to damage relationships significantly.

To break the anger deadlock, it's crucial to take a step back and reflect on why you're angry and what you hope to achieve by waiting for the other person to apologize. It's important to try to understand the other person's perspective, as they may also be experiencing pain and feel just as justified in their anger as you do.

Breaking the deadlock requires someone to take the first step. Be the bigger person and initiate a conversation, even if it feels difficult. Prioritize your relationship over your anger, even if you believe the other party is in the wrong. When you recognize that the relationship is more important to you than your anger, you'll find the motivation to take the difficult steps needed to preserve it.

The anger deadlock is a common but painful situation that can lead to prolonged suffering for everyone involved. By practicing empathy, initiating communication, and offering sincere apologies, you can break the cycle and move toward resolution.

It's also important to note that anger deadlocks aren't limited to just two people. They can occur within groups, where multiple individuals are angry with each other for various reasons, creating an even more complex and challenging deadlock to resolve.

The Good Side of Anger

By now, you may be convinced that anger is a destructive force that we should strive to eliminate from our system. However, the reality is that, while anger is often harmful, it also has a few redeeming qualities that make it worth keeping in check rather than completely eradicating.

Surprisingly, even a demon like anger can have a positive side, leading to beneficial outcomes in certain situations. Let's explore some of the constructive aspects of this often-maligned negative force.

A good example of anger serving a positive purpose is in parenting. Children might avoid engaging in bad behavior because they don't want to provoke their parents' anger. This fear of parental anger can act as a deterrent, encouraging kids to think twice before doing something wrong.

Controlled anger also plays a crucial role in standing up against injustice, exploitation, bullying, and other forms of wrongdoing. In these contexts, anger can be a powerful motivator to take action and fight back against negative forces.

Anger can also drive personal motivation. When you become angry with yourself over a failure, this emotion can push you to become more committed and sincere in your future efforts. The key is to channel this anger in a constructive way, using it to fuel your determination and energy toward achieving your goals.

Furthermore, anger creates discomfort, which can encourage you to take action to resolve the issues causing it, ultimately restoring balance and well-being in your life.

In certain sports, such as boxing, fencing, and wrestling,

controlled aggression—often fueled by anger—is essential. This intensity can help athletes enter a winning state of mind, giving them the edge they need to succeed.

Collective anger can also be a powerful force for good when it unites people against exploitation, injustice, oppression, or any other widespread harm. When channeled appropriately, this collective anger can lead to social change and positive outcomes for the broader community.

However, despite its few positive aspects, it's important to remember that anger is still largely a negative emotion and one of the most damaging if left unchecked. Managing this demon effectively allows us to harness its potential benefits while minimizing its destructive effects.

Mantras for Dealing With the Anger Demon

Now, let's explore some effective mantras to help you manage and overcome the anger demon. By regularly practicing these mantras, you can keep the anger demon in check, transforming it from a destructive force into a manageable and sometimes even constructive aspect of your life.

Mantra 1: Think Before You Speak or Act When You're Angry

Acting out of anger often leads to regrettable words and actions that can harm relationships and escalate conflicts. Just like bullets, once words are spoken, they can't be taken back.

When you're angry and in a heated conversation, it's easy to blurt out hurtful words or bring up old, irrelevant issues that were buried long ago. These outbursts, while quick to deliver, can cause lasting damage—damage that might never be undone.

So, when you're under the influence of anger, resist the urge to immediately respond with whatever comes to mind.

Instead, pause and carefully consider your words, knowing that the first thoughts anger brings are usually harmful. Once spoken, you can't take them back.

In addition to slowing down your response, try to listen to the other person. They might also be speaking out of anger, but by listening, you may gain insights that change your perspective, potentially reducing your own anger.

Anger's worst trait is that it doesn't allow you to think clearly; it pushes you to vent your frustration without considering the consequences. Furthermore, words spoken in anger are seldom kind.

Remembering this mantra during heated moments can help you navigate through difficult conversations with fewer regrets. However, as a human, you may still make mistakes when angry. While this can be unfortunate, it's not the end of the world. You can repair the damage through a simple apology, which can redirect the conversation in a more positive direction.

Often, after your anger subsides, you'll realize that what you said in the heat of the moment didn't hold as much weight for you as it may have for the other person. It's important to clarify this and express your sincere regret for your words.

Similarly, don't take everything others say or do during their moments of anger too seriously.

The mantra here is to recognize the destructive power of anger and consider the impact of your words and actions before expressing them. Managing anger involves pausing, controlling your emotions, reflecting on consequences, seeking understanding, communicating effectively, and maintaining control over your reactions.

Mantra 2: Your Anger Impacts Both You and Those Around You

If not properly managed, anger can have significant negative effects not only on you but also on those around you. Although your anger may reside within you, its impact extends far beyond, affecting everyone in your vicinity— whether they are directly involved in the situation or not.

When you're angry, no matter the source, your anger influences everyone around you. Under the influence of this demon, you become a different person—unhappy, aggressive, and unsettling to those nearby. You might be angry with one specific person or situation, but this emotion often spills over, causing you to behave bitterly toward others who have nothing to do with your frustration.

In any moment of life, you are either happy or not, and when you're not happy, it's difficult to be a positive presence for those around you. Anger, by its nature, takes away happiness and replaces it with negativity.

Under the grip of anger, you might say things you don't truly mean, but those words can leave lasting scars on others. These wounds may fade over time, becoming dormant, but they have the potential to resurface with full intensity in the future, causing more harm.

A crucial and often overlooked truth is that, regardless of the target of your anger, the person most affected by it is you. You become the primary victim of your own anger, bearing the burden of its emotional toll. This can leave deep scars on your mind, leading to regret and self-criticism when you reflect on how you've treated others during those angry moments.

The mantra here is to be aware that your anger affects not just your physical and mental health but also your relationships and the emotional well-being of those around you. Anger is a destructive force that leaves behind negative consequences, making it essential to keep it in check. By understanding the wide-reaching effects of your anger, practicing self-control, and communicating more effectively, you can manage your anger constructively and create a more positive environment for yourself and those around you.

Mantra 3: Anger is Unavoidable, but Don't Let It Linger

Once you understand that anger is a harmful force, and that you are its primary victim, you might aim to avoid getting angry altogether. However, no matter who you are, it's nearly impossible to completely escape the grip of anger.

Even if you're typically calm and possess excellent self-control, there will inevitably be situations, people, or incidents that trigger your anger.

The reality is that there will be moments when you become angry, as anger is a natural and inevitable emotion, and that anger will continue to affect you until you take action. The key question is: what can you do about it?

While you can't prevent anger from arising, you can control how long it stays with you by letting it go as quickly as possible, rather than allowing it to linger and fester. Holding onto anger for too long can negatively impact your mental and physical well-being, as well as your relationships.

However, letting go of anger is easier said than done. When you try to release it, your mind often justifies your anger with seemingly valid reasons, and it will always find plenty of them.

The important thing to remember is that your anger will persist as long as you hold on to these justifications. The truth is, anger is harmful regardless of the reasons behind it. While there may be reasons that trigger your anger, you don't need a reason to let it go—doing so is always beneficial.

Start by acknowledging and accepting your anger as a valid emotion. Suppressing or denying it can actually intensify and prolong the feeling. Next, try to understand what triggered your anger. Identifying the specific event, person, or unmet expectation that caused it can help you address it more effectively.

Forgiveness, whether towards others or yourself, is essential to prevent anger from taking hold and lingering. Forgive, but keep your moments of anger in mind—not to dwell on them, but to learn from them—so you can respond more constructively in the future.

The mantra here is that while you can't stop anger from arising, it's essential not to let it linger. By acknowledging and accepting your anger, identifying its source, practicing forgiveness, and learning from your experiences, you can manage and release your anger in a healthy way.

Mantra 4: Forgiveness is the Key to Managing Anger

When your thoughts are fixated on the cause of your anger and the person responsible, your anger will remain at its peak, continuing to affect you as long as your focus stays on the source of your frustration. However, when you shift your attention inward, you'll realize that, regardless of who or what has caused your anger, it is you who suffers the most from your own anger. This realization makes it crucial to address and resolve your anger sooner rather than later.

Forgiveness is a powerful tool for managing anger because it allows you to release feelings of resentment and negativity, bringing you to a calmer and more peaceful state of mind. It's important to understand that forgiveness is something you do for your own peace of mind; it is primarily for your benefit, not necessarily for the person who may have wronged you.

Consciously deciding to let go of resentment is essential, as holding onto anger harms you more than the person who hurt you. However, forgiveness in this context doesn't mean accepting harmful behavior or forgetting it ever happened. Instead, it's about freeing yourself from the grip of anger.

To facilitate forgiveness, try to understand the perspectives and motivations of others. This can help reduce the intensity of your anger, making it easier to forgive. Additionally, forgive yourself for any mistakes or shortcomings that might be fueling your self-directed anger. Remember that making mistakes is a natural part of being human, and being kind to yourself is essential for letting go of anger.

Accept that some things are beyond your control and that holding onto anger won't change the past. Instead, prioritize your present well-being by letting go of past grievances that continue to fuel your anger.

The mantra here is to recognize that forgiveness is a powerful and effective way to manage anger. By acknowledging and understanding your anger, shifting your perspective, releasing resentment, forgiving both yourself and others, and focusing on the present, you can let go of anger and find inner peace.

Mantra 5: Don't React to Someone Else's Anger with Your Own

There will be countless situations where people get angry with you for various reasons, and it's natural to feel the urge to retaliate with anger. After all, it seems like the natural response to match their aggression with your own. However, while this may provide a brief sense of satisfaction, it's ultimately a superficial and short-lived victory that can cause more harm in the long run.

It's important to recognize that, unlike iron, anger doesn't cut through anger. The idea of "an eye for an eye" might hold some truth in certain contexts, but "anger for anger" only leads to escalation and potential damage to relationships.

When someone directs their anger at you, your first instinct might be to react immediately with your own anger. Instead, try to hold back, take a deep breath, and give yourself a moment to think clearly before responding. Absorbing your initial anger and calming down can make all the difference.

Take the time to understand the reasons behind their anger by listening carefully without interrupting. Remember to stay focused on maintaining self-control and avoid taking their anger personally. Often, their anger is more about the situation than about you as an individual—you might be a part of the situation, but you're not the sole cause.

Assess whether an immediate response is required. In some instances, delaying a response can exacerbate the situation, while in others, taking time before replying might be the most effective approach. Sometimes, silence can be more impactful, letting the other person vent while you act as a calm listener. In other situations, a thoughtful response is necessary to defuse the conflict and prevent it from escalating further.

By not reacting impulsively, you give yourself the opportunity to analyze the situation, consider your options, and craft a more thoughtful response. Always aim to respond with kindness and respect, even when faced with anger, and show a willingness to address the root cause of the issue.

In extreme situations where the other person's anger becomes abusive, it's important to set clear boundaries and be prepared to remove yourself from the situation if necessary.

The mantra here is to never meet someone's anger with your own, as it only intensifies the conflict. Instead, pause before reacting, carefully assess the situation, choose your words wisely, and respond thoughtfully if needed. Reacting to anger with more anger rarely, if ever, leads to a resolution.

Mantra 6: You Can't Control Everything and Everyone That Triggers Your Anger

A significant portion of the anger we experience comes from situations or people that are beyond our control. While you may be able to influence some individuals or circumstances to reduce their impact on you, there will always be others that remain outside your control and continue to provoke anger.

There's only so much you can do to manage the things that trigger your anger. Unfortunately, many of us struggle to accept this reality, often attempting to control everything and everyone to align with our expectations. When things don't go our way, it only amplifies our anger.

The sooner you embrace this mantra and adjust your expectations to reflect this reality, the quicker you'll move toward a life with less anger. Acknowledging and accepting that many of the factors contributing to your anger are outside your control can help reduce frustration and shift your focus to managing your reactions.

After accepting that you can't control the source of your anger, focus on how you'll respond to anger-inducing situations. While you can't control others, you can still set clear boundaries with people or situations that frequently upset you.

Try to understand the perspectives and motivations of those who anger you. This understanding can diminish your anger and lessen the desire to control others. Forgiveness can also help in this process.

The mantra here is to recognize that while you can't control every person or situation that makes you angry, you can control your own responses and emotions. By accepting what is beyond your control, focusing on how you react, and understanding others' perspectives, you can manage this demon more effectively. Remember, your goal should be to focus on what you can control and let go of what you cannot.

Mantra 7: Identify Your Anger Triggers and Address Them Directly

While anger itself is a destructive force, the real culprits are the underlying triggers that provoke this demon. Managing your anger effectively starts with identifying these triggers and developing strategies to deal with them.

If you can learn to respond to these triggers calmly and gracefully, you'll experience greater peace of mind, as fewer anger episodes will disrupt your life. Each anger trigger is unique, and everyone has their own set of triggers that provoke them.

Some triggers may cause mild irritation, while others can make you extremely angry. There are also triggers that no longer affect you because you've learned to manage them and have become immune to their impact. Additionally, the speed at which these triggers elicit a reaction can vary—some may ignite anger instantly, while others build up over time.

To control your anger at its source, start by identifying your specific triggers, prioritize them based on their intensity, and then create a plan to address them. Although you may not be able to eliminate most triggers, you can work on how you respond to them.

The mantra is to focus not just on managing the anger itself, but on understanding and addressing the triggers that provoke it. These triggers are the true sources of your anger. Instead of suppressing, ignoring, or merely coping with your anger, identify what causes it and find ways to effectively manage those underlying triggers.

Mantra 8: Understand Why Others Are Angry With You and Address It Effectively

This mantra focuses on a different aspect of how the "anger demon" can affect you—specifically, when the heat of anger comes from others rather than yourself. When people, particularly those you care about or want to maintain a relationship with, are angry with you due to your actions, inactions, or mistakes, you will inevitably feel the impact of their anger.

Recognizing why they are upset and addressing the root causes can lead to significant improvements in your relationships, fostering a more harmonious environment around you. Often, the reasons for their anger are apparent, making it relatively straightforward to address these issues and reduce the tension.

However, in some instances, you might be unaware of the reasons behind their anger until you actively seek to understand them. Without this effort, you may continue to face their anger without any clear resolution. Sometimes, the cause may be simple and easily manageable, leading to regret that you didn't address it sooner. In other cases, the issue might be something you cannot resolve or choose not to address. In such situations, finding a middle ground or communicating your position honestly can help set the right expectations and ease the tension.

There are times when the expectations others have of you may be unreasonable. These situations are particularly challenging, as you may need to challenge their expectations while they are already upset. The goal here is to help them reset their expectations rather than disappoint them by failing to meet unrealistic demands.

Unmet expectations, whether from others or even your own, are a common source of anger. As you explore the reasons behind their anger, you may discover that you've failed to meet these expectations, acted against their wishes, or caused them some inconvenience—often without even realizing it.

Start by acknowledging their anger, as denying or ignoring it can worsen the situation. Show respect for their feelings by taking their anger seriously and demonstrating your willingness to address it. Approach them calmly, avoiding defensive or angry reactions. Listen to their perspective with an open mind, encouraging them to share their feelings and the reasons behind their anger. Ensure you fully understand their concerns before responding.

Where appropriate, take responsibility for your actions. If you've made a mistake or contributed to their anger, acknowledge it and offer a sincere apology if needed. Be honest about your intentions, feelings, and any limitations you may have in resolving the issue. Transparency can build trust and minimize misunderstandings.

The essence of this mantra is to understand why others are angry with you and to address it effectively. By being patient, empathetic, calm, and open in your communication, you can manage and mitigate the anger directed towards you, ultimately fostering healthier relationships.

Mantra 9: Communication is Key to Effectively Managing Anger

Clear and effective communication is essential for managing anger, whether in yourself or in others. It helps express feelings clearly, prevents misunderstandings, enables understanding of different perspectives, and resolves conflicts constructively. This holds true whether someone else has made you angry or if you have caused anger in others.

When others make you angry, it's important to communicate your feelings clearly without blaming or criticizing them. Be specific about what is causing your anger and take a direct approach—be honest and straightforward, without sugarcoating or hiding your true emotions.

Establish and communicate clear boundaries with people or situations that frequently trigger your anger, and equally, respect the boundaries of others. During these conversations, remain calm and composed. Listen actively and attentively when the other person responds, and avoid raising your voice or making aggressive gestures, even if the other person is upset.

Make an effort to understand the other person's perspective. Give them time to express their feelings without interruption, and exercise patience. Recognize that sometimes a consensus cannot be reached, and be prepared to agree to disagree respectfully.

Similarly, if you sense that you have caused anger in others, take a proactive approach by initiating communication to understand the root cause of their anger and what you can do to resolve it. Often, they may give you hints or direct messages indicating their anger, but it will usually be your responsibility to uncover the true reasons behind it. Sometimes, you might not even realize someone is angry with you because they never express it openly, making it all the more important to remain attentive to subtle cues.

The mantra is that effective communication is crucial for managing anger—both your own and others'. By practicing active listening, staying calm, being honest and direct, setting clear boundaries, being open to understanding, and avoiding blame or criticism, you can handle anger in a more constructive manner.

Mantra 10: Recognize and Address Dormant Anger in Your System

By now, we understand that anger is an unavoidable aspect of life, and there will be times when we find ourselves getting angry. We've also explored various mantras for managing our anger, knowing that while we can't eliminate anger entirely, we should strive to prevent it from lingering.

However, the journey of dealing with anger doesn't end there.

Some anger doesn't simply vanish; instead, it enters a passive or dormant state. The real issue arises when we lose awareness of this dormant anger within us. Often, we mistakenly believe that our anger has dissipated. Over time, we may become so accustomed to the presence of certain dormant anger that we no longer feel its harmful effects.

Dormant anger is akin to a ticking time bomb or a dormant volcano, waiting for the right trigger to erupt. In fact, it's even more insidious than these metaphorical comparisons, as it occasionally manifests in subtle ways, subtly surfacing from time to time.

This dormant anger continues to fester within us, constantly eating away at our well-being, even if we aren't fully aware of it. The root of dormant anger may lie in an unresolved past event that left us with lingering resentment. However, this anger can unexpectedly surface, even when triggered by events that seem unrelated to the original issue.

In today's complex world, it's likely that we harbor multiple forms of dormant anger, some buried deep within us. And unless we actively seek them out, we may never realize their existence in our system.

Therefore, it's essential to regularly engage in self-reflection to identify any dormant anger residing within us. If you uncover such anger, take the time to trace its root cause and seek to resolve or accept it pragmatically.

The mantra here is to acknowledge the existence of dormant anger within your system—anger that you may have grown accustomed to or forgotten about. Though dormant, this anger is still a destructive force, waiting to explode. Regular self-reflection is key to recognizing and resolving these hidden emotions before they cause major harm.

CHAPTER 13

Past, Present and Future - The Demon of Times

You might be wondering why I'm discussing the past, present, and future in the context of this book. Soon, you'll understand that these elements are like deadly demons in our system. For the sake of simplicity, I'll refer to them collectively as one demon.

This demon haunts us by using our own past, present, and future against us. Its primary goal is to steal pleasure from our lives and create stress. It uses our past through haunting memories of previous actions and events, our present by making us struggle with current realities, and our future with the uncertainty and fear of what is yet to come.

If you start thinking about yourself in the context of the constantly changing flow of time, it may look something like this below.

Right now, you exist in the present moment, having already experienced your past and moving towards your future. In other words, at any given time, the present is here, the past is gone, and the future is yet to come.

So, if I ask you which among the three - your past, your

present, or your future - is most important to you, what would your answer be?

Well, regardless of your answer, I request you to hold onto it until you've seen my perspective on this demon.

Let's delve deeper into this demon to understand its presence in our system, how it haunts us, and what we can do about it. Each member of this deadly trio - the past, the present, and the future plays its part in the game of creating disturbances in our lives.

This Demon Exploits Our Troubled Past to Disturb Both Our Present and Future

When you think of your past, it's something you've already lived through, whether it was good, bad, or ugly. Regardless of its nature, the past is done, gone, and finished. If your past was bad, you have already suffered through it. Conversely, if it was good, you might have enjoyed fantastic times with family, travel, food, movies, friends, games, and more. Either way, it exists only in your memories now and will remain there forever.

This demon brings out the bad memories from our past and uses them to scare us with the possibility of those bad experiences happening again. This creates disturbances in both our present as well as future, preventing us from fully enjoying life under the influence of such terror.

The insidious nature of this demon lies in its ability to keep bad memories fresh in our minds all the time. Regardless of how sound our present situation may be, this demon doesn't let us enjoy that by constantly reminding us that since we had a bad experience in the past, it can return at any time. As a result, we start living and doing everything very cautiously, spoiling any fun in the process. This demon plays a significant role in preventing us from living life to its fullest, even if our current condition allows it without any risks.

The effect of this demon's influence is relatively stronger on those who have experienced a bad past involving significant suffering. For example, let's talk about people who witnessed their parents suffering a financial crisis during their childhood. If their family was once affluent but then fell into poverty due to a financial calamity, the struggle for survival and the subsequent poor living conditions leave a long-lasting impact on their future decisions. They become extremely cautious with any financial decisions, always fearing a repeat of past events.

Having witnessed such hardships firsthand, they know how bad things can get, trapping them in the clutches of their bad past. This demon exploits these memories, keeping them from moving forward and living life freely.

They completely forget that their life and circumstances are completely different from those of their childhood where they went through that crisis.

It Doesn't Stop at Examining Only Our Own Past; It Goes Even Further

This demon uses our past to exploit us, but it doesn't stop there. It also seeks out other people's bad experiences to scare us with the possibility that similar events could occur in our own lives. It plants the worry in our minds that if something bad happened to someone else, it could certainly happen to us as well.

But there's a good in this bad, as while this is mostly disturbing, there is a silver lining that it gives us an opportunity to learn from other people's past experiences. By observing and understanding their mistakes and misfortunes, we can prepare ourselves to prevent similar events from happening to us, should we see them as a potential threat.

This Demon Uses Our Present Problems to Trouble Us

The world we live in today is far from perfect, and not everything around us is going well. In fact, our world is becoming more competitive with time, with people fighting for the ever-diminishing resources. Everyone faces challenges in their present life, providing ample fuel for this demon to create disturbances within us.

Beyond exploiting our personal problems, this demon amplifies our fears by bringing in all the bad news happening around the world currently, making us worry that these issues might affect us personally. The reality is that not every bad event will impact us directly or may even be relevant to us, but each piece of negative news has the potential to create a sense of negativity. This can worsen the emotional state of those already burdened by their own problems, dragging their spirits even lower.

This Demon Uses Our Anxieties About the Future to Torment Us

Our future is filled with uncertainties and unknowns, and some of which can be truly frightening. This demon exploits these fears to create disturbances in our present moments. The future is something that hasn't happened yet and is inherently uncertain, leaving us unsure of what will come.

The irony is that even knowing this, the demon still manages to instill fear within us. While some potential future issues may have credible reasons for concern, many should not scare us. Just because something bad could happen doesn't mean it will.

Three Different States

In simple terms, the past is what we've already lived through, the present is what we are experiencing moment by moment, and the future is what we will experience in the times to come, if and when we get there. These represent three different states of time, and physically, we can only be in one state at any given moment.

Upon deeper reflection, it turns out that the state we are in at any given moment is always the present. Any moment in our past was once the present, and the same will be true for the future. Thus, we are always in the present when we are conscious, and our past and future are merely snapshots in our minds.

Problems arise when we defy this physical limitation and try to live in more than one state of time simultaneously. This is when disturbances occur, as one state starts affecting the others, disrupting the natural order.

Among these three states, the past is constant and immutable. No matter what we do, we cannot go back in time and change it. Whatever happened has happened, and this is an important fact to remember.

The present is the most vulnerable of the three, as it is affected by both "bad experiences from the past" and "worries about the future." This is another crucial fact to keep in mind.

The future is mostly an imagination that may or may not unfold as we envision it.

The best way to use the three states is to learn from the past, live fully in the present, and not worry excessively about the future. However, this is much easier said than done.

Now, Later or Never

There's another form of this "past, present, and future" demon that manipulates us by making us oscillate between now, later, or never when it comes to doing something or making decisions. Essentially, "now" is the present, "later" is the future, and "never" is the termination point. The past significantly influences our choices between the three.

The harsh reality is that most of us aren't wealthy, and

this financial limitation brings out this demon, forcing us to constantly decide between now, later, or never in our daily lives. Whether it's buying a TV, planning a vacation, or purchasing a car, this demon heavily influences our decisions.

Life would be simple if we could do whatever we wanted, whenever and however we wished. But the brutal fact is that it isn't! To spend now or not to spend now, that is the question.

If we spend more money now, we might not have enough for later when we might need it. On the other hand, if we save money for the future by sacrificing our present, we might find we never need it.

Let's say we adopt a 50-50 balance philosophy, splitting our resources equally between the present and the future. Not sure if this works for you or not, but it certainly doesn't work for me. It leaves us neither living our lives fully today nor tomorrow. It's a compromise, and we call it a balanced life. Regardless of my views on this, being pragmatic, for most of us this is the best we can do.

Challenging this balance by increasing today's share in the equation adds more comfort to our present but may also add worries for tomorrow. Thus, it's a highly individual choice to find a pseudo-balance between the present and future - not a perfect 50-50, but somewhere close.

Who You Were, Who You Are, and Who You Will Become Are Different People

When discussing the past, present, and future, it's important to understand that time is not the only thing that's changing, we are also evolving with it. As time progresses, we learn new things, update old knowledge, and change both physically as well as mentally.

I'll not be entirely inaccurate if I say that who you are today is a different person from who you were yesterday, and who you'll be tomorrow will be another version of yourself.

So according to this logic, what you did in the past was actually done by a different version of you, based on the capabilities and knowledge you had at that time. If you repeat something you did in the past, it will be executed by the current version of you, with entirely different capabilities and knowledge. Therefore, the outcome is likely to be different as well.

And so comparing yourself with your past self is like comparing apples to oranges.

The Future Exists Only in Our Imagination

When we think about the future, even if there's a strong probability of an event happening, supported by ample data, it may still not unfold as we anticipate, or it might not happen at all.

There are always more parameters influencing future events than those we consider in our predictions, and many of which are beyond our control. While we might be aware of some of these factors, there are likely many others of which we are completely unaware.

Our future predictions are based on analyses that may or may not be accurate. We feel better if our calculations predict a positive future, but if they suggest a bleak one, a demon is born within us that starts to haunt us.

Blinded by the vision of a possible dark future, we often forget the crucial fact that this future is merely a figment of our imagination, and it may or may not happen as we foresee. Instead of treating this as an opportunity to take proactive steps, we start believing it to be true and lose our sleep over it.

Vision of the Future is Shaped by the Lens Through Which We View It

Our vision of the future is largely influenced by the perspective we use to see it. Since the future hasn't happened yet and we can only imagine what it might be like, our perspective plays a significant role in shaping that vision. Changing our perspective will change our vision of the future as well.

If we are currently in a good place, our future may look secure, but we might still find reasons to worry. Sometimes these worries are genuine, but other times we might be manifesting them ourselves influenced by the bad past.

Conversely, even if there is a high probability of a bleak future, we can remain worry-free with the confidence that things could still turn out well, and if not, we'll handle whatever comes our way.

These are two completely opposite perspectives on looking at our future.

The Good in the Past, Present, and Future Demon

While the "past, present, and future" demon often brings challenges, it also offers valuable lessons and opportunities for growth. Recognizing the positive aspects of each time state can help us manage this demon more effectively.

This demon plays a crucial role in our life by reminding us of past mistakes, thus helping us avoid repeating them and landing in similar trouble. As the saying goes, "Learn from your past mistakes and do not repeat them," and this demon is quite instrumental in ensuring that we do just that.

Our past provides us with a wealth of experiences and lessons. Reflecting on our past can help us understand our strengths and weaknesses, enabling us to make better decisions in the present. It's a source of memories, both good and bad, that shape who we are today. By learning from past mistakes and celebrating past achievements, we build a stronger foundation for our future.

Additionally, this demon reinforces the positive aspects of our past. Any good experiences remind us to stay motivated and on the right path. Learning from past successes fast-tracks our progress by saving us from reinventing the wheel.

As for the good in the present—Our present is where life happens. It's the only time we can actively influence or do anything. Living in the present allows us to fully engage with our surroundings and appreciate the moment. It's an opportunity to take action, make changes, and enjoy life.

As for the good in the future—Our future represents potential and hope, and it gives us something to strive for and look forward to. Planning for the future encourages us to set goals and work towards them, giving us a sense of purpose and direction. Even though the future is uncertain, it's a canvas for our dreams and aspirations. Imagining a positive future can motivate us to make the necessary changes in our present to achieve our desired outcomes.

Moreover, if there are potential dark spots in our future, this demon will continually remind us of them. Although this might seem like a method of troubling us with worries about the future, it can be seen as a blessing in disguise. By constantly reminding us of potential future issues, this demon prompts us to find ways to deal with them proactively, effectively preparing us for future challenges.

By focusing on the positives in the past, present, and future, we can diminish this demon's negative influence and create a more balanced and fulfilling life.

These positive aspects and many others make it clear that we cannot completely rid ourselves of this demon. Its presence, though often challenging, serves to keep us vigilant, motivated, and prepared for whatever lies ahead.

Mantras for Dealing With the Past, Present and Future Demon

So despite knowing that this demon is mostly bad, we can not get rid of this from our system because of some of its good qualities. But we can not let this demon control us either, and in fact we need to keep this under control. Now I'm going to talk about mantras for dealing with this demon.

Mantra 1: Don't Be Afraid of Bad Past Repeating Itself

The core message of this mantra is to prevent your past from overshadowing your present and future. By fearing that negative past events might repeat themselves, you're giving undue power to this demon and providing an opportunity for it to potentially disrupt your present and future by giving it more importance than the other two.

When a current situation or incident seems similar to a past one, it's important to recognize that they are two separate incidents. They may look similar but they are not the same. Each event requires a favorable environment with specific conditions to occur, and for a past event to repeat itself exactly, those same conditions must be present again, which is highly unlikely. There's no point living under a fear of something that has a slim chance of happening.

That means past negative events have little or no influence on future occurrences unless you choose to link them. Therefore, you should focus on your present and future, prioritizing them in that order, to prevent your past from influencing your current and future.

When you are worried about past events repeating themselves, remember that current circumstances differ from past ones. Redirect your attention from the past to the present and future, and make decisions based on current realities and future goals, not past anxieties.

The mantra is to empower yourself to live more fully in the present and plan positively for the future, free from the fears of past events repeating themselves.

Mantra 2: Between Your Present and Future, Focus More on Your Present

This mantra emphasizes prioritizing your present over worries about the future. Focusing excessively on potential future problems can prevent you from enjoying the present moment. By focusing on the present, you can prevent future insecurities from spoiling your current happiness.

This demon speculates about all the bad things that might happen to us in future, and uses them to prevent us from having an enjoyable present.

It's true that the present is when you plan for the future, and such planning for the future has become more important with the advances in the medical sciences that's increasing our life expectancy significantly as compared to what it used to be in the past. So future planning is critical but this shouldn't overshadow the importance of enjoying the present.

While it's natural and even necessary to worry and plan for the future, and there's nothing wrong with this as there's no doubt that our future is important for us, we should not overdo this fascination of a better future at the expense of neglecting our present.

It's natural to sacrifice parts of today in pursuit of a better tomorrow, but it's important to strike a balance so that our present doesn't end up suffering as a consequence.

Historically speaking, the traditional teachings on this subject emphasized future over present, which made sense in those tougher times when there were more bad times than good. Now, we should learn from these traditional lessons and adapt them to start giving more importance to our present.

At any given moment, you have a better understanding of your present situation than your future that's mostly uncertain. Keep a bias towards the present while still preparing for the future, and don't let future worries dominate your current life. There is a reason "present is called a present", as it's actually a gift that time gives to us, every moment we are alive.

Furthermore, The notion that today's present becomes tomorrow's past is a powerful reminder that the memories we create now will shape our reflections later. Living fully in the present ensures that when you look back, you'll have a past filled with meaningful, joyful, and purposeful moments.

The mantra emphasizes making your present a priority, enabling you to live a more fulfilling and joyful life while still planning for the future. It's also important to make the most of the present because it will soon become the past, and a well-lived present creates cherished memories for tomorrow.

Mantra 3: Use the Past for Learning, Not for Regret or Fear

Bad experiences from our past keep haunting us, and how you react to them makes a significant difference. You have several options - ignore them, learn from them, fear them, or regret them.

While ignoring the past mistakes might seem like the easiest among these options, it's definitely not the best choice, as there are always some hidden values in past mistakes that can give us valuable learnings. Similarly fear and regret are not good options either, since regret doesn't change or solve anything, and fear is often baseless.

Learning from past mistakes is the most constructive approach among the above choices. By viewing past mistakes as lessons, you can avoid repeating them. Regretting past mistakes doesn't help, as we cannot change what has already happened. Instead, we should focus on learning and applying those lessons to make better choices in the future.

Furthermore, embracing the "sharing is caring" philosophy, don't keep the lessons you've learned from your past to yourself. Share them with your close circle, as they can benefit from your experiences and avoid having to learn everything the hard way through their own firsthand experiences.

The mantra is to focus on using your past experiences as valuable lessons rather than sources of regret or fear. By doing so, you can grow and improve without being held back by negative emotions associated with past events. Let your past be a guide for better decisions and actions, not a source of anxiety or sorrow.

Mantra 4: Don't Expect Future Returns for Present and Past Good Deeds

It's human nature to have expectations of others, and hoping for future returns for present and past good deeds is no exception. The problem arises when you don't receive the expected return, leading to feelings of wasted effort on someone who seemed unworthy of your help.

In these moments, it's easy to forget that while it was someone else's need, helping them was your choice and that you most likely felt a sense of satisfaction from your actions at the time. The act of doing good was a reward in itself, regardless of future outcomes.

Think of your good deeds as choices you made because you wanted to help, not as investments expecting future returns.

The satisfaction and joy you felt while doing these good deeds are returns in themselves.

Moreover everything in life, especially relationships and acts of kindness, should not be treated as investments with expected returns. Instead, they offer immediate rewards through the joy and fulfillment you experience in the moment.

The mantra is to avoid expecting rewards in the future for the good deeds you have done in past and present, and good actions should be performed for their positive impacts, not for anticipated returns.

Mantra 5: Learn From Other People's Past and Present

It's wise to learn from the past, and it doesn't have to be your own. Learning from other people's past and present experiences is a smart approach, and not everything needs to be learned the hard way through personal experience.

By learning from others, you expand your understanding beyond your own experiences. You can be inspired by those who overcame a difficult past to achieve a good present and learn from their journey.

Likewise, you should share your own past experiences to help others learn and grow.

The mantra is to gain wisdom by learning from other people's past and present experiences. Observing their successes and mistakes can provide valuable insights, helping you make better decisions and avoid repeating the mistakes they made. You can use the knowledge gained from their journeys to guide your own path.

Mantra 6: Embrace the Spontaneity and Uncertainty of the Future

We often wonder what the future holds, but the cold hard fact is that there is no reliable way to predict its exact details.

In many areas like health and finances, having some certainty about a good future can help alleviate worries, and the best way to ensure this is to plan effectively in the present.

If you're concerned about some potential future events, it's wise to be prepared to handle them if and when they occur. However, one intrinsic aspect of the future is its spontaneity and the surprises it brings to us, as there are things we can anticipate but can never be completely sure of.

While this uncertainty, spontaneity and unknown about the future can create anxiety, the best way to deal with that is to accept the future as it unfolds, embracing its unpredictability and the opportunities it brings.

The mantra is to accept that the future is unpredictable and full of surprises, and by welcoming the unpredictable nature of the future, you can better adapt and thrive in ever-changing circumstances.

Mantra 7: Find Closure for the Bad Experiences in Your Past

Throughout the journey of our life, we encounter both good as well as bad experiences. While we enjoy the good ones, we often don't remember them for long. On the contrary, this demon makes sure that bad experiences from our past stay fresh in our memory forever, and the more we try to forget them, the more it pushes back to keep them alive.

The best way to handle these bad memories is to find closure for them. Closure doesn't mean forgetting them, which is often impossible with this demon keeping them fresh in your mind. Instead, it involves acknowledging and accepting them as part of your past, and you're neither running away from them nor afraid of them happening again. You should recognize that these experiences happened, but don't let them control your present or future.

Just remember the mantra that the recurrence of past bad

events is highly unlikely. Similar incidents may occur, but they are separate events triggered by different circumstances. By understanding this, you can let go of the fear and regret associated with past experiences and focus on living fully in the present.

The mantra is to close the chapter on the bad experiences in your past. By finding closure, you can move forward without being weighed down by past negativity. Acknowledge those experiences, learn from them, and then let them go, freeing yourself from their clutches.

Mantra 8: Don't Let Fear of a Bad Future Control You - Fight for a Better One

We humans are inherently insecure by nature, especially when it comes to the future. We often worry about potential bad future scenarios, even if they are unlikely. Our instinct is to be prepared for any possible adversity before it occurs. We simply want to be safe and secure all the time with zero exposure, even at the cost of sacrificing our present.

Sometimes you may see a potential bad future, and other times you might feel almost certain of it. Even if you're convinced of a grim outcome, don't start living in that fear before it actually happens. Remember, the future's not set in stone and can always change.

Living in fear of a potential problem only prolongs your suffering. Instead, focus on living in the present and doing your best to prevent that negative future. By remaining hopeful and taking proactive steps, you might find a way to avert the anticipated problems. Even if you can't change the outcome, you'll have the satisfaction of knowing you fought like a warrior.

Your determined efforts may find you a way to prevent or at least weaken potential future problems, making them easier to handle if they do arise. And always remember, there's a chance that the feared future may never happen at all.

The mantra is to understand that even if you are almost certain of a dark future, do not start living in that state yet. Fight for a better outcome, hold onto hope and take proactive steps to change your circumstances. Live in the present and strive to create a brighter future despite any grim predictions.

Mantra 9: Don't Cling to the Past, Present, or Future - Keep Moving Forward

Remember that the past, present and future are three different states of time at any given moment in your life, each with its well defined role. We should not hang on to any one of them for too long with a blind eye toward the other two.

As time progresses, the present becomes the past, the future becomes the present, and new futures emerge. This cycle continues throughout our lives.

When you're fixated on the past, you miss the joy of the present and the possibilities of the future. You may be sacrificing your present and putting your future at risk.

When you're too focused on the present, you might miss valuable lessons from the past and neglect planning for the future. You may be putting your future at risk by not paying required attention to it.

When you're consumed by the future, you miss the enjoyment of the present and the lessons of the past. You may be sacrificing today's happiness for something that may or may not happen.

The mantra is to stay connected to all three, with learning from the past, living in the present, and dreaming for the future. This balanced approach will allow you to move forward with wisdom, joy, and hope.

Mantra 10: Embrace the Significance of the Future in Our

Lives

The past, present, and future each play crucial roles in our lives, each significant in its own way. No matter how our future is shaped by our past and present, the ultimate truth is that the future is yet to unfold, and it remains unknown. What we predict about the future is merely an educated guess, grounded in past data, statistics, and our current situation.

Even the most accurate predictions can fail due to unforeseen and unimaginable factors beyond human comprehension. So, what does this mean for us?

It delivers a powerful message: the future is still in flux, and you have the opportunity to shape it for the better. No matter how the future is depicted, there is always hope embedded within it. We look forward to the future, anticipating its brightest possibilities, even though they are yet to be revealed.

The undeniable and universal truth is that life is challenging. Despite the frustrations of failures and setbacks, even in our darkest moments, there is a small spark within us that clings to hope. This spark fuels our perseverance, driving us to keep moving forward.

In this way, the future plays a vital role in giving us purpose and motivation. Understanding the importance of the future in our lives and holding onto the belief that it will be great is something we must always remember.

The mantra is that the future is our canvas, full of uncertainty yet brimming with possibility. Embrace its significance, nurture hope, and remember that you have the power to shape it for the better.

CHAPTER 14

A Few More Demons

When we talk about the demons in our system, the list is indeed very long. Throughout this book, we have explored many of these internal demons that affect our lives, but there are many more that remain uncovered.

Given the constraints of size and my own life experiences, It's hard for me to encompass all of them in this book. However, I want to briefly touch upon a few more demons, leaving the rest to your own imagination and life experiences.

All of the demons within us, whether covered here or not, have significant impacts on our lives. While this book cannot cover every possible demon, I believe it is crucial to recognize that understanding and addressing these negative forces is a continuous process. Our life experiences and self-awareness are key to identifying and overcoming the demons that reside within us.

Fear: The Demon of Scare

Fear is one of the most common emotions experienced by humans, and it's no less than a demon that haunts us throughout our lives. It presents itself in various forms, affecting us in different ways depending on our circumstances and stages of life.

This demon acts as a significant inhibitor. When we are trying something new or unknown, fear can amplify the potential negative outcomes, making it look more challenging than it may be. This can prevent us from exploring new opportunities. A very good example is where people afraid of public speaking might avoid opportunities to present their ideas.

Fear introduces instability in our otherwise calm environment by bringing in feelings of discomfort and uncertainty. For example, a fear of losing your job can create constant stress, affecting productivity and peace of mind.

Our fear limits us from reaching our true potential by creating doubts about our capabilities and emphasizing obstacles in our path. A very good example is where an athlete might doubt their ability to perform well in a competition due to fear of failure, impacting their performance.

Everyone carries their own set of fears, and the same fear can affect people in different ways. Some common ones include the fear of water, heights, failure, losing, spiders, and public speaking, just to name a few.

This demon starts attacking us from a young age and evolves as we grow older.

As children, many of our fears arise from the unknown. Common sources of fear during childhood include things like thunder and lightning, strict parents or teachers, and difficult school subjects.

During school years, fear of failing in exams, getting bad grades, and social rejection are prevalent.

As adults, we accumulate fears such as losing possessions, fear of public speaking, and fear of failure in general.

There's one important fact that we all should be aware of

is that some fears are valid and based on real dangers, while others are mere manifestations of our mind.

And now let's explore the positive side of fear. Despite its negative aspects, this demon has some positive qualities, making it worthy to be present in us.

At times, fear provides us protection by acting as a warning system, alerting us to potential dangers and preventing harm. For example, fear of heights can prevent us from getting too close to the edge of a cliff, ensuring our safety.

Another good thing that fear has is where it helps us stay within our limits to avoid situations that could spiral out of control. A good example is where fear of overcommitting can help us manage our time better and avoid burnout and failures.

Fear provides a means of maintaining checks and balances in our behavior, ensuring we act responsibly and within limits. For example, fear of legal consequences can deter us from engaging in unlawful activities.

Since fear is primarily a bad demon, we need to manage it effectively to ensure that it serves as a guide rather than a barrier to achieving our true potential.

We should regularly analyze our fears to determine their validity, and remove the ones that are baseless or invalid, as they create unnecessary noise in our lives.

In addition, we should accept the protective qualities of this demon and use them to stay safe without letting them limit our potential.

The conclusion is that fear, though often seen as a negative force, can have beneficial aspects that help us navigate life safely within limits. By understanding the different forms of fear and analyzing their validity, we can keep the protective qualities of fear while discarding the bad ones.

Inferiority and Superiority: The Demons of Complexes

Complex, in the forms of inferiority and superiority, is yet another demon that is deadly in both of these forms, which are two sides of the same coin. They're born when our mental states are influenced by how we perceive ourselves in relation to others.

Our society's structure, which emphasizes comparison and competition, plays a significant role in the development of these complexes, and the constant race to outperform others fuels them further.

During our journey of lives we develop a lot of these complexes, depending on how we are measuring against our competition.

Let's take a closer look at both.

Your superiority complex is all about feeling or pretending to be superior to others, and it compels you to prove your worth and superiority over others continually. This often results in a game of cat and mouse, where your need to feel superior never truly ends. Sometimes you really feel superior while at other times you just pretend that.

Superiority complex makes you inaccessible and isolated, as people tend to avoid those who appear arrogant or boastful, and this can result in missed opportunities for genuine connections and collaborations.

Superiority leads to stubbornness, making it difficult for you to acknowledge and learn from your mistakes, and this becomes an inhibitor in your personal growth and development.

Your superiority complex makes you confined in a bubble of perceived superiority that can blind you to reality, making you oblivious to the flaws and areas where you may need improvement.

But your superiority complex has a positive aspect where it gives you confidence, strength and support during moments of low self-esteem and self-doubt, helping you to focus on your strengths when you feel low.

Your inferiority complex is all about feeling inferior compared to others, and it leads you to feelings of inadequacy and low self-worth. In extreme cases, you may isolate yourself mentally, feeling you are the worst and worthless.

This complex erodes your self-esteem, making you question your existence and capabilities, and discouraging you from seizing new opportunities.

The inferiority complex feeds on your insecurities, magnifying flaws and making you feel incapable and inadequate.

But your inferiority complex has a positive aspect where it brings your weaknesses to the forefront, providing you with an opportunity to address and improve them. It's actually a positive side effect, where the true intention of this demon is to drag you down, but it unintentionally offers a chance for self-improvement.

The first thing that you need to do in your fight with the superiority complex is to acknowledge that no one is perfect, including yourself. In addition to that, engage with others without the need to prove superiority, value their unique contributions and be open to learning from them.

Similarly, in order to deal with the inferiority complex, you should accept your flaws and insecurities as part of your humanity, and focus on your strengths and areas where you excel. In addition, surround yourself with supportive and encouraging people.

The conclusion is that both inferiority and superiority complexes are harmful for personal growth and well-being. However, understanding and addressing these complexes can turn their negative aspects into opportunities for improvement.

Hate: The Demon of Division and Destruction

Hate is one of the most disturbing demons within us, and unfortunately, human history is full of crimes triggered by this demon. The human mind is full of reasons that cultivate hatred for others, and it wouldn't be an overstatement to say that we humans, at times, seem to love to hate.

People harbor hatred for one another for various reasons, including race, color, ethnicity, beliefs, and religion, just to name a few. However, there are countless other reasons that can cultivate hate. Though we have a lot of hatred in our system, we've also been overusing the word "hate" in our daily lives. Whenever we dislike something, we often say we hate it. However, a simple dislike is not the same as hate. Hate is born from an extreme dislike for something or someone, requiring a solid reason for that dislike to escalate to the level of hate.

This demon draws attention to various reasons to plant seeds of hatred in your mind, and as your hatred grows, it consumes your happiness.

Talking about the source of this demon, hate can be the result of some genuine reasons, or external influence and manipulation.

Hatred may have genuine roots, such as personal experiences of injustice or harm. For instance, a person who has been tortured may understandably develop hatred for the torturer.

On the other hand, hate can also be instilled through powerful and convincing rhetoric, without any personal experience to justify it. This is often seen in cases of provoked hatred against particular groups or nations.

Hatred breeds disgust, steals peace of mind, and leaves you

in an unstable state, making you vulnerable to other demons like anger and revenge.

Hate is very strong and has the potential to easily overpower other emotions. It can bury positive feelings deep within, leaving itself at the forefront.

Under the influence of hate, people may act in ways they wouldn't consider in their normal state of mind. This can lead to harmful and destructive behavior.

Unlike some other demons that might have a positive side, hate has no redeeming qualities—at least none that I know of. It serves no constructive purpose and only harms the haters and those around them.

Given the destructive nature of hate, it is crucial to work towards eliminating it from our system.

Understand the root causes of your hatred, and find out whether your hate is based on genuine reasons or external influences. Try to understand the perspectives of those you hate, as that can help dissolve feelings of hatred.

Additionally, forgiveness can help release the hold hate has on you.

The conclusion is that hate is a powerful and destructive demon that offers no benefits. It corrupts the mind, distorts behavior, and destroys peace. By recognizing the roots of hate and actively working to overcome it, we can remove this unwanted demon from our system and improve our overall well-being.

Impatience: The Demon of Frustration and Haste

While patience is an angel that guides us through life's many challenges, its demonic counterpart, "impatience", is the dark side that emerges when patience grows thin. Impatience is a very widely available demon, and it affects us all to varying degrees.

This demon arises from an inability or unwillingness to wait for the right moment, and it can spoil the outcome of efforts by cutting short the time needed for success. The elasticity of patience varies among individuals, meaning everyone has a different threshold for when impatience takes over. This threshold, once crossed, allows impatience to thrive, and impact us negatively.

Impatience often leads to hasty decisions and actions, and just like picking an unripe fruit, premature actions yield unsatisfactory results.

Many failures are attributed to impatience, as success often requires time and persistence, and giving up too soon can result in missing out on imminent success.

This demon can make you abandon efforts just before achieving your goal, causing you to lose in the final stages.

According to my "Theory of the Limit of Patience" (discussed later in this book), everyone's patience has a different threshold. While some people become impatient quickly and frequently, some others maintain patience longer, whether inherently or through experience.

Understanding the elasticity of your patience can help you in managing impatience more effectively.

While mostly considered a bad demon, impatience can have some benefits in certain scenarios.

Impatience encourages quick action, and impatient individuals may act faster, sometimes securing opportunities before others. However, this requires substituting the lost time with increased effort and other accelerating factors.

In competitive environments, waiting too long can mean losing out, and balancing patience with timely action ensures you don't miss opportunities to competitors.

You'll need to maintain a balance between this demon and its angelic counterpart, patience, in order to manage it effectively. In addition, you'll have to understand your impatience triggers and manage them effectively.

You should learn to recognize when patience is beneficial and when it might lead to missed opportunities, and sometimes, taking a calculated risk can be more beneficial than waiting endlessly.

You should assess the situation and decide when it's worth acting swiftly, even if it means accepting less-than-perfect outcomes.

The conclusion is that patience and impatience are two sides of the same coin, each with its role in our lives. While patience is often lauded for its angelic behavior, impatience is considered to be a demon, but it can sometimes push us to act swiftly and seize opportunities. By maintaining the balance between these two forces, and understanding and managing our own elasticity of patience, we can better handle the demon of impatience, to make sure it serves us rather than haunting us.

Arrogance: The Demon of False Pride and Willful Ignorance

Arrogance is a demon that stands shoulder to shoulder with the ego demon. It makes you feel like you're above everyone else, unmatched and unparalleled. This demon fills you with an overdose of superiority complex, making you believe you're at the top of the world and everyone around you is looking up to you.

Arrogant people have a self-belief that they are better, more knowledgeable, and more important than everyone else.

For personal growth, one needs to learn new things and adapt better ways. However, under the influence of arrogance, you'll never feel the need to learn anything new, as you'll see merits in your own ways, even if you lose opportunities as a result of that. This makes arrogance an inhibitor of growth.

Arrogant people often find themselves isolated, and it's hard for them to make true friends, as people generally do not want to engage with arrogance. The only ones who interact with arrogant people are those who need them for selfish reasons, making friendships short-lived and meaningless.

This demon makes you overly confident without any real basis, leading to mistakes and missed opportunities.

Sometimes it's better to let experts handle tasks that they are good at, but arrogance makes people believe they can do everything themselves, often resulting in subpar or inferior results.

Arrogance makes you blind to the good qualities in others and deaf to any suggestions, regardless of whether there's a better way available.

But this demon has a rare positive aspect where it provides a false confidence. In situations where you need to show a backbone to survive, arrogance may temporarily pump you with confidence without any real reasons. Though this won't always work, it might sometimes help when you desperately need confidence and cannot find many reasons to be confident.

The conclusion is that arrogance has hardly anything good in it and is not worthy of a place in your system. You should strive to get rid of this demon for a better social life and personal growth, as it kills your willingness to learn and adapt. By acknowledging others' good qualities and being open to suggestions, you pave the way for true growth and meaningful relationships.

Doubt: The Demon of Hesitation and Uncertainty

Doubt is indeed a pervasive and potent force in our minds, and though primarily it's a demon, it often acts as both a hindrance and a safeguard. This demon can be seen as a double-edged sword, as it serves both as a potential obstacle and as a necessary check in our decision-making processes. Understanding this duality is very important for navigating our life's uncertainties effectively.

Uncertainty is the root cause behind the birth of this demon. When faced with uncertain situations, doubt naturally arises. This is due to the multitude of unknown parameters that we cannot always account for, which creates fertile ground for doubt to be born and flourish in our system.

This demon is sticky by nature, as it's persistent and difficult to eradicate once it takes root in your mind.

Let's explore the dual nature of this demon.

Doubt undermines confidence, making it harder to pursue goals with assurance. It can cause decision paralysis, as it can cripple decision-making by leading to indecisiveness, making it hard to determine the right course of action. A fear of making the wrong choice can prevent any choice from being made.

It makes you second-guess your actions and readiness and an excessive doubt can prevent you from seizing potential opportunities.

There's one form of doubt called self-doubt that erodes self-belief and where your lack of confidence can prevent you from taking actions that could lead to success.

Doubt can cause over-cautiousness. Past negative experiences can amplify doubt, leading to an overly cautious approach that stifles growth and opportunities.

Looking at positive aspects of doubt, it helps us maintain the checks and balances by preventing blind confidence, encouraging you to double-check your plans and actions to avoid rash decisions based on overconfidence.

It prompts you to reassess and ensure readiness, thereby reducing the risk of failure due to unpreparedness.

By introducing a sense of skepticism, doubt helps maintain a realistic outlook, preventing the dangers of overconfidence and encouraging critical thinking and careful evaluation.

The key to harnessing the positive aspects of doubt while mitigating its negative impacts lies in balance. When a doubt arises, understand its source to see if it's based on real risks or unfounded fears.

Learn to differentiate between constructive doubt that prompts necessary caution and destructive doubt that paralyzes action.

Build confidence through preparation and practice. The more you know and the better prepared you are, the less room there is for doubt.

Accept the uncertainty as not all variables can be known or controlled, and focus on what can be managed. Sometimes, taking a leap of faith is necessary. Weigh the potential rewards against the risks and make informed decisions.

The conclusion is that doubt, when managed effectively, can be a powerful ally in making sound decisions and avoiding the traps of overconfidence. While it can hinder progress and create unnecessary hesitation, it also plays a crucial role in ensuring that we approach tasks with due diligence and caution. Recognizing and managing doubt effectively allows you to leverage its benefits without succumbing to its negative impacts.

Assumptions: The Demon of Misunderstanding and Misjudgment

You might wonder how assumptions fit into the concept of internal demons. Assumptions can be double-edged swords. On one hand, they help us navigate ambiguous and unclear situations, enabling us to move forward when information is lacking. On the other hand, wrong assumptions are like a demon that can be destructive, leading us to chaos and conflict.

On the good side, our assumptions play a good role by becoming a necessity in ambiguity by filling in the gaps when we lack complete information, and helping us make decisions to progress in uncertain situations.

And on the bad side, this demon can cause potential harm, as incorrect assumptions can act as internal demons, causing misunderstandings, conflicts, and poor decisions. When assumptions are not validated, they can mislead us.

Assumptions have a deep impact on our behavior and actions, as when our assumptions are wrong, our actions will likely be misguided.

Preconceived notions are often unvalidated assumptions we accept as truth. These mental blocks make us blind to reality and resistant to new information or perspectives.

This demon can have a negative effect on our relationships, as assumptions in relationships can be particularly damaging. Misunderstandings based on false assumptions can lead to conflicts and deteriorate relationships.

Furthermore, wrong assumptions that don't align with expectations can lead to disappointment and undesirable outcomes.

Our assumptions are heavily influenced by past experiences, as quite often, we assume that past experiences will repeat in the future. This can be helpful, but without solid reasoning, it is merely a possibility and not a certainty.

Assumptions about our role in negative events can become a breeding ground for demons like guilt and regret. If these assumptions are incorrect, they can cause unnecessary emotional suffering.

It's very important for you to validate your assumptions, as validating them to the extent possible is crucial to ensure their accuracy. Incorrect assumptions can have significant negative consequences.

While it's not always possible to validate every assumption, making an effort to check their validity can help mitigate potential harm.

The conclusion is that assumptions are both good as well as bad, and recognizing their dual nature and striving to validate them whenever possible can help us harness their benefits while minimizing their potential to cause harm, as unvalidated or incorrect assumptions can become internal demons, leading to misunderstanding, conflict, and relationship issues.

Inaction And Procrastination: The Demons of Stagnation and Missed Opportunities

Inaction and procrastination are two interconnected demons that can significantly impede your personal and professional growth. They are often rooted in fear, uncertainty, and a lack of motivation or discipline, and can lead to missed opportunities, regret, and a diminished sense of accomplishment.

The inaction demon forces us into a state of not taking any steps or making any decisions, often due to fear, doubt, or a sense of being overwhelmed. It can be paralyzing and lead to stagnation.

Our inaction is often driven by feelings like fear of failure, perfectionism, lack of clarity, overwhelm, and low self-esteem, among others.

The fear of making mistakes can hold us back from taking action, while feeling overwhelmed by the magnitude of a task often leads to inaction. Perfectionism can stop us from even starting, and unclear goals or direction can cause indecision and stagnation. Self-doubt can prevent us from taking the initiative.

These inactions may lead to missed opportunities, both personally and professionally, often leaving us with regret for what could have been.

The procrastination demon forces us to delay or postpone tasks or decisions, often by engaging us in less important or more enjoyable activities. It is a common but harmful behavior that impacts productivity and well-being, and quite often leads to regrets by not doing certain things on time.

Procrastination is often driven by factors such as lack of motivation, fear of failure, distractions, poor time management, and a dislike for certain tasks.

A lack of interest or enthusiasm can lead to putting things off, and much like inaction, fear of failure can cause delays. Modern life is full of distractions that can pull focus from important tasks, while poor time management and an inability to prioritize contribute to procrastination. A strong dislike for a task can lead to it being postponed indefinitely, with consistent procrastination negatively affecting both personal and professional relationships.

Delaying tasks often creates last-minute pressure and stress, forcing you to rush and compromising the quality of your work. Missing deadlines can also result in serious professional consequences. Both inaction and procrastination can lower your output, reduce efficiency, and diminish productivity.

To tackle these demons, consider the following strategies: Set clear goals, break tasks into manageable steps, and prioritize by focusing on the most important and urgent tasks first. Eliminate distractions to stay focused and aim for progress over perfection.

In conclusion, inaction and procrastination are powerful obstacles that can prevent you from reaching your full potential. By understanding their causes and consequences, you can transform these negative patterns into motivation for taking action and making progress.

Vengeance: The Demon of Retribution and Revenge

Vengeance is a powerful demon within us, driven by the desire for retribution or revenge in response to a perceived wrong or injustice. It burns inside, sometimes as an intense fire, other times as a smoldering flame lying dormant but still very much alive. This demon compels us to seek harm or punishment against those we believe are responsible for our pain, fueled by the need for justice, reparation, or personal satisfaction.

Vengeance is often triggered by personal injury, betrayal, humiliation, injustice, or loss. For example, physical or emotional harm can ignite a desire for revenge, and broken trust or betrayal can spark an overwhelming urge to retaliate. Perceived unfair treatment, inequality, or public embarrassment can fuel the fire, while the loss of loved ones or property may provoke a deep need for retribution.

However, not every wrong warrants or justifies vengeance. There is often value in letting go of certain grievances, and it's neither practical nor healthy to seek revenge for every offense. The cycle of generational vengeance, where the next generation continues to seek retribution for the wrongs done to their ancestors, only perpetuates conflict and deepens hatred.

While revenge may bring temporary pleasure and a false sense of closure, it often results in further harm. Even when carried out through legal channels, revenge is not the same as justice. Justice, administered by an impartial system, seeks fairness and upholds the law, whereas vengeance is personal and can lead to a cycle of violence. This is why legal systems aim to curb personal vengeance and promote justice through formal processes. Yet, when criminals evade punishment due to lack of evidence or corruption, it can leave us feeling even more wounded.

Assumptions can dangerously fuel the demon of vengeance, and these assumptions are not always accurate. Additionally, third parties may manipulate us, using vengeance for their own interests, turning us into tools for a revenge that may not even serve us. Recognizing the role of assumptions and external manipulation can prevent misguided actions.

To find peace, it is crucial to manage the impulse for vengeance. Forgiveness can play a significant role in quelling the thirst for revenge, but it is also important for those who wronged us to recognize their actions to prevent future harm.

In conclusion, vengeance is a complex and consuming emotion that can drive us to seek retribution for perceived wrongs. It is an internal demon, fueled by a fire that demands satisfaction, whether through immediate retaliation or long-term resentment. Though vengeance may seem to offer closure, it often leads to violence and ongoing conflict, perpetuating cycles of suffering. Understanding its consequences, embracing forgiveness, and promoting justice over revenge can help break this destructive cycle.

Distraction: The Demon of Focus and Productivity Theft

In today's fast-paced world, the distraction demon has become a powerful force, hindering productivity, focus, and personal growth. With the rise of technology, social media, and constant information overload, maintaining concentration on important tasks has become increasingly difficult. This demon not only impacts our efficiency but also takes a toll on our mental well-being and overall satisfaction with life.

Although distractions are not new, they have gained significant strength in modern times due to the ever-growing number of sources vying for our attention. The distraction demon embodies the endless interruptions that divert us from our goals and responsibilities, thriving in environments filled with constant stimuli that compete for our focus.

Here are some common causes of distraction in today's complex and competitive world, where numerous factors fuel this ever-present demon.

Leading the list is technology overload, with gadgets like smartphones, tablets, computers, and gaming consoles offering endless entertainment and information, resulting in constant interruptions. Following closely is social media, where platforms are designed to capture and hold our attention, consuming hours of time with notifications, likes, and comments. Multitasking is another major culprit, as trying to juggle several tasks at once often dilutes focus. Lastly, noisy or cluttered environments can easily disrupt our ability to concentrate on important tasks.

Here are some of the consequences of this demon's presence in our lives. Frequent interruptions and scattered attention reduce efficiency and productivity, while a lack of focus leads to mistakes and below-average performance. Constantly juggling distractions and unfinished tasks increases anxiety and stress, and time wasted on trivial activities leaves little room for meaningful pursuits. Distractions also hinder deep thinking and learning, slowing both personal and professional growth, ultimately leading to a sense of unfulfillment and dissatisfaction with your achievements.

Understanding the nature of the distraction demon and its impact on our lives is the first step toward overcoming it. By identifying the sources and consequences of distractions, we can take proactive measures to regain our focus and productivity. One effective strategy is to start with a digital detox—regularly disconnect from devices to reset your attention and reduce reliance on constant stimulation.

Additionally, try to focus on one task at a time as much as possible.

In conclusion, the distraction demon poses a significant challenge in our fast-paced, technology-driven world. However, by implementing strategies to manage and minimize distractions, we can improve our focus, productivity, and overall quality of life, reclaiming both our time and attention.

Our Fight Against These Demons Within Us is a Never Ending War

All of the demons within us, whether covered here or not, have significant impacts on our lives. While this book cannot cover every possible demon, I believe it is crucial to recognize that understanding and addressing these negative forces is a continuous process. Our life experiences and self-awareness are key to identifying and overcoming the demons that reside within us.

By staying vigilant and reflective, we can recognize these demons as they arise and take proactive steps to address them. Through personal growth, self-compassion, and a willingness to seek help when needed, we can gradually diminish the power these demons hold over us and lead more fulfilling, balanced lives.

CHAPTER 15

Stress: The Master of All Demons

B efore diving deep into the world of this deadly demon called stress, I want to make a simple disclaimer. Stress is one of the most widely recognized and documented problems faced by humans. It is formally acknowledged in the medical field, and there are numerous medications and techniques to address it. I deeply respect these existing efforts. My discussion here is from a different perspective— seeing stress as a demon resulting from various other negative factors within us.

Based on how I look at it, stress is not an isolated demon but the master of all the other demons that exist within us. These other demons are interconnected and support each other, ultimately feeding the master demon, stress.

To control this master demon, it is essential to cut down the supplies it gets from the other demons.

While exploring various demons in this book, we observed that despite their inherently negative core, each demon has a positive aspect that makes it worthy of having a place within us, though in a controlled manner. This dual nature is key to understanding how to coexist with these demons without allowing them to feed their master demon, stress.

Our goal is to maintain a balanced and controlled presence of these demons to leverage their positive sides without being overwhelmed by their negative impacts, thus preventing them from feeding stress.

Throughout this book, we have explored how these demons affect us and contribute to stress. We have also discussed various mantras to deal with them. Now, let's delve deeper into understanding the master demon stress and the mantras to deal with it.

Stress is a complex and powerful force, and it can arise from numerous situations. While some of these situations are within our control, others are not. Acknowledging and accepting this reality of our limitations is crucial in our approach to dealing with this master of all demons.

Good Stress and Bad Stress

Similar to the other demons we've discussed, even this master demon has something good in it if we use it the right way.

Throughout your life, you've likely heard only negative things about stress. Undoubtedly, stress can be a daunting and harmful force, but interestingly enough, there are ways to harness stress positively.

Even the most formidable demon, stress, can be beneficial if leveraged properly. This is where the concept of "good stress" comes into play. I classify stress into two categories: good stress and bad stress. You might wonder how something as demonized as stress can have any positive aspects, but please allow me to clarify on that.

Good stress, also known as eustress, acts as a motivator. It's the kind of stress that pushes you to accomplish tasks and meet challenges head-on. For instance, when faced with a daunting project, you may feel stressed about the complexity and the effort required. This stress, however, can be a driving force, encouraging you to work harder and think creatively to overcome the obstacles.

When you're under good stress, you start exploring new solutions and alternative ways to address the issues causing the stress. Without this pressure, you might not engage in such out-of-the-box thinking.

You can use stress as a tool, by deliberately introducing it into others' systems to motivate them to do the right thing. When managed effectively, this type of stress can foster growth and achievement. For example, a coach pushes an athlete to perform better, and stress in this context serves as a catalyst for improvement and success.

On the other hand, bad stress, or distress, is the type of stress that overwhelms you. It occurs when you face situations where you don't understand what needs to be done or have no clear path forward. This kind of stress is paralyzing, trapping you in a state of anxiety and helplessness. It scares you and keeps you locked in an uncomfortable and unwanted state, with no immediate solution in sight.

So, while stress is primarily a bad demon, good stress can be a powerful motivator, driving you to achieve and grow. By understanding and managing stress effectively, you can use it to your advantage, transforming challenges into opportunities for success.

Stress and Other Demons

We've discussed many of the demons in detail so far, and while the good sides of these demons makes them worthy of living within us, it's their bad side that causes a lot of stress in our lives.

From what we've seen, they all trouble us in many ways, but regardless of how they trouble us, they ultimately end up creating a lot of stress in our system. Let's go over the direct connection between these demons and their master stress, basically the main reasons how they contribute to stress.

Stress From the Guilt Demon

The main reason why guilt causes stress is due to the conflict between your actions and personal value system or standards, and this conflict triggers a range of emotions that contribute to stress.

Guilt demon comes into existence when people believe they have violated their own moral or ethical standards, and this feeling creates internal conflict and emotional distress.

You feel guilty when you have a sense of responsibility for a perceived wrongdoing, regardless of whether it's real or imagined. This responsibility weighs heavily on the mind, contributing to stress.

People tend to obsess over their mistakes or perceived wrongdoings, continuously replaying the events in their minds, keeping the stress active.

Your guilt often leads to self-criticism and negative thoughts about yourself, leading to lower self-esteem and increased feelings of worthlessness and stress, and this stress can become a breeding ground for many other demons.

The inability to forgive yourself and move past the guilt keeps you trapped in a cycle of stress and negative emotions.

Stress From the Worry Demon

The main reason why worry causes stress is due to the anticipation of negative outcomes and a fear of inability to control future events. This anticipation triggers a series of emotions that contribute to stress.

Our worry often stems from uncertainty about the future.

The unknown and fear of negative outcomes create a sense of anxiety and stress.

Similar to guilt, our worry quite often involves repetitive thinking about potential problems and worst-case scenarios, keeping the stress active in our system.

Our worries often lead to imagining the worst possible outcomes, amplifying the sense of anxiety and stress.

Worry is fueled by a feeling of helplessness or lack of control over issues in our lives, which heightens stress levels.

Stress From the Expectations Demon

The main reason why expectations cause stress is due to the pressure they create to meet certain standards, whether they are self-imposed or imposed by others. When people set high or unrealistic expectations for themselves or feel the weight of others' expectations, it can lead to feelings that contribute to stress.

People who impose high expectations on themselves often feel they must perform flawlessly, and this relentless pursuit of perfection becomes a significant source of stress for them. In addition, the fear of not meeting expectations can lead to anxiety and stress.

When people fail to meet expectations, they may engage in harsh self-criticism, leading to feelings of inadequacy and increased stress.

Expectations from parents, teachers, employers, or peers can create external pressure to succeed. Fulfilling these expectations can be stressful, especially if they are unreasonable or unattainable.

The anticipation of having to meet high expectations can cause anxiety, even before any actual performance or task is undertaken, and this anxiety is a significant source of stress.

Expectations can strain relationships, especially if there is a constant pressure to meet the expectations of others, and this strain can lead to conflicts and stress within relationships.

Stress From the Envy and Jealousy Demons

The main reason why envy and jealousy cause stress is due to the negative emotions and distortions they create, which can lead to feelings of inadequacy, resentment, and fear of loss. These emotions and thoughts trigger a range of physical and mental responses that contribute to stress.

Envy and jealousy often come to life when you compare yourself to others and feel inferior. This sense of inadequacy can lead to low self-esteem and self-worth, and resentment and bitterness towards others, contributing to stress.

Jealousy, in particular, involves a fear of losing something valuable, such as a relationship or status. This fear creates anxiety and stress.

Envy and jealousy can strain relationships, by leading to conflict, distrust, and distancing from others, and this can result in social isolation and additional stress.

These demons can foster an unhealthy sense of competition, leading people to constantly try to outdo others, which is exhausting and stressful.

Envy and jealousy can lead to aggressive behavior, creating further interpersonal conflicts and stress.

Stress From the Anger Demon

The main reason why anger causes stress is due to the physical and behavioral responses it triggers in your system. When a person feels angry, their body undergoes a series of changes designed to prepare them for a "fight or flight" response, which can contribute significantly to stress.

Anger can result in distortion in the thought process, making you unable to think clearly, which can enhance feelings of frustration and stress.

People often replay anger-inducing events in their minds, leading to prolonged periods of anger and stress.

When you feel wronged or unjustly treated, it can intensify your anger and contribute to ongoing stress.

Acting out in anger can lead to conflicts with others, damaging relationships and creating additional sources of stress.

Anger can cause people to withdraw from social interactions, leading to feelings of loneliness and increased stress.

Stress From the Regret Demon

The main reason why regret causes stress is due to the feelings of conflict that arises from thinking about past decisions and wishing they had been different. This internal struggle leads to a range of negative emotions and thoughts that contribute significantly to stress.

Regret often involves looking back at past decisions with the benefit of hindsight, leading to feelings of guilt and self-blame. This can create a constant stress due to internal conflict between what was done and what could have been done differently.

When you focus on missed opportunities or paths not taken, it can create a sense of loss and dissatisfaction, fueling stress further.

Under the influence of regret, people harshly criticize themselves for their perceived mistakes, and get feelings of sadness and frustration over unmet expectations and lost potential, which contribute to stress.

People have a habit of looking at the discrepancy between their current situation and their ideal or desired outcome, and that creates a state of mental discomfort with internal conflicts that contributes to stress.

Stress From the Ego Demon

The main reason why ego causes stress is due to the constant pressure it creates to protect and maintain one's self-image and identity. This often leads to a range of emotional and behavioral responses that contribute significantly to stress.

Ego drives people to avoid failure at all costs to protect their self-image, and this fear creates significant stress, especially when they're facing challenging situations.

This demon often leads to unrealistic expectations and perfectionism, and the constant striving for flawlessness and fear of making mistakes can be a major source of stress.

Under the influence of ego, people become resistant to change and new ideas, creating stress in dynamic or uncertain environments.

Ego makes it difficult for people to accept constructive criticism, leading to defensiveness and stress when receiving feedback. In addition, this demon can lead to conflicts in relationships due to a need to always be right or dominant. This can strain personal and professional relationships, creating ongoing stress.

An inflated ego can lead to social isolation, as people with big egos may push others away or struggle to form genuine connections, resulting in loneliness and stress.

Stress From the Relationships Demon

The main reason why relationships cause stress is due to the complexity and emotional investment involved in maintaining and managing them. Our relationships require constant attention, communication, understanding, and compromise, which can be quite stressful at times.

Relationships are a very complex phenomena, and all of them differ from one another in all kinds of ways, and at any given moment in our lives we'd be juggling through many different relationships at the same time.

There is no way we can maintain the same level of relation with everyone around us, as there'll always be conflicts and catch twenty two's. It'll never be too easy for you, and you'll have to choose one over the other in more situations than you may want.

When you try to maintain a perfect and healthy relationship with everyone around you, while it may be the right thing to do, it'll become the biggest source of stress for you as it's an almost impossible ordeal.

So it's not the relationships but the balance and management of all the relationships that we have to maintain in our lives, that's the root cause of stress.

When you're close to someone, it often involves opening up and sharing personal feelings and experiences. This vulnerability can lead to fear of rejection, judgment, or betrayal, causing significant stress.

When you're relying heavily on someone for emotional support, it can lead to stress if that support is inconsistent, unreliable or withdrawn.

Misunderstandings and poor communication, which are not that uncommon in relationships, can lead to conflicts and frustration, causing stress. Similarly, ongoing disputes and unresolved issues can create a persistent source of tension and stress.

Unrealistic or unmet expectations of yourself or the others in the relationship can lead to disappointment and stress.

The demands of maintaining a relationship, such as spending time together, providing support, and fulfilling commitments, can be overwhelming and stressful.

Stress From the Comparison Demon

The main reason why comparison causes stress is due to the negative impact it has on self-esteem and self-worth. When you compare yourself to others, you often focus on your deficiencies or shortcomings, which can lead to feelings of inadequacy, jealousy, and dissatisfaction, and this focus on perceived shortcomings can result in further lowering your self-worth.

Feeling inadequate compared to others can lead to social withdrawal, isolation, and a decrease in social support, which can exacerbate stress.

When you compare yourself with others who appear to have more success, happiness, or desirable qualities, it can lead to jealousy and envy, which are emotionally draining and stressful.

Continuous comparison can lead to frustration and resentment towards yourself and others, creating additional emotional turmoil.

As a result of a comparison, you may have a desire to match or surpass others, which can result in perfectionism, which is a significant source of stress due to its unattainable nature.

Stress From the Over-Encouragement Demon

The main reason why over-encouragement causes stress is due to the unrealistic expectations and pressure it can create. While encouragement is generally positive, excessive encouragement can lead to a range of emotional and behavioral responses that contribute to stress.

Over-encouragement can set excessively high standards

and expectations, making people feel that they must always perform at an exceptional level. This can lead to stress as they struggle to meet these expectations.

The pressure to meet high expectations can create a fear of failure, and people may worry that they will disappoint those who have encouraged them, leading to anxiety and stress.

Over-encouragement can foster perfectionism, where people feel they must be flawless in their efforts, which is a significant source of stress.

Excessive encouragement can lead to self-doubt if people feel they are unable to meet the expectations set for them. They may question their abilities and worth, leading to stress.

And at times, people may develop impostor syndrome, feeling that they do not truly deserve the praise and encouragement they receive, which can create ongoing stress for them.

Stress From the Needs, Wants and Greed Demon

The main reason this deadly trio causes stress is rooted in our relentless pursuit of needs, wants, and unchecked greed.

Modern life's demands make it increasingly difficult to differentiate between what we genuinely need, what we desire, and where greed begins to take control. This ongoing struggle becomes a significant source of stress, as we constantly strive to fulfill these cravings, often at the cost of our peace of mind.

The Needs, Wants, and Greed Demon is a metaphorical representation of this struggle. It feeds on our dissatisfaction, pushing us to seek more, achieve more, and accumulate more, regardless of the toll it takes on our mental and emotional well-being.

This demon thrives on our endless quest for fulfillment, leading to a cycle of stress that can be difficult to escape.

Stress From the Past, Present and Future Demon

The main reason why the past, present, and future cause stress is due to the different types of concerns and pressures each time frame brings to us, which can lead to a continuous cycle of worry and anxiety. At any given moment in life, we'd be dealing with the stress from our past, present and future at the same time. Let's see how each of these time frames contributes to stress.

Stress From the Past

Overthinking about past mistakes, failures, or missed opportunities can lead to feelings of regret and guilt, and this emotional burden can cause significant stress as people ruminate over what they could have done differently.

Unresolved conflicts or traumas from the past can continue to affect people's mental and emotional state, leading to stress.

Recalling negative experiences can trigger stress responses, as the mind and body react similarly to the initial event.

Stress From the Present

The demands of our daily lives, such as work, family obligations, and personal responsibilities, can create a high level of stress as we try to manage everything effectively.

Ongoing issues or crises that require immediate attention can cause acute stress.

The pressure to meet current expectations and perform well in various aspects of life can lead to stress, especially when we feel we are not meeting these expectations.

Stress From the Future

A fear of the unknown and uncertainty about what the

future holds can cause anxiety and stress, and worrying about potential problems or changes can be overwhelming.

Anticipating future challenges, such as career changes, financial concerns, or health issues, can lead to stress.

Setting and striving to achieve future goals can create stress, especially if people feel unsure about their ability to succeed or fear failure.

Mantras for Dealing With the Master Demon Stress

To effectively confront the stress demon, it's crucial to first recognize the other demons that reside within you and understand how they contribute to your overall stress. Strive to maintain a balanced relationship with these demons, harnessing their positive aspects while preventing them from overwhelming you. Additionally, find ways to minimize the negative impact these demons have, as they ultimately feed to their master.

Up to this point, we've been exploring the various demons within us and identifying mantras to deal with them, all with the goal of weakening their master—stress.

Now, let's delve into some powerful mantras that can help us directly confront and overcome this master demon.

Mantra 1: Stress May Originate Externally, But You Allow It Into Your System

It's common for people to claim that certain individuals or situations cause them a lot of stress. While it's true that much stress originates from external sources, there's often a reason why you accept this stress rather than rejecting it. Additionally, The real impact of stress depends on how you absorb and react to it, which is why different people experience varying levels of stress even when faced with similar challenges.

People and situations create environments where the stress demon can take root and grow within you. When someone or something causes you stress, you always have the option to reject its entry into your system. However, despite having this option, you may find it difficult to exercise it due to various reasons. Often, you take on stress because you want to prevent things from falling apart or fix what is already broken. Essentially, you choose to engage with the stressful situation, even if it means accepting the accompanying stress.

So, while it may seem like someone or something is giving you stress, it's actually you who allows that stress to take hold —whether by choice or due to external pressures. The source of stress may be external, but its presence in your system is ultimately up to you.

Stress is fundamentally a state of mind. While the situations that cause stress may be real, the stress itself depends entirely on how you respond to those situations. If you internalize the impact of a situation, you'll likely feel a high level of stress. Conversely, if you focus on absorbing the shock and concentrate on the path forward, your stress levels will be significantly lower.

By recognizing that the impact of stress is influenced by your reaction, you can take proactive steps to manage and reduce stress in your life. It's possible to control the stress that arises from various situations. Although it may not be easy, it's certainly achievable.

The first step in managing stress is to recognize when you're accepting it and understand why you're doing so. You need to shift your mindset to view stressful situations more positively and realistically, preventing them from having a significant impact on you.

The essence of this mantra is to recognize that while stress may come from external sources, ultimately it's your choice to accept or reject it from entering your system. Furthermore, its power over you is something you control, and that totally depends on how you react to it.

The essence of this mantra is to understand that, although stress may originate from external sources, it is ultimately your choice to accept or reject it from entering your system. Moreover, the power stress holds over you is entirely within your control, determined by how you choose to react to it.

Mantra 2: Don't Carry Stress from One World to Another, Unless It's Intentional

We experience different kinds of stress in various aspects of our lives. Each "world" we inhabit—be it personal, professional, or social—comes with its unique share of stress. However, sometimes stress can spill over from one world to another, affecting our ability to handle the challenges of the moment.

There are two outliers in this case.

The first is that every stress we encounter in any of these worlds inevitably has a counterpart in our inner world. This happens because we are always simultaneously present in our inner world, regardless of where we are physically. Our inner world is constantly processing and reflecting the stress from all the other worlds we navigate.

The second outlier is that our fabricated world—the world we personally create in our minds—is typically free of any stress. This is because it's a space we consciously manifest, often as a refuge from reality, and we tend to keep negativity out of this imagined realm. In this world, we have complete control, allowing us to shape it into a stress-free environment where we can retreat and recharge.

The stress unique to a particular world is relevant only in that context, so it's important to leave it there when transitioning to another world—unless there's a specific reason to carry it with you.

For example, when transitioning from work to home, it's beneficial to leave work-related stress behind and focus on your personal life. Likewise, personal issues should ideally be set aside when you enter your professional world. The challenge arises when we drag stress from one world into another, which can lead to neglecting the stressors that are more relevant in the current context. Our capacity to handle stress is limited, so when part of that capacity is occupied by stress from another world, it diminishes our ability to manage the stress of the present world.

However, the biggest challenge in managing this context-switching lies in our inner world, which is always aware of what's happening across all our worlds. With practice, though, you can learn to shift your focus from one set of stressors to another as you move between different worlds you inhabit. Moreover, this isn't about forgetting stress but rather about redirecting your attention to the stress that is most relevant to your current situation.

There are exceptions, though. Sometimes, carrying stress from one world to another can be helpful, especially if you need a change of context to work on a problem. Additionally, you might need to discuss stress from one world with someone in another world, seeking advice or support.

A common exception is in the social world, where we often share stress from other worlds with friends to gain relief or gather insights.

The mantra is that you shouldn't carry stress from one world to another unless it serves a specific purpose. Instead, focus on the stress relevant to the world you're in. Your carrying stress across the worlds may result in you neglecting the stressors relevant in the current world you are in.

The mantra is not to carry stress from one world to another unless it serves a specific purpose. Instead, focus on the stress relevant to the world you're in. Carrying stress across worlds can lead to neglecting the stressors that are most important in the current world you are navigating.

Mantra 3: Don't Run Away From Stress, Confront It

It's quite common to hear advice from well-meaning individuals suggesting that you should distract yourself with other activities to avoid situations that cause stress. While this approach might offer temporary relief, it comes with significant drawbacks and is not a long-term solution for dealing with the stress demon. Instead of fleeing from stress, you should confront it head-on.

When you use distractions to escape stress, you're merely postponing the inevitable and often turning a blind eye to the underlying issue. Although this strategy might work for a while, it's not a permanent fix. Sooner or later, the stressful situations will reemerge, often with greater intensity.

If you continue to run from stress, you'll find that life keeps presenting you with similar challenges more frequently. Moreover, this avoidance tactic won't be feasible for every stressful situation. In fact, this approach only adds to your list of unresolved stressors, compounding the problem over time.

Instead, you need to change your strategy and tackle stress directly. You can't keep hiding from it forever; facing stress with determination will strengthen you and better equip you to handle stress in general.

To do this, you must first recognize and acknowledge that you are under stress, accepting it as a natural part of life. Then, resolve to confront this stress to the best of your ability. Identifying the specific cause of your stress is crucial, as it will enable you to address it more effectively.

The essence of this mantra is that running away from stress is neither sustainable nor effective. By facing stress directly, acknowledging its presence, and addressing its root causes, you can manage it more successfully. Embrace stress as a part of life and view it as an opportunity for growth and self-improvement.

Mantra 4: Release What You Can't Control, and Trust Time to Heal

We humans often have a tendency to stress over anything that crosses our minds, even those things far beyond our control. It's crucial to recognize that in any situation, there's only so much we can do, and the rest are factors outside our influence.

Accepting that we have limited control over many aspects of life allows us to focus on what we can change and let go of what we cannot. Understanding this is key to dealing with this demon effectively.

We've all heard the saying, "Time is the greatest healer," and while it may seem cliché, it holds true even when dealing with stress. Sometimes, the best remedy is to allow time to address the issues that are causing you stress. After you've done everything within your power, let time take over as your ally, trusting it to handle what you cannot.

This approach may feel like a leap of faith, and in many ways, it is. But remember, this leap is often the most logical step when you've exhausted all other options.

Stressing over things completely beyond your control is a waste of energy—energy that could be used for more constructive pursuits. However, remain aware of the stress you've handed over to time. If it feels like it's lingering indefinitely, you may need to reassess your approach and apply a more direct solution. But don't let it fall into dormancy.

The essence of this mantra is to stress over only on what you can influence, and for the rest, trust in time. By doing so, you conserve your energy for more productive activities. Trust in the healing power of time, be patient, and stay vigilant in case some issues require more than just waiting. Also, ensure that the stress you've entrusted to time doesn't quietly slip into a state of dormancy.

Mantra 5: Be Mindful of Creating Stress in Others

It's safe to say that a significant portion of the stress we experience comes from external sources, such as other people and situations. We humans are interconnected in various ways. While we often focus on managing our own stress, we may inadvertently or intentionally introduce stress into other people's lives.

Sometimes, we deliberately create stress in others to motivate or correct them. In certain situations, stress can be a catalyst for action or change, and when done with good intentions, it may be necessary. However, this approach should be used with caution, as it can have unintended negative consequences. It's important to weigh the long-term effects of creating stress in others and ensure that the benefits outweigh any potential harm.

Instead of relying on stress as a motivator, it's often better to find positive ways to encourage and support others. Positive reinforcement can be just as effective, if not more so, in inspiring change and growth.

More often than not, we are unaware of how our actions or words can cause stress in others. This unintentional stress is something we need to be particularly mindful of, as it can introduce unnecessary burdens into other people's lives. We may unknowingly introduce various "demons" into others' systems through our actions.

To avoid creating stress in others, it's essential to evaluate your actions by considering their perspectives and feelings. Putting yourself in their shoes can help you understand the impact of your behavior on them.

Taking this extra step can prevent you from unintentionally adding stress to others' lives. By being mindful of how our actions affect others, we can reduce the stress we might introduce into their systems.

The essence of this mantra is to be aware of how your actions impact others. Evaluate your interactions to ensure that you are not unknowingly contributing to their stress, and strive to foster positive, supportive relationships instead.

Mantra 6: Share Your Experiences to Help Others Manage Their Stress

This mantra embodies the core message of this book. My motivation for writing about stress management stems from the realization that the methods and theories I've developed to deal with stress have been more effective than those used by many people around me. By documenting my experiences and theories, I hope to offer support to others who may be facing similar struggles.

We have all encountered the stress demon in various forms throughout our lives. While we may have succumbed at times, we have also discovered our own unique ways to tame this demon. The essence of this mantra is the understanding that your personal techniques for managing stress, which you might consider ordinary, could be incredibly valuable to someone else—potentially even life-changing.

Rather than keeping these insights to yourself, why not share them with others? By doing so, you can help create a supportive community where people assist each other in dealing with their stress demons. Since stress is a universal experience, sharing how you manage it can foster connections with others who are going through similar challenges.

There are two primary ways to share your experiences to

help others: unsolicited sharing and targeted assistance.

Unsolicited Sharing: Share your methods and ideas for dealing with stress, even when no one specifically asks for them. In today's digital age, there are countless platforms for doing this—blogs, social media posts, or even casual conversations. Someone might come across your advice and find it incredibly helpful. Often, unsolicited advice can provide unexpected solutions to people who didn't even realize they needed it.

Targeted Assistance: Actively look for opportunities to offer your experiences to those who are seeking help. Whether through community events, or interactions with friends, family, or colleagues, you can share your knowledge with those who ask for it.

Helping others with their stress not only benefits them but also offers advantages for you. By assisting others, you create a network of mutual support, gain a sense of fulfillment and purpose, and may even reduce your own stress levels. Engaging with others about their stress can also provide you with new insights into managing your own challenges.

The mantra here is that sharing your personal experiences in dealing with stress can significantly benefit both others and yourself. Whether through unsolicited sharing or targeted assistance, your unique methods can offer valuable support to those in need.

Mantra 7: Don't Let Stress Paralyze You—Keep Moving Forward

The impact of the stress demon varies from person to person, affecting individuals with different intensities and durations. Some people are able to absorb stress and move on quickly, experiencing only a short-lived impact, while others may become overwhelmed, frozen, and unable to handle anything else going on in their lives.

This mantra emphasizes the importance of acknowledging stress but continuing to move forward despite it. It's crucial to recognize the presence of this demon without letting it halt your progress. You must keep moving and manage other responsibilities even when stress is weighing on you.

People respond to stress in different ways. While some may completely succumb to it, others manage to find positive aspects even in stressful situations, which helps them keep moving forward. The key is to remember that dealing with stress is just one of many priorities in your life at any given time, and the other priorities won't pause just because you're stressed.

If you neglect these other issues while you're stuck in a state of stress, they can grow stronger and create more problems, leading to even greater stress. One effective strategy is to delegate tasks to others to lighten your load, allowing you to focus on addressing the most pressing problems. Additionally, don't hesitate to seek support from friends, family, or professionals, as sharing your burdens can provide relief and new perspectives.

The essence of this mantra is to understand that dealing with stress is just one of many priorities in your life, and you shouldn't allow it to freeze you in place. By acknowledging stress and continuing to address your other responsibilities, you can prevent additional problems from arising, which in turn strengthens your ability to manage stress. Keep moving forward, and over time, you'll find that stress becomes more manageable and less overwhelming.

Mantra 8: Acknowledge and Address Dormant Stress in Your System

Stress is a powerful and dangerous demon, and it becomes an even greater threat when it lies dormant. The problem is that, despite often sensing its presence, we tend to deny or ignore it, and sometimes we're entirely unaware that it's lurking within us.

Dormant stress is the kind of stress that has embedded itself so deeply into your system that you barely notice it anymore. You may unknowingly accept its permanent presence, allowing it to remain hidden and unacknowledged. This stress keeps subtly influencing you over time and only surfaces when triggered by certain events or situations.

When multiple demons are contributing to your stress, some unresolved stress can quietly slip into a dormant state. It's crucial to understand that dormant stress, although less intense and harder to recognize, can still have a significant impact on your well-being. It may operate quietly, but it remains a persistent threat to your happiness.

Ultimately, dormant stress is like any other stress—the sole purpose of its existence is to haunt you and strip away your happiness. Recognizing and acknowledging dormant stress is vital because denying or ignoring it allows it to grow stronger and more harmful over time, tightening its grip on you.

To prevent stress from becoming dormant, regularly check in with yourself to assess your stress levels. Don't allow stress to become a normal, accepted part of your life. Address it as it arises. Even if you can't resolve a particular stressor immediately, keep it in an active state by continually seeking ways to resolve it. This will help prevent it from slipping into dormancy.

Additionally, make an effort to probe deeply into yourself to identify any dormant stress that may not be evident in your conscious mind.

The essence of this mantra is that dormant stress is a hidden burden with the potential to significantly harm your well-being. By recognizing and acknowledging its presence, you can take proactive steps to address it effectively. Remember, ignoring or denying dormant stress only allows it to grow stronger over time.

Mantra 9: Everything is Solvable—You Just Need to Tweak Your Definition of "Solvable"

In our everyday lives, especially in this complex and competitive world where all these demons are constantly at play, we often find ourselves facing situations that can lead to significant stress. While we manage to solve many of these challenges to some level of satisfaction, there are always a few that remain unresolved, stuck in a state far from what we would consider satisfactory. These unresolved issues often cause us stress, primarily because they seem open-ended with no clear path forward.

The reality is that everything is solvable—you just need to adjust your definition of "solvable."

The problem often arises when we try to resolve everything from our own perspective, marking something as solved only when it meets the satisfaction level we've set. While there's nothing inherently wrong with this approach, as it reflects our unique values and goals, it can lead to frustration when things don't turn out the way we expect.

The truth is, not everything will end up the way we want. Sometimes, solutions seem elusive because we're too focused on our own desired outcomes. However, if we broaden our perspective and consider the bigger picture, we might find that a solution exists—it just doesn't align perfectly with our original expectations. This solution may not be ideal for us, but it could be favorable for someone or something else. By accepting this broader, more inclusive definition of a solution, we can resolve the issue and remove it from our list of stressors.

In its unresolved state, the problem was only causing you stress because it didn't meet your criteria for resolution. But by adjusting your definition, you can find closure, even if the outcome isn't exactly what you had hoped for.

This approach doesn't mean you should apply it to every unresolved issue, as each challenge is unique and requires its own time and circumstances to resolve. However, if an issue has remained unresolved for a long time with no good end in sight, it might be better to change your approach rather than letting it linger indefinitely, where it might silently slip into dormancy.

The mantra is to recognize that everything is solvable if you're willing to broaden your perspective and adjust your definition of what "solvable" means. Sometimes, accepting a solution that works for others—even if it's not ideal for you— can be the key to finding peace and moving forward.

Mantra 10: The Idea of a Stress-Free Life is Just a Utopia

The cold, hard truth is that the concept of a completely stress-free life is nothing more than a utopian fantasy. It simply cannot exist in reality. Even if, hypothetically, you managed to control every aspect of your life and solve all your problems, these achievements would only be a few among many prerequisites for attaining a truly stress-free existence.

Let's imagine for a moment that you've mastered control over your life and resolved all your issues. While these are certainly important steps toward reducing stress, they are far from sufficient. The fact is, stress is an inherent part of life, shaped by both internal and external factors that are often beyond your control. The stress demon, along with its many servant demons, will always find ways to infiltrate your system. The key is not to eliminate stress entirely but to learn how to coexist with it while maintaining control.

Remember, your life doesn't exist in isolation. It's deeply interconnected with people, situations, and environments— all of which can contribute to your stress. Even if you solve all your personal problems, external factors like the actions of others, unforeseen situations, and unpredictable events can still introduce stress into your life.

Stress can arise from countless sources, including relationships, work, health, and virtually anything else that plays a role in your life. There's no shortage of situations that can invite the stress demon into your system, and it's impossible to control all these variables.

The first step is to accept that stress is a natural part of life. This acceptance can actually reduce the additional stress that comes from chasing an unattainable, stress-free existence. Instead of striving to eliminate stress entirely, focus on finding ways to manage it effectively and leverage its positive aspects when possible.

The essence of this mantra is to recognize that a completely stress-free life is an unrealistic goal. Rather than aiming for a life without stress, learn to live with these demons in a way that keeps you in control. Accept stress as a natural part of life and focus on coexisting with it, making the most of the positive aspects it can sometimes offer.

CHAPTER 16

Angels - The Defense
Against Our Demons

Fortunately, demons are not the only forces at work within us!

Throughout this book, I've discussed the various inner demons that feed on us and, in turn, fuel their master —stress. We've also seen that many of these demons have redeeming qualities, making them necessary in certain ways, preventing us from fully eradicating them from our system. However, despite their positive aspects, their core nature remains harmful. So, while we allow them to exist, we must ensure they remain under our control.

Just as every good contains a bit of bad, and every bad has a trace of good, the presence of demons in our system implies that something positive must also reside within us.

The answer is yes: we are blessed with many angels within us. These angels, much like the demons, inhabit our system. But unlike demons, their purpose is to protect and support us. They act as our internal defense, helping us combat the harmful influences of the demons. By nurturing these angels, we empower them to assist us in our fight against stress and its servant demons.

Think of these angels as an internal immune system, a force of good that stands against the negative forces within us. They form an inner army, helping us resist and balance out the demons in our system.

However, it's important to recognize that while these angels exist within us, many of them lie dormant. They can only help us manage our demons if we awaken and strengthen them, allowing them to grow and reach their potential.

Ironically, despite being gifted with these protective angels, many of us neglect or fail to tap into their full power, leaving them underdeveloped.

There's a balance we must understand: just as demons have redeeming traits, these angels are not without flaws. They, too, have their shadows.

Additionally, not all of the angels I've mentioned may fit the traditional image of an angel. Some might simply be positive aspects of our human experience. I refer to them as angels because of the vital role they play in helping us combat our inner demons, keeping those negative forces in check. They assist us in preventing these demons from becoming more destructive.

This balance between good and bad, between angels and demons, is a central part of the human experience. It reminds us that even amidst challenges, we possess inherent strengths and positive qualities that can guide us through tough times.

And finally, just as all demons serve their master, stress, all angels work to empower their guardian, peace. Peace is a state of bliss, the ultimate source of supreme strength, and the very essence we all seek in our lives.

In the following chapters, let's dive deeper into these angels and explore their nature.

CHAPTER 17

Patience: The Angel of Waiting Calmly

Patience stands as one of the strongest angels within us, providing the power to endure and wait for the right moment without being overwhelmed by the challenges we face along the way. This angel is so powerful that mastering the art of patience can shield us from many disturbances caused by the inner demons we wrestle with.

The Power of Patience

This angel can work wonders if we acknowledge its presence, nurture its strength, and tap into its potential when facing inner demons. Patience brings the ability to wait for the right opportunity, and in doing so, that moment is far more likely to arrive. In times of sorrow and hardship, patience becomes the endurance needed to remind us that nothing lasts forever—bad days, too, will pass.

Time plays a crucial role in every aspect of life. If the timing isn't right, things may not work out, leading to struggles and setbacks. Patience is the guiding force that gives us courage to face these challenges and the resilience to wait for brighter days. When we're in pain and have done all we can, patience makes the pain diminish or become bearable.

Sometimes, letting things unfold at their own pace is necessary. Rushing for a resolution often leads to poor results. With age and experience, patience typically grows, but it requires conscious effort to develop. It is not an automatic gift —it must be practiced and cultivated.

How Patience Helps Us Combat Our Demons

Patience is a powerful defense against anger. When we learn to be patient, we stop reacting impulsively and reduce both the frequency and intensity of our anger. This angel also counteracts two daunting demons: regret and guilt. By being patient, we make fewer mistakes, leading to fewer regrets and less guilt.

In relationships, patience is key. It fosters time for growth, understanding, and connection, helping us navigate relationship challenges with grace. Patience also helps us deal with the past, present, and future demons. By practicing patience in difficult moments, we create a better future for ourselves.

Patience diminishes the negative effects of unhealthy comparisons by allowing us to trust in our own journey and wait for our moment to shine. Instead of feeling envy toward those in more favorable positions, patience reassures us that our time will come. This same quality also helps to counter the demon of worry—rather than dwelling on difficult situations, patience encourages us to remain calm and trust that things will eventually improve.

Expectations, too, are better met with patience. Often, others need time to understand, agree, and meet our expectations. Being impatient only hinders that process. Likewise, when we're expected to fulfill someone else's expectations, patience ensures a more thoughtful and timely response.

Patience can also help combat the demon of self-doubt. By giving us the time to reflect and validate our concerns, patience gradually weakens the grip of self-doubt, allowing us to gain clarity and confidence in ourselves.

Balancing Patience with Action

It's important to understand that patience should not be confused with weakness. Others may perceive it that way if we don't actively show that we are still in control of the situation. Patience should have limits. It's essential to establish a threshold and prepare an action plan when that limit is reached.

It's also critical to remember that while we can control our own patience, we cannot expect others to do the same. Relying too heavily on everyone else being patient is unrealistic and can lead to disappointment.

The Dark Side of Patience

Like all good things, patience has its downsides. While its benefits are plentiful, waiting indefinitely for something that may never happen can be harmful. It's essential to establish realistic timeframes and recognize when it's time to take action, rather than patiently waiting indefinitely.

The two primary causes of the negative aspects of an angel like patience are impatience and excessive patience, and the line between the three is very thin. Patience can easily shift into either impatience or excessive patience, so we must remain mindful of this delicate balance.

Impatience rarely brings any positive outcomes and can actually give rise to several demons within us. It often leads to inferior results by not allowing enough time for better outcomes to unfold. Likewise, impatience may push you to settle for a suboptimal choice before better opportunities have a chance to appear.

On the other hand, excessive patience can cause missed opportunities. Waiting for the perfect moment that may never arrive could leave us regretting that we didn't seize smaller chances along the way.

Moreover, others may misinterpret patience as weakness or passivity. Setting clear limits and having an action plan can prevent others from taking advantage of our patience. Expecting everyone around us to be patient can also be unrealistic, leading to frustration and anger.

As our patience reaches its limits, the demon of anger often begins to grow, resulting in an outburst when our patience finally runs out.

Summing Up

Patience is a powerful angel that helps us manage the various demons within us. By cultivating patience, we can better navigate life's challenges, reduce stress, and build resilience. However, it's essential to ensure that our patience has boundaries, and we must be ready with a plan of action when the time is right.

CHAPTER 18

Hope: The Angel That Saves Us From Drowning

Hope is an angel that reaches out and holds our hands, keeping us afloat when we feel as if we are drowning in the sea of life's problems. It's a beacon of light that guides us through darkness, making us believe in possible outcomes even when we are completely surrounded by negativity. This angel fills us with the endurance needed to face life's setbacks, disappointments, and challenges.

The Power of Hope

Hope equips us with resilience, enabling us to endure tough times and confront challenges head-on. It is a form of blind faith that drives us forward, even in the bleakest moments. It's the delicate thread we cling to, trusting it won't break no matter how heavy the burden. Hope requires no logic or proof —it simply exists as a force that propels us through difficulties.

Often, life's constant setbacks can turn people pessimistic, yet hope emerges as a rescue force. It instills a belief in us that things will improve, urging us to hold on. In situations where failure seems certain, hope brings a glimmer of light, nudging us to persevere and remain open to better outcomes. When reason and effort fall short, hope becomes the last lifeline to cling to.

How Hope Helps Us Combat Our Demons

When it comes to our life and its demons, hope is one angel that proves to be an effective force in fighting life's inner demons.

Hope plays a major role in combating the comparison demon. It helps us when we feel inadequate through comparisons with others, showing us that our situation can improve. It bridges the gap between where we are and where we wish to be, keeping our spirits high with the possibility of positive change.

Hope helps us confront the worry demon by offering reassurance that difficult times are temporary. It instills confidence that the sources of our worries will eventually fade, encouraging us to believe that brighter days are ahead. Instead of being overwhelmed by fear of the unknown, hope provides a sense of calm, reminding us that things can and will improve with time. By focusing on the possibility of positive outcomes, hope helps us manage our worries and face challenges with greater resilience.

Hope helps us fight the demons of regret and guilt by encouraging us to make thoughtful choices and avoid shortcuts that often lead to poor decisions and lasting remorse. It also softens anger by reminding us that our current circumstances are not permanent and have the potential to improve with time. Through hope, we are motivated to stay patient and focused, trusting that better outcomes are within reach, which allows us to navigate challenges with a clearer, more positive mindset.

This angel plays a crucial role in our fights against the past, present and future demons. It offers comfort by easing our fears about the past repeating itself, the challenges of a difficult present, or the uncertainty of a bleak future. Hope reassures us that things can and will improve, and it encourages us to draw strength from positive experiences in our past, reminding us that we have overcome obstacles before and can do so again.

In relationships, hope plays a pivotal role in keeping connections intact, even during turbulent times. Many relationships endure severe trials but remain alive as long as hope lingers. The loss of hope often marks the beginning of their downward spiral.

Hope protects us from jealousy and envy, keeping our spirits elevated and reducing the impact of these negative feelings.

There are moments when, due to challenging situations and circumstances, we lower or abandon expectations of both ourselves and others. In these times, it is hope that keeps those expectations alive, offering the possibility of them being fulfilled, even if only partially. Hope sustains the belief that positive outcomes are still possible, helping us remain open to progress, no matter how small.

The Dark Side of Hope

Even a powerful force like hope carries a shadow, reminding us that even the purest good often comes with a touch of darkness.

Sometimes, hope raises unrealistic expectations, leading to disappointment when those expectations aren't met. This is where hope can become dangerous. Our hope from others can be mistaken for demands and expectations, creating pressure on them. This is a side of hope we must be careful with.

Another risk is passively relying on hope without taking necessary actions. Hope should inspire us to act, not replace the effort required for success. If we simply rely on hope without making efforts, failure becomes much more likely.

Excessive hope can also be damaging. Too much hope in someone's success can create undue pressure on them. Likewise, hoping for positive outcomes in unlikely situations can backfire, leading to crushing disappointment if things don't go as planned. This reliance on hope can set us up for even more painful losses in the future.

Another drawback of hope is that when it prevails against all odds, it can lead to an unhealthy reliance on it. This dependence is risky, as something that worked once or twice doesn't guarantee it will work again in the future.

When faced with numerous disappointments in life, it's easy to lose faith in hope and fall into pessimism. However, to maintain your belief in hope, it's important to view each disappointment as an isolated event rather than letting them accumulate and cloud your perspective.

Using Hope Effectively

To use hope effectively, it must be paired with action. Hope shows us the possibilities, but it is our job to act on those possibilities and move toward our goals. At the same time, we must develop resilience to handle disappointments. Hope offers assurance during dark times, but it doesn't guarantee results.

To maximize its potential, hope should be anchored in reality. While hope encourages us to dream, maintaining realistic expectations helps to prevent unnecessary heartache.

However, there are exceptions where hope becomes a last resort when everything else has failed. In such situations, hope might not be grounded in reality, but it serves as a lifeline, helping you stay afloat during life's storms.

Summing Up

Hope is a powerful force that guides us through life's

storms, giving us the strength and resilience to persevere. While it has its risks—like raising unrealistic expectations—the good far outweighs the bad. By combining hope with effort, managing expectations, and preparing for setbacks, we can fully harness this angel's power to face life's challenges and keep moving forward with a positive outlook.

CHAPTER 19

Love: The Most Powerful Angel in Our System

L ove is one of the most powerful angels within us, yet we often fail to tap into its full potential. This angelic force has the ability to solve our most difficult challenges and vanquish many of the demons we face. Love, in its truest form, goes beyond logic and reason, existing as something entirely unconditional. When love comes with conditions, it becomes more of an arrangement—a reality we commonly see today. True love, however, brings selflessness and joy in giving.

The reach of love is vast, present within each of us and in every realm we inhabit. Its presence is strongest in our personal and inner worlds, where love is often unconditional. Unfortunately, as we move through our materialistic lives, love can become conditional. This includes love for ourselves, our families, and life partners—those closest to us by birth or choice.

In our social world, love extends to friends, but it tends to come with conditions. These are the people we choose to bring into our lives. In the professional world, love may manifest as passion for our work or affection for colleagues, but this too is shaped by circumstances and decisions. While love exists in all facets of life, its purest form is rare and often tainted by materialistic influences.

The Strength and Fragility of Love

Despite its immense power, love is fragile. It is blissful to experience pure love, yet maintaining it can be challenging. In truth, most forms of love in our lives are tinged with imperfections. In its purest state, love is invulnerable to expectations or conditions. But in reality, love is influenced by external factors and is often shaped by the behaviors and actions of those involved.

When love is based primarily on arrangement, it becomes delicate and prone to breaking when the terms of the arrangement aren't met.

Love instills in us a sense of responsibility toward those we care about and gives us the strength to shoulder these responsibilities without growing weary. It provides endurance to overcome life's challenges and offers healing, comfort, and solace during difficult times.

How Love Helps Us Combat Our Demons

Love has the power to conquer many of the internal demons that plague us, if we nurture it and allow it to work. Here's how love helps us fight various demons within us.

This angel aids us in overcoming the demon of expectations by transforming them into acceptance, allowing us to more easily embrace and tolerate others as they are. It also motivates us to meet the expectations of others when we truly care for them.

Love conquers the ego demon by giving us the strength to follow our hearts, even when our egos try to block the way. It gives us the strength to act in ways that go against our pride and self-interest.

When it comes to the demons that can arise in relationships, love is the glue that holds our relationships together, keeping them strong even in the face of challenges. Without it, relationships become transactional, devoid of deeper meaning.

Love helps overcome the comparison demon by diminishing the power of harmful comparisons. When we love someone, we are more likely to accept their flaws and avoid comparing them to others.

When love drives our actions, we approach them with complete devotion, leaving less room for mistakes and, as a result, reducing regret and guilt.

Love has the power to suppress anger. When someone does something that upsets you, your love for them enables forgiveness, which in turn lessens your anger toward them. Similarly, when someone is angry with you, regardless of the reason, your expression of love has the power to calm their anger and bring it to a more manageable level.

There's an interesting connection between love and anger. When you become angry at someone you love, it's often because there's a good intention behind it—something meant for their benefit, though they might not realize it at that moment.

The connection between love and worry is a bit different. Love can often amplify worry, especially when we care deeply for others. However, this worry stems from concern and good intentions, making love's presence a positive force behind it.

The Dark Side of Love

The strange yet undeniable truth is that even something as angelic as love has a dark side.

Excessive love can lead to overprotectiveness or over-forgiveness, causing unintended harm. For instance, you might over-encourage someone without assessing their true abilities, setting them up for disappointment. Similarly, you may be blind to someone's selfish actions because of your love for them, allowing them to exploit you.

Unconditional love, while beautiful, can lead to being taken for granted by the very people you care about. It's important to maintain mutual respect and appreciation, even in unconditional love.

One-sided love can also be painful, as it often leads to heartbreak when the feelings are not reciprocated. Love cannot be forced, and it's crucial to accept this reality.

Conditional love can lead to disappointment when the conditions aren't met, and in extreme cases, love can blind people to the difference between right and wrong. They may even harm others in the name of love.

A lack of love where it's expected can sometimes become a significant issue. When someone anticipates your love and you don't offer it, whether intentionally or because you're unaware of their unspoken expectations, it can lead to misunderstandings and hurt feelings.

When someone you love deeply leaves, it leaves a permanent scar, as love never truly dies—it only becomes dormant. Lost love lingers, haunting you throughout your life. While love is a beautiful emotion, losing it becomes a wound that never fully heals.

Summing Up

Love is a powerful angel that helps us confront and conquer the demons within us. By embracing love in its purest form and being mindful of its potential downsides, we can harness love's strength to improve our lives and relationships. Love brings joy, resilience, and healing, making it an invaluable force in our journey through life.

CHAPTER 20

Logic: The Angel of Reason

L ogic is one of the most valuable angels we humans are blessed with. It serves as a powerful tool, helping us make sense of countless events in our lives, both seen and unseen. In the world of science, logic is paramount, but beyond its boundaries, logic has its limitations. There are aspects of life that defy explanation, either because our logic isn't yet advanced enough to comprehend them, or because they're part of a larger, mysterious design. Logic relies on the strength of reasoning and plays a crucial role in every facet of our lives.

The Role of Logic in Our Lives

An interesting aspect of human nature is that when things are going well, we rarely rely on logic to explain why—we simply enjoy the moment. However, when things go wrong, we turn to logic to search for reasons and explanations, helping us process difficult situations and supporting us emotionally in tough times.

Logic is essential in our decision-making process. When you think about it, life is made up of a series of choices, and its quality is shaped by the decisions we make along the way.

Logical thinking enables us to make better decisions, leading to a higher quality of life. Without it, our choices would be based on superficial judgments or gut feelings, which might not always be reliable. This makes logic a critical angel in our system.

How Logic Helps Us Combat Our Demons

When it comes to the demons that plague our lives, logic is an angel that guides us toward making better decisions, helping us fight many of these inner negative forces.

Logic helps manage our expectations of others. Not all of our expectations will make sense to others, but by using logic, we can refine and eliminate the unreasonable ones, making them more acceptable and easier for others to meet. This same principle applies when we're on the receiving end of others' expectations.

This angel is also useful in battling the comparison demon. Many of the comparisons we make are irrational, and logic can help eliminate those that are invalid, improving the accuracy of our assessments. By reducing the influence of illogical comparisons, we decrease the power this demon holds over us.

Similarly, envy and jealousy often arise from faulty comparisons. By applying logic to these comparisons, we can weaken the grip of these destructive demons.

Logic also helps diminish the impact of guilt and regret demons. When we feel guilty or regretful about past actions, logic allows us to understand that the choices we made were the best possible given the circumstances at the time. This perspective helps reduce feelings of guilt and regret. Furthermore, thinking logically in the present reduces the likelihood of making mistakes, thus minimizing future regret and guilt.

When it comes to anger demon, logic reminds us

that getting upset over irrational reasons is unwise. This understanding helps us manage our temper and reduce the frequency of anger outbursts.

The ego demon thrives when we abandon logic. By applying logical thinking, we start to chip away at our ego, helping us regain perspective and humility.

The Dark Side of Logic

While logic is a helpful angel, there are situations where we must exercise caution in relying on it.

In relationships, for instance, relying solely on logic can create friction. Sometimes, we need to make exceptions, accepting things that aren't entirely logical to show love, understanding, and a willingness to prioritize the relationship over reason.

Expecting everyone to behave logically all the time is also unrealistic and can lead to disappointment and strain in relationships.

It's also crucial to recognize that logic has its limits. Not everything can be explained logically, and when we encounter situations where logic fails, it's important not to become fixated on finding explanations. In such cases, taking a leap of faith may be necessary.

Just because you can't find a logical explanation for something doesn't mean it's inherently illogical. You may simply be missing pieces of the puzzle, and relying on incomplete logic leading to faulty conclusions.

Logic that perfectly explains one situation may not work in another, even if they seem similar, as each event has its unique circumstances. Blindly trusting logic can sometimes do more harm than good.

Additionally, logic that once explained something may not hold true over time. Circumstances change, and relying on outdated logic can lead to undesirable outcomes.

There's no shortage of situations where we should be careful when placing our trust in this angel.

Summing Up

Logic is a powerful angel that aids us in decision-making and helps us confront many of our inner demons. However, it's essential to recognize its limits and maintain flexibility, especially in relationships and situations where logic alone doesn't provide all the answers. By balancing logic with empathy, intuition, and understanding, we can address our inner struggles more effectively and navigate life's challenges with greater wisdom.

CHAPTER 21

Forgiveness: The Angel of Healing

F orgiveness is a powerful angel that we are blessed to have in our system. It extends its healing touch to both the person we forgive and ourselves, bringing emotional release and inner peace. This angel appears when we are wronged, and instead of seeking revenge or holding onto bitterness, we choose to forgive.

The Power and Benefits of Forgiveness

Forgiveness has a profound impact, offering healing to all involved. It not only helps the person being forgiven but also brings relief to the one who forgives. By choosing forgiveness, we free ourselves from negative emotions like vengeance, bitterness, and resentment, leading to emotional liberation and peace.

While punishment may offer temporary satisfaction, forgiveness brings true closure. It's often easier to punish someone for their wrongs, but it takes courage to forgive. The act of forgiveness sets us apart and elevates us beyond the desire for retribution. Moreover, the feelings that come from forgiving are much more fulfilling than those that follow punishment. Where punishment may quell our anger temporarily, forgiveness eradicates it entirely, offering a deeper sense of peace.

How Forgiveness Helps Us Combat Our Demons

Forgiveness is a powerful tool in our battle with inner demons. By forgiving ourselves and letting go of self-blame, we can release the grip of guilt and regret demons.

When it comes to battling the demon of expectations, this angel urges us to forgive others when they fall short of our expectations and to show the same compassion to ourselves when we fail to meet our own.

Forgiveness also plays a crucial role in mending and improving relationships. It fosters understanding and gratitude, often transforming strained relationships into positive, respectful ones.

Moreover, when we forgive someone, it often inspires genuine gratitude, fostering a positive and respectful relationship. Additionally, it also frees them from their guilt, leading to genuine gratitude for your forgiveness.

By leading us down the path of forgiveness, this angel diminishes the influence of anger and resentment, preventing them from controlling our actions and freeing us from the weight of grudges and the desire for vengeance. Additionally, it saves us from the mental anguish of contemplating revenge.

By guiding you to forgive yourself for past mistakes, this angel helps you overcome guilt and regret, allowing you to release self-blame and accept your errors, recognizing that mistakes are a natural part of life.

This angel challenges our ego, encouraging us to move beyond a self-centered view and consider the perspectives of others. When we forgive those driven by envy or other negative emotions, it can transform their feelings and even inspire them.

After wronging others, people often worry about repercussions and revenge. However, when they are forgiven, they are freed from the grip of the worry demon.

The Dark Side of Forgiveness

Surprisingly, even an angel as powerful as forgiveness carries a potential dark side.

Over-forgiveness can be perceived as weakness, leading others to exploit or harm us, knowing we may forgive them. Additionally, forgiving someone without addressing their mistakes denies them the opportunity to learn and grow, potentially leading to repeated wrongdoings.

Silent forgiveness, too, can be harmful. When we forgive without communicating it, we rob the other person of the chance to understand and improve. Similarly, excessive self-forgiveness without accountability can inhibit our personal growth. Instead of learning from mistakes, we may find ourselves stuck in a cycle of errors.

There's also the risk of developing a superiority complex through forgiveness, feeling elevated above those who lack the strength to forgive. This sense of superiority can be detrimental, both to our humility and our relationships with others.

Summing Up

Forgiveness is a powerful angel, bringing healing and peace to everyone it touches. By embracing forgiveness, we can overcome many of our inner demons, improve our mental health, strengthen relationships, and foster personal growth. However, it's important to balance forgiveness with accountability and communication to ensure it leads to positive change and not repeated harm.

CHAPTER 22

Appreciation: The Angel of Gratitude and Acknowledgment

Appreciation is a guiding force in our lives, encouraging us to recognize and express gratitude for the efforts of others, making them feel valued and important. Additionally, this angel allows us to focus on what we have, rather than dwelling on what we lack. One of the beautiful aspects of appreciation is its ability to highlight the positive, leading to encouragement and motivation for continued good work.

When we are on the receiving end, being appreciated boosts our morale, making us feel recognized and valued. This, in turn, elevates our happiness and motivates us to keep moving forward.

Appreciation in Different Worlds

The influence of this angel extends to all spheres of life. Whether it's our inner, personal, professional, or social world, appreciation plays a pivotal role in acknowledging others and making them feel valued. This also encompasses self-appreciation.

In personal and social circles, we appreciate the efforts of family and friends, which strengthens bonds and fosters closeness.

In the inner realm, practicing self-appreciation helps us stay grounded and resilient, especially during tough times.

In the professional world, appreciation often takes a more formal tone—manifesting in promotions, financial rewards, or public recognition. However, even in this setting, a few sincere words of acknowledgment can go a long way.

How Appreciation Helps Us Combat Our Demons

Appreciation is a powerful tool against the negative forces that can plague our lives. In many areas of life, this angel can help us escape the grasp of various negative emotions and situations.

Appreciation helps us break free from the hold of the comparison and envy demons. We often compare ourselves to those we perceive as better, leading to feelings of inadequacy and envy, but this angel helps us shift our mindset. By appreciating others' success, we can turn envy into inspiration, allowing us to set new goals while feeling positive about others' achievements.

This angel weakens the influence of the relationship demon by strengthening bonds, as recognizing others' efforts encourages deeper connections.

Appreciation also leads to greater fulfillment of expectations because people are often more motivated to meet the needs of those who value and acknowledge their contributions. This helps reduce the influence of the expectations demon. The same applies when we are meeting both others' expectations and our own.

By appreciating our past efforts, regardless of the outcome, we can deal with feelings of regret or guilt. This doesn't mean justifying mistakes but rather valuing the effort we put in despite the results.

Appreciation also curbs envy and jealousy demons by shifting our focus from what we lack to what we already have. When we are thankful for the present, the worry about the future lessens, and we become more centered in the now.

The Dark Side of Appreciation

While appreciation is inherently positive, it does have a shadow side if not kept in balance.

Over-appreciation, for instance, can turn into flattery, losing its sincerity and value. If appreciation is not genuine, it can be perceived as manipulative or deceitful.

Excessively appreciating someone's every action, regardless of its merit, may lead to overconfidence, causing them to believe everything they do is correct. This can result in failure or disappointment when their actions don't live up to inflated expectations.

This is a typical example of misguided parenting, where parents constantly praise everything their children do, believing it to be encouraging. While their intentions are good, the outcomes can be harmful.

Lack of appreciation can be equally harmful. When people feel undervalued, it can lead to resentment and a decrease in effort. On a personal level, the absence of acknowledgment can sow seeds of self-doubt, making us question the value of our actions and contributions.

People may become addicted to appreciation, and when it is absent, they can experience a sense of emptiness, a drop in motivation, and increased self-doubt.

Expectations can also cause issues; when others expect appreciation and don't receive it, they may feel disappointed or resentful. Furthermore, when one person receives appreciation, it may ignite envy in others who feel they deserve recognition but are overlooked.

Finally, appreciation can be misused. Some may employ it as a tool for manipulation, using excessive praise to serve their own interests.

Summing Up

Appreciation is a powerful and uplifting force that nurtures gratitude, motivation, and positive relationships. It helps us fight inner demons by keeping our focus on the positive and by recognizing the efforts of others. However, like all good things, it requires balance. Appreciation must remain sincere and measured, avoiding excess or neglect, to prevent its potential downsides from causing harm.

CHAPTER 23

Kindness: The Angel of Compassion and Generosity

Kindness is an angel within us that encourages friendliness, generosity, consideration, and compassion toward others. True kindness, often referred to as altruism, is a selfless act performed without any expectation of receiving something in return.

The Essence of Kindness

This angel is driven by pure and positive intentions, inspiring in us a genuine desire to contribute to the happiness and well-being of others. Kindness nurtures compassion in our thoughts, promoting an authentic concern for the needs and feelings of those around us.

It brings out our generosity, encouraging us to give time, attention, assistance, or support to those in need, sometimes requiring personal sacrifice. Its influence extends beyond human interactions, fostering compassionate connections with all living beings and the world around us.

Kindness also plays a vital role in strengthening relationships, serving as a catalyst for growth in personal, social, and professional bonds.

Kindness in Different Worlds

This angel has a presence in all the worlds we live in.

Kindness in our inner world means showing kindness to ourselves, and though it may seem insignificant, it profoundly impacts our emotional stability and overall well-being. It helps us combat self-blame, self-doubt, and the pressures of unrealistic self-expectations.

Kindness in the personal realm deepens connections, strengthens family bonds, and enhances trust, creating a nurturing and supportive environment.

In the social world, acts of kindness build trust and encourage positive relationships in the broader social sphere. They create a ripple effect, inspiring others to be kind and fostering a more harmonious society.

In the professional world, kindness promotes teamwork, collaboration, and a positive work environment. It can reduce the toxicity that often arises in competitive settings, making work more comfortable and supportive.

How Kindness Helps Us Combat our Demons

In our internal battles against negative forces, kindness is a powerful ally.

Kindness weakens the grip of the ego demon by expanding our thoughts beyond self-interest and shifting our focus to the well-being of others, reducing selfish tendencies.

This angel helps us manage the demon of expectations by fostering understanding and patience when things don't go as expected, allowing us to consider others' perspectives and circumstances.

In confronting the relationships demon, kindness acts as

a catalyst in all types of relationships—personal, social, and professional—by building trust, fostering understanding, and creating a supportive environment.

When others upset us, kindness helps us avoid reacting with anger. Instead, it encourages us to understand the circumstances or emotions behind their actions, weakening the grip of the anger demon and easing our initial frustration.

Kindness helps keep the needs, wants and greed demon in check. By focusing on the needs of others and embracing selflessness, we minimize our needs and wants and avoid falling into the trap of greed.

Kindness toward oneself, especially when forgiving personal mistakes, reduces the impact of regret and guilt demons. Instead of fueling self-blame, it promotes healing and growth.

The Dark Side of Kindness

Interestingly, even a powerful angel like kindness has a dark side, which manifests as potential pitfalls that we should be mindful of.

Kindness can open the door to exploitation, as some people may take advantage of it, seeing your generosity as an opportunity for selfish gain.

In certain situations, kindness may be misinterpreted as weakness, particularly by ruthless individuals who view kind people as incapable of taking decisive or strong actions.

Kindness can lead to forgiving others without holding them accountable. If people are forgiven without realizing their mistakes, they may repeat harmful behaviors instead of learning from them.

Excessive help born out of kindness can create dependency in others. When they no longer receive that help, they may feel unsupported or fear failure.

Acts of kindness toward one person may be misinterpreted by others as favoritism, potentially sparking feelings of envy or jealousy.

While kindness is selfless and expects nothing in return, the reality is that the world isn't always as kind as those with generous hearts. Even kind people, being human, often have an unspoken expectation of at least being appreciated. When they go unacknowledged for too long, their patience may run out, causing them to lessen their kindness, and in extreme cases, withdraw entirely. This shift—from being exceptionally kind to withdrawing help—can be disheartening and often has negative consequences.

Summing Up

Kindness is a powerful angel that fosters compassion, generosity, and positive relationships. It helps us combat various internal demons by promoting selflessness and understanding. While there are potential pitfalls—such as exploitation, dependency, and perceived weakness—balancing kindness with discernment ensures its positive impact. Through practicing kindness, we can cultivate a more compassionate, supportive, and harmonious world.

CHAPTER 24

Acceptance: The Angel of Embracing Reality

A cceptance, by definition, is the act of willingly embracing or acknowledging something or someone as they are. Yet, it is much more than a simple act—it is an angel that helps us in our battles against the many demons within. We humans have a natural tendency to resist change at first, but over time, we evaluate and usually embrace it if it seems beneficial or unavoidable. Acceptance is woven into the very fabric of our lives, influencing how we manage unmet expectations, differing viewpoints, and life's challenges.

Acceptance fosters a positive and open attitude towards reality, whether it involves a situation, person, or circumstance, without the need to change or resist it. This angel gives us the ability to see things from other people's perspectives, deepening our understanding and appreciation of their views. It also strengthens our adaptability by helping us navigate changes and new realities, providing the inner resolve to overcome resistance to change.

Acceptance in Different Worlds

Acceptance plays a vital role in every aspect of our lives.

Within our inner world, self-acceptance is crucial for resilience and a healthy self-image. It involves embracing our strengths, weaknesses, successes and failures.

In the personal realm, acceptance strengthens family bonds by allowing us to embrace differences in behavior and temperament, fostering deeper connections despite our variations.

In our social world, this angel helps us appreciate diversity in people, cultures, and ideas, leading to a more respectful and understanding society.

In our professional world, acceptance promotes inclusivity in the workplace, helping us value diverse perspectives and ideas. It allows us to collaborate effectively with people of different backgrounds, leading to mutual recognition and respect.

How Acceptance Helps Us Combat Our Demons

In the struggle against life's inner demons, acceptance is a key ally.

It's common for the anger demon to arise when things don't go as expected, but acceptance helps us embrace reality, easing the intensity of that anger.

When people or situations fall short of our expectations, disappointment often follows. Acceptance allows us to embrace reality and understand the reasons behind these unmet expectations, helping us handle the disappointment with grace.

Many of our worries come from situations beyond our control, yet we dwell on them constantly. Acceptance allows us to recognize our limitations and prevents these unnecessary concerns from disrupting our peace.

Negative comparisons can diminish our self-esteem and make us feel inadequate. Acceptance helps us embrace and appreciate our own circumstances and abilities, reducing the impact of the comparison demon on our well-being.

The demons of regret and guilt often haunt us over past mistakes, but by accepting and learning from them, we can lighten the burden these demons place on us.

This angel is vital in building healthy relationships, as it helps us accept others as they are and acknowledge our own mistakes. These two key factors are essential for fostering deeper, more meaningful connections.

The Dark Side of Acceptance

While acceptance is a powerful force for good with many admirable qualities, it can have potential downsides if misunderstood or misapplied. Here are some of the negative aspects of acceptance.

Excessive acceptance can backfire, leading others to take you for granted, as they feel no fear of resistance regardless of their behavior. Additionally, they may interpret your acceptance as a sign of weakness.

Over-acceptance can lead to complacency, where you become too comfortable with your situation and lose the drive for improvement or growth. It may also cause you to settle for lower standards, resulting in mediocrity or poor performance.

Acceptance can sometimes be mistaken for resignation, where people stop attempting to improve a negative situation, believing it to be unchangeable.

Likewise, acceptance may hinder you from taking the necessary steps to improve your situation, resulting in inaction.

Silently accepting someone's harmful or toxic behavior without addressing it can encourage them to continue acting that way.

When someone accepts all your flaws without addressing them, it hinders your personal growth by depriving you of the opportunity to recognize and improve upon those flaws.

Summing Up

Acceptance is a powerful angel that guides us through life's challenges by promoting a positive attitude, fostering understanding, and helping us adapt to realities. However, it's essential to recognize its potential downsides and ensure mindful application. By practicing conscious acceptance, we can harness its positive aspects to improve our lives without falling into its potential traps.

CHAPTER 25

Willpower, Grit, and Tenacity: The Angels of Not Giving Up

The dynamic trio - willpower, grit, and tenacity are closely connected angels, and we are blessed to have them in our system as they play a significant role in helping us achieve our goals and overcome challenges and lucrative looking shortcuts. While they share similarities, they also have distinct qualities of their own that contribute uniquely to our determination, perseverance and resilience.

Willpower: The Guardian of Self-Control and Temptation

Willpower is a guiding force within us, helping us resist temptations, maintain self-control, and stay focused on our long-term goals. It empowers us to overcome short-term desires and impulses, especially when distractions threaten to derail our progress.

This angel strengthens our mental resilience, enabling us to stick to decisions, plans, and goals despite challenges. By enhancing our self-control, willpower helps us manage our emotions, behaviors, and thoughts—key elements for maintaining discipline and focus.

Grit: The Angel of Passion and Perseverance

Grit is a powerful angel within us, granting the perseverance and passion needed to pursue long-term goals. It enables us to endure challenges and setbacks without losing motivation or determination.

By definition, grit is a blend of passion and perseverance toward lasting objectives, emphasizing consistent effort despite difficulties. It fills us with the resolve to keep moving forward, no matter how tough the journey becomes.

This angel equips us with the mental toughness to bounce back from failures, learn from setbacks, and continue our path. Driven by a deep passion for long-term success, grit fuels our motivation and commitment to persevere, no matter the obstacles.

Tenacity: The Angel of Persistence and Determination

Tenacity is a powerful angel within us, blessing us with the ability to hold firmly to a course of action, belief, or purpose despite difficulties or setbacks. This angel keeps us steadfast and committed to our goals, no matter how challenging the journey.

Defined as the determination to continue pursuing something even when it seems impossible, tenacity embodies unwavering persistence and a refusal to give up, regardless of the odds.

This angel instills in us the persistence to maintain effort, the determination to stay committed, and the endurance to keep pushing forward, no matter the challenges we encounter.

Interplay Between Willpower, Grit, and Tenacity

Together, willpower, grit, and tenacity form a powerful trio that mutually reinforce each other to guide us through life's challenges. Willpower helps us make the right choices in the moment by exercising self-control, grit keeps us driven with passion and perseverance, and tenacity ensures we remain committed over the long term.

The willpower angel gives us the initial strength to resist immediate temptations and distractions, laying the groundwork for sustained effort. The grit angel builds on this by fueling our passion and perseverance through ongoing challenges and setbacks. The tenacity angel then reinforces both, ensuring long-term persistence and unwavering commitment to our goals.

While they work in harmony, each plays a distinct role. Willpower helps us conquer immediate temptations and stay focused in the short term. Grit sustains passion and perseverance over time. Tenacity provides the sheer determination to push forward, even in the face of overwhelming obstacles. Together, they provide a complete framework for achieving success in both the short and long term.

How They Work Together to Help Us Combat Our Demons

When we are tormented by the demons within us, the trio of willpower, grit, and tenacity unite to help us fight back.

This dynamic trio helps us combat the procrastination demon by working in harmony. First, willpower pushes us to begin tasks and resist the temptation to delay. Then, grit steps in to keep us motivated, helping us push through challenges along the way. Finally, tenacity ensures we stay committed and follow through, completing the tasks and achieving our goals.

When the despair demon clouds our lives and fills us with hopelessness, these angels come to our rescue. Willpower gives us the strength to resist giving up immediately, grit builds resilience to push through the feelings of despair, and tenacity ensures we hold on to hope and continue our journey, regardless of the challenges.

In moments when the self-doubt demon makes us lose confidence, this trio comes to our aid. Willpower helps us resist negative self-talk, maintaining our belief in ourselves. Grit fuels perseverance and helps us rebuild our confidence, while tenacity ensures we remain steadfast in our trust in our abilities, even in the face of doubt.

During rough patches in relationships, this trio provides the strength to withstand negative energy, resist taking impulsive actions, and hold on to hope for better times. Willpower keeps us from making rash decisions, grit motivates us to keep working toward healing, and tenacity ensures we stay committed to rebuilding the broken bonds.

When facing the demons of guilt, regret, or worry, these angels give us the strength and courage to confront them. Willpower helps us resist succumbing to their grip, grit encourages us to keep moving forward, and tenacity ensures we hold on to the belief that we can rise above their torment.

And the list goes on! In every battle with our inner demons, this powerful trio works together to protect, guide, and empower us.

The Dark Side of Willpower

One often overlooked reality is that willpower, unfortunately, is not an infinite resource. It can be depleted over time, especially when we're constantly bombarded by challenges or temptations, leading to diminished self-control and a higher chance of giving in to those urges.

Relying too heavily on willpower can also make you rigid and overly strict with yourself, which can result in burnout, stress, and a lack of balance in life. When your willpower falters and you give in to temptations, you may feel a sense of failure, damaging your self-esteem and fostering feelings of guilt and inadequacy.

Moreover, not all temptations are harmful. Some can serve as quick stress relievers in a demanding world, and strictly rejecting every temptation might mean missing out on brief moments of relaxation and relief.

The Dark Side of Grit

While grit focuses on the pursuit of long-term goals, it can sometimes turn into an unhealthy obsession, leading you to neglect other important aspects of your life. The relentless drive to persevere can cause you to ignore signs of burnout and exhaustion, leaving you drained before reaching your goals.

Grit can also make you overly stubborn, pushing you to pursue goals that may no longer be viable or beneficial. In doing so, you could miss opportunities to invest your time and energy in something more realistic or worthwhile. Over time, some goals lose relevance, and continuing to chase them blindly can result in wasted effort.

It's important to recognize that not everything is possible. Blindly following grit while ignoring red flags can lead to inevitable failure. If you spot warning signs along the way, it's wise to pause and reevaluate your goals. Deciding to redirect your energy based on hard facts is not giving up—it's a strategic choice to focus on more achievable and meaningful pursuits.

The Dark Side of Tenacity

The tenacity angel, though a powerful source of strength, can sometimes lead to inflexibility. Its emphasis on holding on steadfastly may stop you from adapting or adjusting your course, even when doing so would be the wiser option.

Relentless determination in the face of all challenges can

take a toll on the overall quality of your life, leading you to overlook other important aspects. Under tenacity's influence, the drive to hold on at all costs can cause you to neglect priorities that need attention.

Over time, some goals lose their relevance. Clinging to them solely out of tenacity can result in wasted time and energy that could be better spent on more meaningful pursuits.

Summing Up

Willpower, grit, and tenacity are interconnected forces that work in harmony to help us achieve our goals and overcome challenges. Willpower offers the initial strength to resist temptations, grit sustains long-term passion and perseverance, and tenacity ensures unwavering commitment. Together, they create a powerful trio that supports us in battling our inner demons, helping us navigate life's complexities with resilience and determination.

However, while these angels are powerful allies, it's crucial to recognize their potential downsides. Understanding their limits helps us avoid falling victim to burnout, rigidity, or misplaced persistence.

CHAPTER 26

Trust - The Angel of Confidence and Security

Trust is like an angel in our lives, providing us with immense convenience and peace of mind. When this angel is absent, we find ourselves stuck in a cycle of doubt and verification, leading to inefficiency and anxiety. But when trust is present, we move with confidence and ease, making our interactions smoother and more productive.

By definition, trust is the confidence we have in the reliability, integrity, and honesty of a person, group, product or system. However, it's not something we offer immediately or at first glance. Trust is developed gradually over time, through consistent positive actions, dedication, and open communication.

The Role of Trust

Trust plays a vital role in building and maintaining relationships. Once it's established, this angel enhances the quality of our connections, encourages cooperation, and creates a sense of security and well-being. Trust simplifies our lives by eliminating the need for constant validation, allowing us to act with peace of mind and confidence.

We often borrow trust that others have already established, saving time and effort. For instance, when we rely on reviews to make decisions about a company, product, or even a person, we're leveraging the trust built by others. This system of reviews rests on the belief that others' experiences are trustworthy, guiding us in our choices—whether it's purchasing an item or choosing a movie.

How Trust Helps Us Combat Our Demons

Trust is also an essential ally when facing our internal demons.

In our fight against worry, for example, trust helps diminish the impact of this demon. When we trust someone, it removes much of the need for constant concern, freeing us from the mental burden of doubt.

Trust is the foundation of any relationship. Without it, relationships can deteriorate, developing toxic and harmful traits. Trust not only strengthens bonds but also keeps them healthy and stable, helping to prevent the emergence of many demons and conflicts that arise from broken or strained relationships.

Trust in oneself can help neutralize the demons of envy and jealousy. When you're confident in your abilities, insecurities lose their power, and these demons cannot cause as much harm.

In the same way, self-trust shields you from the regret and guilt demons. When you trust your decisions, you recognize that negative outcomes are often shaped by circumstances beyond your control, not just personal mistakes, which weakens the grip of these demons on you.

Trust also helps combat expectations—both those you have of others and those others have of you. When you trust in yourself, you feel more confident in meeting the expectations placed on you. Likewise, trust in others can reassure you that they'll meet your expectations.

Trust helps us defend against the demons of past, present, and future demon. It gives you the confidence that you can navigate future challenges, allowing you to confront potential worries of the future with greater resilience.

The Dark Side of Trust

Though trust is a powerful force, it has its vulnerabilities.

Trust is as fragile as it is powerful. It takes time and effort to build but can be shattered by a single breach, causing emotional pain and making it hard to trust again. A broken trust can lead to missed opportunities where trust might have made life easier.

If you break someone's trust, even unintentionally, you may be labeled untrustworthy. This is why businesses prioritize customer satisfaction and good reviews—one negative review can tarnish their reputation and cost them dearly.

Trusting the wrong person, like a scammer or someone with bad intentions, can lead to betrayal or harm. Overextending trust can also create pressure on others, leading to anxiety in relationships. When someone feels the weight of your trust, they may fear letting you down, which can strain the relationship.

Explicitly telling someone they've broken your trust can introduce guilt in their system, which may harm the relationship further.

Trust can also raise expectations, and when those expectations aren't met, it can damage relationships and lead to disappointment. Placing excessive trust in someone who fails to meet those expectations can also lead to feelings of regret.

Another danger is rushing trust. If you place too much trust in someone too soon, it can backfire if the person isn't reliable. Excessive trust in oneself can also breed overconfidence and ego, making you blind to your weaknesses and the risks you face, potentially leading to mistakes and regret.

On the flip side, a lack of trust—whether in yourself or others—can give rise to doubt, leading to missed opportunities, constant anxiety, and strained relationships. The delicate balance of trust is crucial.

Summing Up

Trust is a powerful angel, fostering confidence, security, and efficiency in our lives and relationships. While its benefits are immense, misapplying trust or taking it to extremes can lead to negative consequences. When balanced properly, trust helps us navigate life with greater ease, strengthens our connections, and contributes to our overall well-being and success.

CHAPTER 27

Morals - The Guiding Angel of Right and Wrong

Morals serve as a guiding angel in our lives, providing us with a moral compass that helps us stay on the right path. They are the principles or rules of behavior that guide us in distinguishing right from wrong, influencing the choices we make, the actions we take, and how we interact with others.

Every day, we are faced with numerous decisions—some clearly right, some wrong, and others falling into a gray area. Ironically, the wrong choice often seems more appealing due to its ease or the shortcuts it promises. However, this option typically leads to harm for ourselves and others. The right choice, though often more difficult and time-consuming, is the one that aligns with our moral compass. This angel gives us the wisdom and strength to make the right decision, even when the wrong path seems more tempting.

The Role of Morals

Morals act as our guiding star, offering us a framework to navigate through life's choices, especially when faced with difficult or ambiguous situations. They encourage us to practice honesty, sincerity, and integrity in our actions and relationships. Yet, this path isn't always easy, as the wrong option often appears more attractive with its promises of ease and quick rewards.

In every realm of life, this angel pushes us to uphold fairness, justice, and equality. It ensures that we treat others with respect, consideration, and kindness, even when it's challenging.

How Morals Help Us Combat Our Demons

Morals play a key role in combating our internal demons, helping us stay on the right side of life and minimizing the influence of harmful negative forces.

With morals guiding us, we are more likely to make choices that align with our values, reducing opportunities for guilt and regret demons to haunt us. This angel also helps keep the ego demon in check by fostering humility, empathy, and respect for others.

Morals encourage generosity and sharing, helping to restrain the greed demon. They teach us patience, forgiveness, and understanding, which diminishes the anger and expectations demons, and prevents our relationships from becoming toxic.

By instilling contentment and gratitude, this angel weakens the jealousy and envy demons, helping us appreciate what we have and respect the achievements and possessions of others.

The Dark Side of Morals

While morals are essential for guiding us through life, they can reveal a darker side when misapplied or taken to extremes.

If you cling too rigidly to your moral principles, it can make you intolerant, judgmental, and inflexible in complex situations. In some cases, strictly following your morals may not be practical and can even harm you or others.

Believing your moral standards are superior to others can create a sense of moral arrogance, leading to the rise of an ego demon. Additionally, when you fail to live up to your own moral expectations, it can create feelings of guilt, shame, and a diminished sense of self-worth.

Conforming to society's moral standards at the expense of your own beliefs can lead to resentment and a lack of personal fulfillment. Conversely, imposing your own moral standards on others through judgment or punishment can foster an oppressive environment, where people feel constantly pressured and judged.

Summing Up

Morals are a guiding angel, helping us navigate the complexities of life with integrity, fairness, and compassion. They enable us to combat various demons by promoting honesty, empathy, and respect for others. However, it's important to be mindful of the potential dark side of morals, ensuring we don't become rigid, judgmental, or arrogant in their application. Balancing moral principles with flexibility and understanding helps us avoid the negative consequences of their extreme use.

CHAPTER 28

Peace: The Guardian of All Angels

To say that peace is the ultimate nirvana for humanity is no overstatement. In the fast-paced world we live in, peace of mind has become a rare and highly desired state. Just as demons serve their master, stress, all angels work to strengthen their guardian—peace. Peace represents the ultimate positive energy that angels nurture within us, bringing harmony to our thoughts, actions, and emotions. It is the foundation upon which all angels thrive.

Peace is the guardian of all angels, the calmness that nourishes their strength. Just as all rivers flow into the ocean, the energy of angels culminates in peace. It is the state of balance and inner tranquility we all seek. While stress breeds chaos, distraction, and exhaustion, peace fosters mental clarity, emotional stability, and physical well-being.

In the presence of peace, the angels are most effective, guiding us to navigate life's challenges with grace and resilience. It's the final destination we all long for—a state of serenity where we are aligned with our purpose, grounded in our values, and equipped to face life's storms with unwavering calm.

However, peace is not merely the absence of stress or

conflict; it is the presence of an inner stillness that empowers us to navigate the world with confidence, strength, and compassion, even amid the chaos. Ultimately, peace is the true bliss we all seek, and the angels are our guides, helping us achieve this state of harmony and wholeness.

The Path to Peace

Nearly everyone is searching for peace, each on their own journey to reach this blissful state. While most follow a familiar path in pursuit of peace, some take roads that make us question their intentions—are they truly after peace, or something else?

Looking at the world's turbulent history, one might wonder: if everyone seeks peace, why do some choose the path of violence? Countless wars have been fought over wealth and power—where is the peace in that?

While answers may vary, I believe that everyone, in their own way, is in pursuit of peace. Those who resort to violence in the quest for wealth and power are, in their minds, seeking their version of peace. The key difference is that their pursuit is selfish—they aim for personal peace at the expense of the world's harmony, satisfying only their own desires.

Peace is a Journey, Not a Destination

Many of us are chasing peace, mistakenly seeing it as an ultimate goal. In truth, peace is not an end point but a journey —one experienced through small and large moments of joy, fulfillment, and contentment that resonate deeply with our inner selves.

Peace can come from a variety of sources, both material and spiritual—whether it's through the activities we enjoy, the food we eat, the books we read, or the goals we accomplish. Some people experience peace by giving and sharing, while others find it in receiving what they've longed for. Anything that touches the core of our being, where true calmness resides, can become a source of peace.

Ultimately, it is the accumulation of these small episodes of peace that defines the journey, not an elusive final destination. Those who understand this simple truth are able to enjoy moments of peace throughout life's journey, rather than endlessly striving for nirvana as an unattainable goal.

The Materialistic World and Peace

While true peace often comes from spiritual fulfillment, materialistic desires also play a role in contributing to our peace, from a pragmatic perspective.

The satisfaction of materialistic needs may seem superficial, but realistically, they do provide a sense of peace in our conscious state. As humanity has evolved, we've accumulated more to meet our needs, desires, and even our greed. While the meaning of peace remains constant— providing inner stillness—the ways in which we access it have changed.

The materialistic world may offer only fleeting happiness, yet it remains a key pillar that supports our journey toward lasting peace. While happiness is not synonymous with peace, it helps sustain us on the path to the ultimate guardian of all angels—peace.

Everyone's Definition of Peace Is Unique

We are all different in countless ways, and so are our definitions of peace. Each person's path to peace is unique, yet we often fail to recognize this. Instead, we impose our ideas of peace onto others, and they do the same to us.

With so much variety in the world, only a small fraction of it will align with your personal definition of peace—and what brings peace to us may create friction for others. For example, people in a car together may find peace from different music genres, yet only one genre can play at a time. While some may enjoy the music, others may simply tolerate it, finding peace in the shared experience of being with loved ones rather than the music itself.

True peace is impossible to achieve perfectly, and so we must adjust our expectations, finding peace in the moments we can, and accepting that no one path fits all.

The Reality and Compromise

As we've explored throughout this book, stress and its servant demons live within us, often tolerated due to their occasional benefits. Similarly, angels help us combat these demons, but they, too, have their own dark sides we must remain wary of to avoid their traps..

With both demons and angels present, achieving perfect peace in its purest form is an unrealistic goal. Not everything that brings us happiness or peace is practical in our day-to-day roles. For instance, a career you love may bring you joy, but if it doesn't pay the bills, that joy may be short-lived. We must balance the pursuit of peace with the practical demands of life.

The key lies in embracing compromise. Rather than striving for a completely stress-free life, we should aim for a balance in which peace outweighs stress, creating a more harmonious state within us.

The war between peace and stress is an eternal conflict. Our task is to nurture the angels, empowering their guardian, peace, to help us in the never-ending struggle against the demons within, and to prevent them from feeding their master, stress.

Summing Up

Peace is the guardian of all angels, the force that helps us combat the stress and chaos of life. It is not a final destination but a journey—a series of moments that bring us closer to our inner selves. By nurturing peace within, we empower the angels to guide us toward a life of clarity, fulfillment, and balance.

CHAPTER 29

My Theories That Help Me Combat These Demons

Throughout my life, I've observed that people, including myself, go through a lot of stress. However, one thing that I've noticed is that there's a significant difference in the way I handle stress as compared to others, and that led me to explore this subject further.

I discovered that whenever I encounter stressful situations, a defensive system of thoughts triggers automatically as a reaction to that stress. So just like everyone else, I too get stressed but this defensive system reduces the frequency, magnitude, and lifespan of my stress significantly.

This defensive system of thoughts is nothing but some theories I've developed over time, and they work wonders for me. I'm sharing these theories with the hope that they help you in combating your own demons, and inspire you to identify your own coping mechanisms for dealing with these demons that you might not have recognized yet.

I encourage you to reflect on your own experiences and identify the theories or coping mechanisms that work for you. By doing so, you can build your own defensive system to combat stress and lead a more fulfilling life.

Let's explore my theories that help me deal with stress and its servant demons in my system in the next few chapters.

CHAPTER 30

Theory of the Limit of Patience

My theory of the limit of patience highlights that while patience has an elastic quality, there's a limit to which it can go, as it also has a breaking point. When this limit is reached, various demons such as anger, frustration, resentment, and despair are unleashed in our system. Following this theory prevents me from taking people for granted indefinitely and also guards me against others doing the same to me.

Key Concepts of This Theory

The elasticity of our patience is such that it can stretch as well as adapt, but only to a certain extent.

Everyone has a different limit to their patience, which, when exceeded, can result in the birth of many demons in our system, leading to negative emotions and behaviors. Also this limit is not set in stone and can change over time and in different circumstances.

A person will have different limits to their patience for different people.

The age and depth of a relationship has a significant influence on the elasticity of patience. Over a period of time, people in long-term relationships often develop greater patience for each other, and in many cases it gets to a point where it becomes almost unbreakable.

How This Theory Helps Me Combat My Demons

This theory encourages me to be mindful of my patience limits, which helps me manage my reactions and avoid reaching a breaking point. By recognizing and respecting these boundaries, I can prevent negative outcomes, such as triggering unwanted emotions and behaviors in both myself and others.

It also aids in combating relationship issues, as I remain attentive to the patience levels of those I interact with. By being proactive and not pushing others to their limits, I help maintain harmonious relationships and avoid unnecessary conflicts. Understanding that everyone has different thresholds for patience allows me to adopt a more tailored approach in my interactions, which fosters mutual respect and strengthens my connections with others. Recognizing these varying limits also enhances my empathy and compassion in my relationships.

When it comes to my own patience with people and situations, I strive to be more accommodating by stretching my limits. This helps prevent the internal demons that would otherwise arise when my patience runs thin.

Anger, for example, is a demon that grows as patience reaches its limit. This theory equips me to address anger proactively, both in myself and in others. By recognizing when someone's patience is wearing thin, I can prepare for the possibility of an anger response and manage the situation more effectively.

Worry is another demon that emerges when someone's patience is tested, especially if they are anxiously waiting for something important. When the wait extends too long, worry can start to take hold. This theory helps by encouraging timely communication with others before their patience reaches its limit, allowing them to reassess the situation and take action to prevent worry from overwhelming them.

The same principle applies when I have expectations of others, or when others have expectations of me. Both sides have patience limits. This theory reminds me to acknowledge these limits, so if I'm unable to meet someone's expectations, I don't delay in delivering the news to avoid disappointing them later. Similarly, I communicate my own patience limits with others, so they can either meet my expectations or manage them proactively, avoiding frustration.

Lastly, working on extending my patience helps me grow personally, improving my ability to handle stress and adversity more effectively. By expanding my patience limits, I strengthen my resilience and overall well-being.

Summing Up

The theory of the limit of patience helps me navigate relationships and personal challenges more effectively by understanding that patience may have elasticity but it has a breaking point, a limit to which it can stretch. By being aware and respectful of these limits in myself and others, I can prevent the negative consequences of impatience and foster stronger, healthier relationships. This theory has been instrumental in saving me from the stress and its servant demons that arise when patience is pushed beyond its limits.

CHAPTER 31

Theory of Gray, Not Just Black and White

This theory of mine highlights that not everything in our world is perfect, and any such expectations are unrealistic, and will end up remaining unmet mostly.

In the context of this theory, "Black and White" represents absolute perfection or crystal clarity, while "Gray" signifies things that are not perfect, with varying degrees of deviation from perfection. According to this theory, achieving perfection in our complex world is extremely difficult, and almost everything has a shade of gray, which is a blend of black and white. However, the intensity of this grayness varies from one situation to another, making them unique in their deviation from a perfect black and white.

Key Concepts of This Theory

There is nothing wrong in expecting things or situations to be perfectly "Black and White", but imperfection is inevitable, as in our complex and ever-changing world, perfection is rare, and in fact nearly impossible, due to the multitude of parameters required to align perfectly for that to happen.

In order for something to achieve perfection, it requires numerous parameters to be in the right state, intensity and order, which thinking realistically, is quite difficult to attain and maintain consistently, as sometimes certain parameters would be missing, while at other times they won't be in the right state or order, and some other times they would simply lack in intensity that is needed for them.

However, when you recognize this variability of parameters, it'll help you in accepting that perfect conditions are nearly impossible. In addition to that, your understanding that deviations from perfection are normal will help you in setting realistic expectations.

When you adapt your expectations to align with reality, it prevents you from disappointment and frustration. This adaptation will help you in managing your expectations and reduce the impact of unmet expectations.

Also in this constantly changing world of ours, which is not a controlled experimental setting, it's almost impossible for all parameters to remain constant as expected. So it's almost a fact that things will never turn out to be exactly perfect as expected, and even if they do, they won't remain the same. There'll always be a deviation from perfection. Only the degree of deviation will vary depending on how many parameters are in your favor.

Setting Realistic Expectations

This theory helps me in setting my expectations that are closer to reality, that may not be perfect but practical for sure. This helps me reduce disappointment and complains, when things do not turn out perfectly, as my expectations are aligned with reality.

Accepting that things will not always be perfect helps me in managing stress and frustration, and leads to greater satisfaction and reduced emotional disturbance, saving me from many demons that might have been born as a result of my unmet expectations when they were unmatched with reality.

Dealing with Others' Expectations

There's one exposure in following this theory that while I may accept the "Gray" in others, they might expect "Black and White" perfection from me, and these unrealistic expectations may end up creating several demons in my system, if I don't deal with them.

Helping others understand the practicalities and deviations from perfection, and a proper communication can help align their expectations with reality to reduce conflict and disappointment in relationships.

How This Theory Helps Me Combat My Demons

By embracing the gray areas and letting go of the expectation that everything must be black and white, this theory helps me combat several of my inner demons, and here are a few of them.

This theory helps me combat regret and guilt demons, as only perfection can prevent anyone from making mistakes. However, since I can not be perfect, I will make mistakes, so when these demons haunt me for my mistakes, my acceptance of mistakes help me in reducing the intensity of their attacks.

I no longer expect flawless outcomes and am less likely to feel disappointed by setbacks.

Similarly, this perspective prevents me from over-encouraging others, as I understand that imperfections make mistakes inevitable, and my excessive encouragement might lead them to set unrealistic expectations for themselves.

This theory helps me combat the expectations demon by making me understand that perfection is nearly impossible, and adjust my expectations to be more realistic. This reduces the frequency and intensity of disappointment from unmet expectations.

Following this theory I deal better with the worry demon, with the understanding that perfection is unattainable, as it reduces the worry about achieving perfect outcomes. This enables me to take a more relaxed and realistic approach to life's challenges.

Another inner struggle this theory helps me manage is the anger demon. When I stop expecting things to be perfectly black and white, I no longer get angry, as I'm prepared to accept the possibility of gray outcomes.

Summing Up

The Theory of Gray, Not Just Black and White, helps in setting realistic expectations and accepting imperfections in our constantly changing world. By adapting this perspective, I can reduce the impact of unmet expectations, and manage demons like stress, regret, guilt, anger and worry more effectively. This theory promotes a practical and compassionate approach to life, helping me navigate complexities in relationships and personal challenges with greater ease and understanding. Proper communication with others is essential to manage their expectations and maintain harmony.

CHAPTER 32

Theory of Balance in Give and Take

According to my theory of balance in give and take, everything that happens to us is part of a greater system that maintains equilibrium between us and our world, including its people and circumstances. This theory assumes that whatever we give eventually returns back to us in some shape or form, and whatever we receive or enjoy is either a return for past actions or an advance for future actions. So this balance is not limited to individual transactions of gives and takes, but extends to the collective experiences of our lifetime as well as of those around us.

The harsh truth of life is that everything is about give and take, and this holds true in all of our worlds, whether it is inner, personal, social, professional or fabricated.

You'll receive your fruits based on what you're willing to give. The more you work hard, the more success you'll get, assuming all other required parameters are in place.

Key Concepts of This Theory

Things in our life have a reciprocal nature, as everything we give comes back to us in one way or another, and everything we receive is linked to what we have given in the past or will give in future. This understanding encourages me to have a mindset of generosity without immediate expectation of return and leave this settlement to destiny.

This balance of give and take is a collective balance that includes not just your own individual transactions of give and take, but also the collective actions of your family and others close to you. That means, benefits and obligations can extend beyond your personal actions to those of your loved ones, like for example results of good deeds done by your father may come back to you, and similarly you may have to give back for something that was given to your mother or brother.

Another way to view this theory is that everything in life comes with a trade-off. When we gain something, we inevitably lose something else. If we're fortunate, we may have the option to choose what to sacrifice, but something will always have to be given up. Life is a constant balance of give and take. Understanding this helps me set realistic expectations about the trade-offs that come with my desires.

How This Theory Benefits Me

This theory helps me develop patience and understanding by making me recognize that returns on good deeds may not be immediate. This helps me manage expectations and reduces frustration, encouraging patience and perseverance in the face of delayed rewards.

Under the guidance of this theory I understand that perfect balance is rarely visible on the surface, and that helps me in accepting situations that seem unfair.

This theory comes to my aid when I experience a loss, reassuring me that something good may eventually come from it or that the loss might be a payback for a past gain.

This theory helps me accept the loss that accompanies certain gains by allowing me to see that loss as part of a larger balance, which reduces its emotional impact.

On the other hand, when I experience unexpected gains, this theory reminds me that they might be rewards for past actions or an advance for future sacrifices.

When I don't see proper returns despite my sincere efforts during challenging times, this theory helps me stay calm by fostering a long-term perspective on effort and reward. It reduces my stress and encourages a steady, balanced approach to navigating life's highs and lows.

This theory encourages me to keep doing good without expecting immediate rewards, trusting that balance will be restored over time.

How This Theory Helps Me Combat My Demons

There are very few situations where this give-and-take will appear perfectly balanced from a surface-level perspective, and that imbalance often becomes a breeding ground for various inner demons.

One of the roles our past, present, and future play in life is to maintain this balance between what we give and receive over the course of our lifetime. However, instead of trusting this natural process, we often interfere with it, making room for additional demons to enter our system.

Now, let me explain how this theory helps me combat stress and its servant demons.

With every act of giving, the expectation demon is born within us. This theory helps me combat that demon by reminding me that not every good deed will bring an immediate return. It reduces the frequency and intensity of disappointment and frustration caused by unrealistic expectations, helping me maintain a healthier perspective.

When we don't see a perfect return for our efforts, disappointment sets in, allowing the regret demon to enter our system. Similarly, when we receive something and can't give back immediately, the guilt demon creeps in. This theory helps me understand that not every give-and-take will have an immediate response, lessening the power of both the regret and guilt demons.

The greed demon drives us to take more and more without considering the need to maintain balance by giving back. By understanding the importance of giving in return, this theory weakens the influence of the greed demon, fostering a more generous mindset and encouraging a balanced approach to both acquisition and generosity.

Similarly, the ego demon disregards our obligation to maintain balance and only focuses on taking from others. This theory helps me combat the ego demon by making me recognize the importance of giving. It helps keep my ego in check, reduces selfish behavior, and encourages humility.

This theory helps me manage the worry demon by encouraging me to trust that good will eventually result from sincere efforts, even if delayed. This trust helps alleviate my worry and anxiety, allowing me to remain calm and focused.

It's not uncommon for us to over-encourage others by assuring them of success without truly understanding or considering their efforts and abilities—what they are giving. This can become a breeding ground for various inner demons within them, as unrealistic expectations and undue pressure begin to take root.

Summing Up

The Theory of Balance in Give and Take emphasizes the reciprocal nature of actions and the inevitability of trade-offs in life. It encourages accepting imperfections, and cultivating a mindset of generosity and patience. By embracing this theory, I can manage stress more effectively, maintain emotional equilibrium, and diminish the influence of inner demons like expectation, regret, guilt, greed, and worry. It promotes a balanced approach to life, highlighting the interconnectedness of our actions and their long-term consequences.

CHAPTER 33

Theory of Reality and Its Multiple Perspectives

Throughout this book, I have applied this theory to support my thoughts and insights. According to this theory, every reality has multiple perspectives, each deviating from the core reality to varying degrees of distortion. These perspectives represent individual versions of reality, shaped by the unique lens through which they are viewed. As individuals, we all possess distinct lenses, resulting in different perspectives, even when we are observing the same reality.

Key Concepts of This Theory

Every reality has multiple perspectives, so when different people observe the same thing, each views it through their own unique lens, creating distinct versions of that reality. While they may seem to be looking at the same object or situation, they are actually seeing their personalized interpretation, which differs both from others' views and from the objective reality itself. In effect, they are all seeing something different. It's rare for two people to perceive the same thing in exactly the same way. Even when an individual looks at the same thing at different times, their perspective will shift, reflecting changes in their mindset or circumstances.

Recognizing this helps me understand that everyone's perspective is valid, shaped by their unique experiences and viewpoints. It fosters empathy and open-mindedness, allowing me to appreciate the diversity of perspectives even when they differ from my own.

It may sound strange, but there are situations where it's better to follow a perspective rather than the harsh reality itself. A difficult reality might inhibit your progress, while an empowering perspective can provide the motivation you need to move forward in the right direction. In these cases, a positive or hopeful outlook can drive growth and resilience, even when reality feels discouraging.

Sometimes, more than one perspective can be correct, each offering different benefits and drawbacks. In such cases, you need to choose the perspective that aligns best with your circumstances at the time. The problem arises when people assume their perspective is the only reality, leading to conflicts and misunderstandings. Recognizing the validity of multiple viewpoints can help avoid these issues and promote better communication and cooperation.

How This Theory Helps Me Combat My Demons

When it comes to our lives and the inner demons we face, this theory serves as a powerful tool to help me combat those negative forces within. By acknowledging the multiple perspectives that shape our reality, it allows me to confront and manage these demons more effectively, offering a balanced and nuanced approach to navigating life's challenges.

The ego demon convinces us that our perspective is the only reality and that others should abandon their viewpoints in favor of ours. This theory helps me keep my ego demon in check by reminding me to recognize and respect the validity of other perspectives, fostering humility and open-mindedness.

This theory helps me reduce the impact of the worry demon by offering alternate perspectives that reveal different angles to a problem, which can ease concerns. Additionally, it allows me to focus on less worrisome aspects of situations, helping to overcome the anxiety demon and approach challenges with a calmer mindset.

The regret and guilt demons often attack by reminding us of past mistakes. This theory comes to my aid by helping me understand that those mistakes were based on the specific perspective I held at the time. Furthermore, it offers alternate perspectives, which help reduce the intensity of the regret and guilt demons, allowing me to view the past with more understanding and less self-blame.

The expectation demon strikes when others fail to meet our expectations. This theory helps me manage disappointment by encouraging me to consider others' perspectives, allowing for a more understanding and balanced response. By doing so, it reduces the negative impact of the expectation demon, making it easier to cope with unmet expectations without unnecessary frustration.

The comparison demon fosters the growth of many other inner demons, but this theory introduces new perspectives that can prevent negative comparisons. By offering alternative ways of viewing situations, it helps minimize the impact of demons born from comparisons, such as envy, insecurity, and self-doubt, allowing for a healthier and more balanced mindset.

Whenever I feel greed taking hold, this theory helps by offering different perspectives that highlight the irrelevance and futility of greed. These alternate viewpoints reduce the influence of the greed demon, reminding me of the value of balance and contentment over excessive desire.

Summing Up

This theory helps me understand the fundamental truth about perspectives: that all perspectives on any reality are simply different versions of the same reality, each valid in its own way. As a result, I become more open to considering and valuing others' viewpoints, and I no longer assume or argue that only my perspective is correct. This shift fosters greater empathy and understanding in my interactions with others.

CHAPTER 34

Theory of Multiple Factors Behind Any Success or Failure

My Theory of Multiple Factors Behind Any Success or Failure highlights that there are several factors responsible for contributing to any outcome, whether it's a success or a failure. While some factors are apparent and within our control, others may be hidden or completely out of our control. This theory emphasizes that our role in any outcome is only a fraction of all the factors responsible, and so we cannot solely blame ourselves for failures nor take full credit for successes. It fosters a more balanced understanding of outcomes and relieves undue pressure or self-criticism.

Key Concepts of This Theory

There are multiple factors behind any outcome, and its success or failure is determined by a combination of visible and invisible factors, some of which are beyond our control. This understanding helps distribute the weight of responsibility.

We are only partially responsible for any outcome, and our actions are just one part of the whole equation. Realizing this brings peace of mind for my failures and prevents me from becoming arrogant for my successes, reducing feelings of self-blame or arrogance.

While we play a significant role in our outcomes, it's not the sole determining factor, and this knowledge encourages us to give our best effort without getting overwhelmed by the outcome.

How This Theory Helps Me Combat My Demons

This theory helps me combat several of my inner demons by reminding me that while I do play a concrete role in my successes and failures, it is only a limited role, influencing just a fraction of the outcome. This understanding reduces the burden of self-blame for failures and tempers the temptation toward arrogance in success, fostering a more balanced perspective.

When the regret and guilt demons haunt me by resurfacing past mistakes or failures, this theory comes to my aid by helping me recognize that I am only partly responsible for those outcomes. This realization reduces the weight of these demons, easing the burden of regret and guilt and allowing me to move forward with a clearer perspective.

When others fail to meet my expectations, this theory helps me recognize that they are only partly responsible for fulfilling them and should not be fully blamed. This understanding prevents the expectation demon from haunting me, fostering a more compassionate and realistic view of others' roles in my life.

Anxiety about potential failures or adverse outcomes can create fertile ground for the worry and fear demons. This theory helps me recognize that I am only responsible for my part in any situation, encouraging me to focus on what I can control and let go of the rest. By doing so, it reduces the influence of these demons and helps me manage anxiety more effectively.

When I encourage others, this theory helps me avoid over-encouraging by reminding me to convey an important message: they are only responsible for their part. As long as they give their best with full honesty, and if all other factors align in their favor, they will achieve good results. This balanced approach fosters realistic expectations while still offering support and motivation.

Success can inflate my ego, giving rise to arrogance. This theory protects me from these demons by reminding me that I am only partly responsible for my success, and therefore cannot take full credit. This understanding helps me stay grounded and maintain humility, even in moments of achievement.

This theory encourages me to be confident once I'm assured that I've done my part with honesty, preventing the self-doubt demon from taking over. It reinforces trust in my efforts and helps me move forward without second-guessing myself.

Summing Up

The theory emphasizes the role of various elements in determining outcomes. By recognizing that our role is only a fraction of the whole, we can reduce the impact of demons like regret, guilt, worry, fear, and arrogance. This theory suggests a balanced approach to understanding success and failure, encouraging us to focus only on what we can control while letting go of factors beyond our influence. This mindset fosters inner peace and a healthier perspective on both achievements and setbacks.

CHAPTER 35

Theory of Order Within Chaos

According to my Theory of Order Within Chaos, chaos will always surround us. The harsh reality is that this chaos is here to stay, embedded in our lives in various forms. Sometimes it will be active, other times dormant, and often, it will be quietly building in the background.

For a long time, I blamed the chaos in my daily life for my failures and procrastination, believing it was the root cause of my setbacks. But then I realized that this chaos is never going to disappear. If I wait for it to subside before taking action, I'll be waiting forever. To create any sense of order, we must learn to live and thrive amidst the chaos. In essence, we need to discover the order that exists within the chaos itself.

Key Concepts of This Theory

Chaos is primarily characterized by unpredictability, confusion, and a lack of order. This lack of structure and stability creates an environment where various internal "demons" can easily emerge—whether they be fear, doubt, anxiety, or procrastination. Since this chaos is not going anywhere, the conditions that allow these demons to thrive will always remain fertile. As long as chaos persists, so too will the potential for these negative forces to surface and grow.

According to this theory, even in the most chaotic situations, there is an underlying order or pattern waiting to be uncovered. By identifying and understanding these hidden patterns, we can navigate chaos more effectively and counteract the internal demons it tends to unleash. Recognizing that chaos is not entirely random but contains elements of order allows us to regain a sense of control and stability, even in the midst of uncertainty.

And when it's getting hard to find this order within chaos, we need to create one from scratch to remain in control of the chaotic situation instead of succumbing to it.

And when it becomes difficult to find the underlying order within chaos, we must create one from scratch to maintain control over the chaotic situation, rather than succumbing to it. By actively imposing structure or patterns where none are apparent, we can regain a sense of direction and purpose. This act of creating order, even in small ways, can help us stay grounded and prevents us from being overwhelmed by the confusion and unpredictability around us. It empowers us to shape the chaos, rather than letting it dictate our actions.

This shift in perspective empowers me to manage chaos, rather than be overwhelmed by it, and find clarity in what initially appears to be disorder.

How This Theory Helps Me Combat My Demons

While chaos may give rise to many internal demons—such as fear, doubt, and anxiety—this theory helps me combat them by bringing a sense of order within the chaos. By identifying patterns or creating structure amidst the disorder, I can counteract the negative effects that chaos unleashes. This process allows me to manage the chaos more effectively, reducing its hold over me and providing clarity and focus where confusion once reigned. Through this approach, I'm able to face the demons head-on and regain control.

Chaos disrupts our sense of control and predictability, often giving rise to demons like anxiety and worry within our system. This theory can help by allowing us to recognize patterns within the chaos, bringing a degree of predictability to what initially seems random. By identifying these patterns, we can restore some sense of order, which in turn reduces the influence of anxiety and worry. The ability to find or create structure amidst uncertainty helps mitigate the impact of these negative forces, allowing us to navigate chaotic situations with greater confidence and calmness.

The unknown elements of chaos often invite the fear demon into our system, as unfamiliar and potentially threatening situations disturb our minds. In the midst of chaos, our instinctive response to the unknown can heighten this fear. However, this theory helps by allowing us to recognize familiar patterns within the chaos, which can neutralize the fear demon. By finding these patterns, we introduce a sense of familiarity and predictability, which helps calm the mind and reduce the power that fear holds over us. In essence, recognizing the familiar within the chaos restores a sense of stability and control.

Decisions made under pressure in chaotic situations can often lead to mistakes, giving rise to guilt and regret demons within our system. This theory, however, helps us acknowledge that mistakes are an inevitable part of navigating chaos. By understanding the patterns within chaos, we can learn from those mistakes and make more informed decisions in the future. Recognizing that errors are a natural outcome of chaos, we reduce the emotional weight of guilt and regret, using them instead as lessons for growth.

Chaos can heighten our tendency to compare ourselves to others who appear to manage disorder more effectively, leading to feelings of inadequacy. This theory helps us recognize that everyone has their own unique skill set and experience in finding order within their chaos. By embracing this understanding, we can prevent the comparison demon, reducing the urge for unhealthy comparisons and fostering self-acceptance instead.

When others fail to meet my expectations, this theory protects me from the attacks of the expectation demon by helping me understand that it's difficult for anyone to fulfill expectations while navigating their own chaos. It reminds me that they may be struggling to find order in their own chaos, just as I am in mine, fostering empathy and patience instead of disappointment.

Summing Up

This theory helps me combat various demons by recognizing that chaos is not entirely random, but contains underlying patterns—an order within the chaos. By identifying and understanding these patterns, I can reduce the impact of demons like anxiety, fear, guilt, unmet expectations, and other negative emotions, allowing me to regain a sense of control and stability even in chaotic situations.

It also helps me accept the reality that there will rarely be a day when everything is perfect and nothing goes wrong. Instead of dwelling on the chaos in my life, I should focus on finding order within it and carving a path forward despite the disorder.

CHAPTER 36

Theory of Survival in The Worst Case

The Theory of Survival in The Worst Case is simple yet powerful. It helps me stay calm in situations where my inner demons would otherwise overwhelm me. When things are going wrong and spiraling downward, this theory proves highly effective against demons like worry.

The idea is to imagine the worst possible scenarios and assess how you would survive in those challenging moments. If you can identify ways to endure the worst, worry loses its power to scare you. However, if your assessment shows that you would face significant challenges during the worst times, it signals the need to work on mitigating those risks. Otherwise, you'll remain vulnerable to those potential threats.

Key Concepts of This Theory

Imagining worst-case scenarios allows you to closely examine what they might look like, how you could end up there, and what you can do to prevent them from happening or to survive if they do happen. The goal is to identify vulnerabilities during challenging times so that you can plan to avoid or mitigate them effectively.

If I can survive even my worst possible scenario, then there's no need to worry beyond what's within my control. This kind of reflection also helps filter out unnecessary wants and greeds, revealing what my true needs are in those situations. It's a way to focus on what truly matters and gain clarity amidst uncertainty.

How This Theory Helps Me Combat My Demons

This theory helps me combat my demons by shifting my mindset from fear and anxiety to preparedness and control. By imagining the worst-case scenarios, I face my fears head-on rather than letting them control me. This proactive approach diminishes the power of demons like worry, fear, and uncertainty, because instead of being overwhelmed by "what-ifs," I have a plan for even the toughest situations.

By identifying vulnerabilities, I can focus on strengthening those areas, reducing the impact of guilt and regret demons when things go wrong. The regret demon haunts us for being unprepared or making mistakes. This theory allows me to anticipate potential challenges, consider preventive actions, and be ready to face tough situations. The confidence that comes from knowing I've done my best to prepare for the worst significantly reduces the power of the regret demon.

It also helps me separate true needs from wants, quieting the comparison and expectation demons by reminding me of what is truly essential. Ultimately, the theory gives me a sense of control, allowing me to manage chaos more effectively and combat my inner demons with clarity and resilience.

This theory is deeply connected to our past, present, and future. We learn from past experiences—where we succeeded and where we struggled during tough times—apply that wisdom to our present challenges, and use it to build confidence and preparedness for any potential worst-case scenarios in the future. By integrating lessons from the past into our present actions, we equip ourselves to handle future difficulties with greater resilience and clarity.

This theory allows me to envision the worst possible scenarios, helping me understand what they could look like and devise ways to prevent or survive them. By doing so, it reduces the fear of the unknown and weakens the influence of the worry demon, allowing me to remain calm. Without this theory, I would be overwhelmed and consumed by my worries.

The greed demon drives me to crave more, often beyond what is necessary or beneficial. This theory helps me filter out those excessive desires by prompting me to imagine worst-case scenarios, highlighting my true needs in those moments. It also weakens the greed demon's influence by fostering contentment with the essentials, showing me that I can survive without the excess that my greed might demand. This realization brings clarity and reduces the hold of unnecessary desires.

It also lessens the influence of the comparison, envy, and jealousy demons by fostering contentment and shifting my focus to what truly matters—the essentials.

This theory makes me less vulnerable to the expectations demon, as growing confidence in my ability to survive tough times reduces my reliance on extra expectations of others. Furthermore, being prepared for worst-case scenarios helps shield me from the disappointment of unmet expectations, making me more resilient in the face of uncertainty.

Summing Up

This theory helps me maintain my calm and focus during challenging times by imagining worst-case scenarios and preparing for them, should they actually occur. By identifying ways to survive and understanding my essential needs, it helps me tackle inner demons like worry, greed, expectations, regret, comparison, envy, and jealousy.

CHAPTER 37

Theory of Adaptability

The Theory of Adaptability emphasizes that change is unavoidable, whether we choose it or it is imposed upon us. If not managed effectively, change can create a breeding ground for many demons in our system. Adapting to change, new circumstances, and unexpected outcomes—regardless of personal preference—has allowed me to avoid potential negative consequences that could have arisen from resisting those changes.

This theory has shown me that adapting doesn't mean losing who I am. Instead, it signifies broadening my ability to accept change while staying true to my core identity. Through adaptation, I've integrated new behaviors into my existing self, representing growth rather than a fundamental transformation. The most significant challenge in embracing this theory is the internal resistance to change and fear of the unknown. However, recognizing and accepting the inevitability of change can help overcome these obstacles.

How This Theory Helps Me Combat My Demons

This theory helps me in combating my demons by enabling me to adapt to changing circumstances and unexpected outcomes.

Often, the outcomes differ from what we anticipated or fall short, leading the expectations demon to haunt us. This theory helps me adjust to varying results, lessening the influence of the expectations demon and helping me manage disappointment.

When others don't act as we wish, it can awaken the ego demon within us. This theory helps me adjust to those around me, diminishing the ego demon's grip and enabling me to handle unwanted behaviors without feeling offended.

Comparing myself to others, especially those who seem better, can fuel the envy and jealousy demons. This theory helps by guiding me to align my desires with my abilities and circumstances, minimizing the harmful effects of comparisons.

Uncertainty and changing circumstances can create the perfect environment for the worry demon to thrive within us. This theory helps me adapt to change, boosting my confidence and diminishing the influence of the worry demon.

Resistance to change can lead to actions or decisions for which we may have regret or guilt later. Conversely, when I adapt to the changes, it can help us prevent making mistakes, reducing the growth of regret and guilt demons in our system.

Resisting change can result in actions or decisions we may later regret or feel guilty about. However, by embracing change, I can avoid mistakes and limit the growth of regret and guilt demons within us.

Following This Theory

One caveat of following this theory is that your adaptability might be seen as a weakness by others, leading them to take you for granted. Therefore, it's important to maintain assertiveness and set clear boundaries while applying this approach.

Additionally, not all changes are beneficial, so it's crucial to carefully evaluate whether adapting to a particular change or unexpected outcome is the right decision.

Summing Up

This theory helps me navigate the inevitability of change, preventing it from nurturing internal demons like worry, regret, guilt, envy, and ego. By embracing adaptability and remaining flexible without losing my core identity, I can gracefully navigate change and manage expectations. While adaptability is a powerful tool, it requires careful evaluation and assertiveness to ensure it's used effectively and not mistaken for weakness.

CHAPTER 38

Theory of Protecting The Inner Core at All Costs

My Theory of Protecting Inner Core at All Costs emphasizes the importance of safeguarding our inner self from external negative influences. Our inner core represents the real, unchanging essence of who we are. When external disturbances penetrate this core, they can unleash many demons within us, leading to significant emotional turmoil. This theory recommends maintaining the integrity of our inner core to ensure emotional stability and resilience in our system.

Key Concepts of This Theory

Within each of us lies an inner core that embodies our true essence, untouched by outside forces. It reflects our most profound values, beliefs, and core identity. Safeguarding this inner core preserves our authentic self, no matter how much the world around us may change.

An intriguing fact is that many of us lead dual lives: one shaped by our inner essence and the other by the outward persona we present to the world. This external persona often aligns with societal norms and expectations, acting as a façade for how others perceive us. It's essential to find a balance between these two aspects of ourselves, ensuring that the inner core remains intact without being overshadowed by the external image.

While others may believe they understand our inner selves, their knowledge is limited, often based on assumptions. Only our inner world has full access to the depths of our true core.

We must address negative influences and inner demons at the surface level, preventing them from reaching our inner core. By doing so, we can better manage stress and negative emotions, keeping them from taking control.

How This Theory Helps Me Combat My Demons

Unlike my other theories, this one acts as a guardian or watchman, helping me protect my inner core from the invasion of various demons. If they reach my core, they could threaten the integrity of my inner self.

Worry and anxiety can disturb our peace and infiltrate our inner core if left unchecked. This theory serves as a constant reminder to safeguard my inner core, keeping these negative forces on the surface and preventing them from taking root. In doing so, I can stop worry and anxiety from causing deeper disruptions within.

The fear demon can become a paralyzing force when it invades our inner core, disrupting our sense of identity and shaking our core. This theory helps me build a mental shield, keeping the fear demon from penetrating my core and gaining control over it.

The demons of guilt and regret can erode our inner core if they are allowed to sink in too deeply. This theory encourages me to address these feelings at the surface through reflection and proactive steps, preventing them from reaching and damaging my core.

The demons of comparison, envy, and jealousy can distort our self-perception when they penetrate our core. This theory encourages me to acknowledge and confront these negative forces, ensuring they don't take root within me or grow too powerful.

Unmet expectations often lead to frustration and disappointment, which can affect our core beliefs and self-esteem. According to this theory, by setting more realistic expectations and managing disappointments at a surface level, we can lessen the emotional burden that comes from unfulfilled desires, preserving the strength of our inner core.

Strengthening and Protecting Our Inner Core

Regularly reflect on your core values and beliefs to fortify your sense of self, creating a clear boundary between your inner identity and external influences. Keep a strong distinction between core values and surface-level concerns.

Set and maintain healthy boundaries to shield your inner self from negative external forces and stressors. Continuously nurture positive aspects of your core through affirmations and self-compassion, boosting self-esteem and minimizing the effects of negative emotions.

Summing Up

This theory emphasizes the importance of safeguarding our innermost self from external negative influences. By keeping a clear boundary between the inner core and surface-level issues, we can prevent stress and its servant demons gaining root inside our core. This approach helps combat various demons such as worry, fear, guilt, regret, comparison, envy, jealousy, and expectations at the surface level when they haven't become too strong yet.

CHAPTER 39

Theory of Right and Wrong

My Theory of Right and Wrong highlights that while we are taught to differentiate between right and wrong from an early age, the reality of these concepts is far more complex. Our world is not black and white, and it consists of many shades of gray. This complexity stems from the fact that even what seems wrong can contain elements of good, and what appears right can carry its own flaws. Understanding and navigating these nuances is essential for making balanced decisions.

If only the world was as straightforward as "right is right and wrong is wrong," but the truth is far more complicated. From our earliest lessons in school, we're instructed to choose the right path, even when the wrong one may seem more tempting or rewarding. We're encouraged to be good and ethical individuals from the start.

There's nothing inherently wrong with this idea; in fact, it's a crucial foundation for a moral and ethical society. However, the challenge comes when sticking to the right path is difficult, especially when the wrong path appears faster, easier, and more appealing. The allure of shortcuts often makes the wrong side more attractive, demanding more of our attention.

Key Concepts of This Theory

The concept of right and wrong is inherently complex, as these notions are not absolute; they often contain elements of each other. This awareness helps us navigate the moral and ethical challenges of real-life situations.

Our inner demons thrive on the fact that every wrong decision contains some good, and every right choice carries some drawbacks. In a world full of trade-offs, these demons tempt us towards poor decisions by emphasizing the positive aspects of wrong choices and the negative sides of right ones, creating a constant struggle. Otherwise, we would simply choose what is right. Acknowledging this internal battle allows us to make more informed choices.

Interestingly, these demons also make us aware of the flaws in right decisions. Without their influence, we might only focus on the positives and be blindsided by the downsides. By highlighting these shortcomings, we can address them and make better decisions.

Perspective also plays a key role in understanding right and wrong. What one person sees as right, another might view as wrong, and considering different perspectives allows for a more balanced and nuanced view. Moreover, circumstances can shift the moral balance. What seems right in one situation may appear wrong when conditions change, illustrating that right and wrong are often a matter of context.

How This Theory Helps Me Combat My Demons

This theory has been a powerful tool in helping me confront several inner demons, especially by enhancing my understanding of the complex nature of right and wrong.

A common struggle is the fear of making wrong choices and being overwhelmed by their potential consequences. This theory helps me address that fear by recognizing that all decisions come with trade-offs. By acknowledging this, I feel less paralyzed by the idea of choosing incorrectly. It reminds me that no decision is entirely free of flaws, reducing my anxiety over the "right" or "wrong" choice.

Even when I'm confident I've made the right decision, I sometimes feel disappointed when the outcome falls short of my expectations. This theory helps ease that disappointment by reminding me that even the best decisions can have imperfections. Understanding that right choices can still lead to less-than-perfect results weakens the power of unrealistic expectations.

Another demon I often face is comparison—especially when it involves others I perceive as superior. Envy and jealousy can creep in, leaving me feeling inadequate. This theory helps by showing that while comparisons may seem right on the surface, they often overlook crucial flaws in perspective. Recognizing this helps alleviate some of the weight of these feelings, making me realize that my envy or jealousy is not entirely justified.

Sometimes, I stand firm in what I believe is right, but when others challenge my perspective, it causes me to question myself leading to self-doubt. This theory reassures me by emphasizing that right and wrong often depend on perspective, and it's possible that others' judgments may not be entirely correct. However, it also encourages me to re-evaluate my stance, confirming my perspective to ensure its validity.

Sometimes, I knowingly choose a path that feels wrong, but I do so because I see potential long-term benefits or find some good within that wrong. This theory helps me navigate these moments by assuring me that as long as no harm is done to others and I am mindful of the consequences, it's acceptable to take that path. It reminds me, though, to be cautious and ensure that my actions don't hurt anyone along the way.

The regret and guilt demons often arise when I reflect on past decisions I now perceive as wrong. This theory comforts me by suggesting that what seemed like a right decision at the time should not be harshly judged in hindsight. This perspective reduces the burden of guilt and regret, allowing me to move forward with less emotional baggage.

The ego demon can be particularly destructive, making me believe that my perspective is the only right one. This theory confronts my ego by reminding me that even my views may have their own imperfections. It encourages me to consider multiple perspectives, fostering open-mindedness and reducing arrogance.

In addition to helping me navigate these negative forces, this theory boosts my confidence in making complex choices painted with rights and wrongs. It reduces my anxiety and fear of making mistakes, promoting more confident and thoughtful decision-making overall. Through this understanding of right and wrong, I feel more empowered to face the challenges that come my way, with less fear and more clarity.

Summing Up

This theory emphasizes the complexity and intermingling of right and wrong. By understanding that right and wrong are not absolute and that perspectives play a crucial role, we can make more balanced decisions. This theory helps combat various demons such as expectations, comparisons, regret, guilt, worry, fear, and ego by recommending realistic expectations, self-acceptance and informed decision-making.

CHAPTER 40

Theory of "It's Okay to Not be Okay"

This is my ultimate—kind of a "catch-all"—guiding principle, the theory that helps me navigate the ups and downs of life. The idea that everything will always be okay is an unrealistic expectation. Even when life is smooth, there will inevitably be moments where things aren't quite right.

In the same way, it's impossible for me to avoid doing things that aren't always okay. There will inevitably be moments when I make choices that fall short of what's ideal. However, as long as I take responsibility for my actions and ensure I'm not causing harm to others, I can accept that it's okay.

Expecting everything—including my own behavior—to always be perfectly okay is like chasing an unattainable dream. While striving for perfection is a worthy goal, it's equally important to accept that life will sometimes offer less-than-ideal outcomes. The key is to learn from those moments and keep moving forward.

Some might see this approach as promoting mediocrity, but from a practical standpoint, it helps me manage disappointment when things are not okay. It's better to be realistic than to live in a fool's paradise.

Key Concepts of This Theory

When you consider life in its entirety, it's a complex blend of many elements—physical health, wealth, mental well-being, relationships, and more. It's impossible for all these aspects to be perfectly okay all the time.

Moreover, your life isn't just about you; it also includes the people around you, both near and far. No matter how much you try to control things, striving for everything and everyone to be okay, there will always be someone or something that isn't okay. This adds to your list of not-okay things, simply because you care.

There will always be something or someone you dislike, creating situations that aren't okay for you. Life will always be a mix of okay and not-okay moments, and that's just the reality.

How This Theory Helps Me Combat My Demons

The theory of "It's Okay to Not Be Okay" has been instrumental in helping me face and overcome my inner demons by reshaping how I view challenges, setbacks, and imperfections in life.

One of the major demons I face is comparison, and I'm fully aware that many forms of it are not okay. Comparing myself to others, especially those I perceive as better, often leads to feelings of inadequacy and sadness. On the other hand, when I compare others' downs to my ups, I may feel a temporary sense of superiority, but this can quickly turn into complacency. Being human, it's nearly impossible to avoid such comparisons completely, but I've learned that as long as I limit them, it's okay to indulge in them occasionally, even if it's not okay and the best thing for me.

Similarly, making mistakes never feels okay. Mistakes often bring feelings of guilt, regret and disappointment. However, I've come to understand that it's part of being human. As long as I acknowledge my mistakes, learn from them, and strive to make amends, I'm okay—even if making mistakes is never entirely "okay."

Anger is another demon I wrestle with. Left unchecked, it can escalate situations and make things worse. While I know it's not okay to lose control, I also recognize that anger is a natural emotion that can't be avoided. As long as I manage it most of the time and remain mindful, I can accept that occasional outbursts are okay, even if they aren't ideal.

Envy and jealousy are also demons I try to keep at bay. Although I know it's better for my peace of mind to avoid them, I can't always resist. Still, as long as I manage these feelings most of the time, I've learned to accept that it's okay to feel them occasionally, even if they aren't positive emotions.

Sometimes, I over-encourage others or even myself, creating unnecessary pressure. I know this isn't always okay, but at times it gives me a sense of involvement and caring. The theory of "It's Okay to Not Be Okay" has helped me accept that it's alright to sometimes push a little too much, even if it's not ideal.

Ultimately, life is filled with situations that aren't perfectly okay, and my response to them may not always be either. These imperfections create fertile ground for many of my inner demons to grow. But this theory offers me a lifeline, reminding me that sometimes, it's okay to not be okay, and that's part of life's journey.

Summing Up

This theory doesn't advocate for settling for mediocrity; rather, it encourages a practical approach to navigating life's complexities. I no longer expect everyone and everything around me, including my own actions, to be perfectly okay and flawless. This perspective has helped me maintain balance, build resilience, and better prepare myself to handle whatever challenges come my way.

CHAPTER 41

A Tale of Three Families: Confronting Their Demons With the Guidance of Their Angels

I n the complex and competitive world like ours, people face a myriad of internal demons and find guidance through a host of benevolent angels in their system. These demons and angels are interconnected, constantly influencing the lives of everyone in their path.

Let me walk you through a fictional short story exploring the lives of three distinct families from different financial backgrounds battling their inner demons while seeking solace in the angels guiding them. In this story, the affluent Browns, the middle-class Millers, and the poor struggling Smiths are shown navigating their unique challenges, learning valuable lessons along the way while dancing between these demons and angels.

This story shows only a glimpse of their lives highlighting only a few of their demons and angels, and there's a whole lot more to them than what's covered here.

My primary purpose of categorizing the families by their financial status and affluence is to challenge the widespread belief that wealth can solve all problems and that everything is always perfect in the lives of the rich. Both the wealthy and the poor face their own distinct challenges, but they each have their own demons to contend with.

The Brown Family: Demons and Angels in the World of the Affluent

The Brown family is part of rich and affluent class of society, comprising Robert Brown, a successful CEO; Emily Brown, a philanthropist and socialite; and their teenage son, Lucas Brown. Despite their wealth, the Browns are not immune to the demons that haunt them, but they also find strength in the angels within their lives.

Robert, driven by ambition, battles demons like superiority, overconfidence, and ego, which are often associated with his social class. He also struggles with the expectation demon, placing undue pressure on Lucas, who feels overwhelmed and inadequate as a result of that. By doing comparisons between his own journey and his son's, he invites the demons of comparison and over-encouragement, causing strain rather than inspiration.

Emily faces the demons of greed and desire, spurred by her social circle's emphasis on luxury and status, which sometimes leads to tension at home. Additionally, she becomes a source of envy for friends and relatives, and she is occasionally plagued by the guilt demon for not spending more time with her family due to her social commitments.

Lucas, too, wrestles with demons such as anger, envy, and comparison, struggling under the weight of his father's expectations. Anxiety takes hold as he worries about meeting these high standards, and he often finds himself the object of envy among less fortunate peers.

How the Browns Found Balance

Despite the pressures they face, the Browns' love for one another remains their guiding force. Emily often relies on the angel of patience, while Robert learns to temper his expectations with understanding. Lucas holds onto hope that his parents will one day see him for who he truly is, without the burden of their expectations.

Robert begins to accept Lucas's individual path, guided by the angel of acceptance, and forgives himself for being overly demanding. He recognizes that both he and Lucas have their unique journeys and stops comparing them.

Emily's philanthropic efforts are driven by the angels of love, kindness, and morality, and she instills in Lucas the importance of giving back to society. Lucas, free from the weight of his father's expectations, begins to help underprivileged children, inspired by the kindness angel within him.

In summary, Emily's kindness inspires Lucas to volunteer, finding fulfillment beyond academic success. Robert's acceptance of Lucas's choices strengthens their relationship, easing the pressure on him. The Browns come to realize that their love and trust are far more valuable than material wealth.

The Miller Family: Demons and Angels in the World of the Middle Class

The Miller family, representing the middle class, consists of John Miller, a dedicated office worker; Sarah Miller, a schoolteacher; and their teenage daughter, Megan Miller. Their lives revolve around stability and daily struggles, confronting various demons while drawing strength from the angels within.

John, as the primary breadwinner, is often haunted by demons like worry, anxiety, guilt, and anger, concerned about job stability and his ability to provide for his family. He also struggles with the demons of comparison and envy when he sees others who are more financially secure. Additionally, he often regrets over missed opportunities that adds to his burden.

Sarah is similarly haunted by worry and guilt, feeling torn between her work and the desire to spend more time with Megan. Financial concerns weigh heavily on her, as do regrets about not pursuing more opportunities in her youth, which she believes have contributed to their current struggles.

Megan, growing up in a middle-class household, grapples with the demons of comparison and envy, longing for the wealth and privileges of her friends. Anger often takes hold as she resents the compromises that she and her family must make, such as missing out on expensive school trips and luxury items.

How the Millers Found Harmony

Despite the challenges, John draws on the angels of hope and willpower, striving for a better future and working hard to maintain family stability. Sarah, meanwhile, finds solace in the angels of love and hope, creating a warm and nurturing home environment and teaching Megan to appreciate the small things in life.

Megan, despite limited resources, works hard and smart, earning scholarships through perseverance and determination. Together, John and Sarah use logic and trust to plan their finances, teaching Megan to live wisely within their means.

In conclusion, John and Sarah's open communication fosters a stronger family bond, and Megan discovers joy in activities that don't require wealth. The Millers realize that hope, love, and careful planning can overcome financial worries and bring them closer as a family.

The Smith Family: Demons and Angels in the World of the Struggling

The Smith family, part of the struggling lower class, includes Michael Smith, an unemployed father; Lisa Smith, a part-time waitress; and their young son, Tommy Smith. Their lives revolve around survival and resilience, facing numerous demons while seeking strength from the angels within.

Michael battles demons such as anger, frustration, envy, and worry as he struggles to provide for his family. His sense of guilt and anger stems from his inability to meet even their basic needs, compounded by regrets over missed opportunities and the lack of support during his youth.

Lisa, the sole breadwinner, is haunted by worry and anxiety, constantly struggling to make ends meet. She feels guilty for not being able to fulfill Tommy's wishes and envies those who have more. Tommy, too, is plagued by jealousy and envy, feeling inferior to his wealthier peers and fearing that his friends will abandon him because of his family's poverty.

How the Smiths Found Strength

Despite their hardships, Lisa holds onto the angels of patience and love, keeping her family united. Michael draws on the angels of hope and willpower to stay motivated in his job search, believing in a better future for his family.

Lisa accepts their situation with the help of the angels of kindness and acceptance, encouraging her family to find joy in the small moments. Tommy, seeing his parents' struggles, learns the value of hard work and money, guided by the angel of kindness and a resolve to one day fight poverty.

In summary, Michael finds a job through a community program, regaining his sense of purpose. Lisa's kindness inspires their neighbors to support them, creating a strong community bond. Tommy, learning from his parents' resilience, finds joy in simple, creative play. The Smiths discover that love, hope, and patience can help them overcome financial hardships and lead a fulfilling life.

Summing Up

The journeys of the Brown, Miller, and Smith families highlight a universal truth: regardless of financial status, ethnicity, or family structure, we all carry within us both demons and angels. These forces shape our lives, influencing our thoughts, actions, and interactions. By understanding and navigating these internal struggles, we can face life's challenges and emerge stronger, fortified by the bonds of family.

CHAPTER 42

Closing Thoughts

As we reach the final chapter of this book, I want to take a moment to express my gratitude to you, the readers. Throughout these pages, I've discussed various demons, angels, and shared my personal theories, but my primary goal has always been to spark new thoughts in your minds and to empower you in your own battles against the demons you face. Thank you for embarking on this journey with me.

The ideal state for us is to achieve a stress-free life, as our purpose on this earth is to enjoy our time here, not to be burdened by stress. However, when we think practically, expecting a completely stress-free existence might be unrealistic. Instead, if we can reach a state where stress is managed and kept under control, that's a very positive and worthwhile place to be.

The Demons

Demons such as anger, greed, need, want, greed, ego, worry, expectation, relationships, envy, jealousy, comparison, past, present, future, regret, and guilt represent the darker aspects of our human experience. They are born out of our fears, insecurities, and desires. These demons can cloud our judgment, strain our relationships, and hinder our progress. However, they also serve a purpose: they reveal the areas of our lives where we need to grow, learn, and heal.

Stress is the master demon that feeds on all these other servant demons in our system.

The Angels

On the other hand, angels like love, hope, patience, willpower, kindness, forgiveness, acceptance, logic, trust, and morals are the guiding lights that help us navigate through life's challenges. These angels provide us with the strength to overcome our demons, fostering resilience, compassion, and understanding. They remind us of our potential for goodness and our capacity to connect with others on a deeper, more meaningful level.

Embracing the Balance

The concept of demons and angels within us underscores the importance of balance. It is unrealistic to expect a life free from demons creating challenges or negative emotions. Instead, our goal should be to recognize and manage these demons while nurturing and strengthening our angels. By doing so, we create a harmonious inner world that reflects in our outer lives.

Personal Growth and Resilience

Personal growth often arises from our struggles with internal demons. By facing and understanding these darker aspects of ourselves, we develop resilience and a deeper sense of self-awareness. This journey is supported by our angels, who provide us with the tools and guidance needed to navigate our challenges.

The Role of Relationships

While I've depicted relationships as demons in the context of this book, I want to call out that our relationships play a crucial role in this dynamic. Through our interactions with family, friends, and community, we encounter both demons and angels.

These relationships can trigger our fears and insecurities, but they also offer opportunities for love, support, and growth. By fostering positive relationships, we can amplify the presence of angels in our lives and create an environment that mitigates the influence of demons.

Final Reflection

In the end, the concept of demons and angels within us serves as a powerful metaphor for the human experience. It reminds us that life is a complex interplay of challenges and triumphs, fears and hopes, darkness and light. By acknowledging both our demons and angels, we embark on a journey of self-discovery and personal growth, leading to a more balanced, fulfilling life.

As we navigate this journey, let us remember the lessons learned from the Brown, Miller, and Smith families. Let us embrace our inner struggles with courage and compassion, guided by the angels of love, hope, patience, and understanding. In doing so, we not only enrich our own lives but also contribute to a more compassionate and connected world.

Thank You!

Made in United States
Orlando, FL
24 February 2025

58861405R00256